A True Story

LEO WINOKUR WINN

AuthorHouse™
1663 Liberty Drive
Bloomington, IN 47403
www.authorhouse.com
Phone: 1-800-839-8640

© 2014 Leo Winokur Winn. All rights reserved.

No part of this book may be reproduced, stored in a retrieval system, or transmitted by any means without the written permission of the author.

Published by AuthorHouse 02/06/2014

ISBN: 978-1-4918-4278-2 (sc)
ISBN: 978-1-4918-4279-9 (e)

Library of Congress Control Number: 2013922703

Any people depicted in stock imagery provided by Thinkstock are models, and such images are being used for illustrative purposes only. Certain stock imagery © Thinkstock.

This book is printed on acid-free paper.

Because of the dynamic nature of the Internet, any web addresses or links contained in this book may have changed since publication and may no longer be valid. The views expressed in this work are solely those of the author and do not necessarily reflect the views of the publisher, and the publisher hereby disclaims any responsibility for them.

*In memory of my beloved
Parents, sister and my entire family
that perished in the Holocaust*

Contents

Introduction ix
Prologue xi
The Cast Of Characters xvii

Chapter 1	The Voyage	1
Chapter 2	A Late Summer Morning	5
Chapter 3	Grandparents' Home	11
Chapter 4	The Gypsy	16
Chapter 5	The Smell Of War	20
Chapter 6	Our Place	23
Chapter 7	Good Neighbors?	27
Chapter 8	Last Calm Day	29
Chapter 9	Headaches And Candles	31
Chapter 10	My Education	34
Chapter 11	Our Gentile Neighbor	37
Chapter 12	My Father's Family	41
Chapter 13	Retreat	48
Chapter 14	A Bit Of History	52
Chapter 15	A Wedding	58
Chapter 16	Visiting School	64
Chapter 17	Our American Connection	68
Chapter 18	Business Talk	74
Chapter 19	Surrender	79
Chapter 20	Army Parade	83
Chapter 21	New Masters - New Policies	93
Chapter 22	Getting To Know Death	99
Chapter 23	The Burning Altars	104

Chapter 24	A New Home	115
Chapter 25	The Ghetto	120
Chapter 26	Our Mr. R.	123
Chapter 27	First Death In The Family	126
Chapter 28	Hitting The Streets	131
Chapter 29	Bubbe's Wish	134
Chapter 30	Life Is Fickle	136
Chapter 31	The Art Of Surviving	141
Chapter 32	Typhus And Rumors	147
Chapter 33	A New Front	150
Chapter 34	Deportations	157
Chapter 35	Vegetables And Sewing Machines	160
Chapter 36	Rations And News	167
Chapter 37	A Painful Departure	171
Chapter 38	Where Is God?	175
Chapter 39	Chaos	180
Chapter 40	One Solution	191
Chapter 41	The Trains	193
Chapter 42	A God-Send	195
Chapter 43	A False Alarm	200
Chapter 44	The Camp	211
Chapter 45	Selection	215
Chapter 46	Getting Out Of Hell	222
Chapter 47	In Germany	225
Chapter 48	Another Leader, Another Camp	229
Chapter 49	A New Order	232
Chapter 50	Staying Alive	241
Chapter 51	The Last Gasp	252
Chapter 52	Escape	257
Chapter 53	Liberation	262

Epilogue 279

Introduction

The topic of World War Two, and the horrible punishment it impaired on many lives, appears to be inexhaustible. A plethora of books, films, and philosophical theses has been published on this subject, and yet almost 65 years later new information appears on an almost weekly basis and every book or treatise on this subject helps to shed more light on it.

Although historians may have reached a modus vivendi and established a series of facts related to WW2, the individuals caught up in the process are frequently inclined to differently interpret experiences acquired under situations that appear to have been almost identical, and draw different conclusions from them. This is particularly true of people who experienced the Nazi onslaught and managed to come out alive.

For most of the time since my liberation, by the US Army in Southern Bavaria, I have tried to forget my past experiences. I immigrated to the United States, acquired a good education, got married, had three great children, and developed a good reputation in the specific engineering branch that I specialized in. Yet, almost every night before falling asleep I keep on recalling my family which has been almost totally annihilated. War-based nightmares haunt me to this day. It was only after my retirement in 1991 that I began to give some thought to writing a book on my experiences. It took me ten years to bring it to fruition. It seemed to me that the best way to express my feelings and experiences was in the way of a simulated diary. Memories of my childhood and the war are still fresh in my mind in spite of the decades that have since elapsed. This book is thus a biographical sketch of a youth of 16 caught up in the war. I was 21 when the war ended. I have intentionally refrained from checking out the facts on which this book is based. I wanted it to be truly representative of my feelings at that time as I remembered them.

I have also avoided, whenever possible, the use of one word to describe what happened. I simply do not believe that one word can describe or stand for the history of atrocities performed by the Nazis. There is no word to describe this. There is no single word that will keep the memory of those times alive. Single words are subject to definitions which from a semantic standpoint may be easily misinterpreted and changed.

I hope that this book will, in its own way, add to the illumination and better understanding of the Nazi era experience.

Prologue

Lodz, Poland, August 1939. Europe is filled with rumors of an impending war. The Jews of Poland are restless and frightened. Yet life goes on .The general feeling of the Jewish populace can best be described by the songs they are singing. Two songs, in particular, stand out at this time: One, in polish, called: *Pinia Nojman*, is about a girl who still looks for love in Pinczew. It describes this little town as being a heavenly town, where people live in security, peace, and without worries. They produce the most delicious cheese, eggs and butter. In one word Pinczew is paradise. The other song delivers a warning. The words are in Yiddish. It calls for people to wake up. Can't they see that their little town is burning? Instead of standing there with folded arms they should pull out the hoses and begin to extinguish the fire which is about to engulf them. It is called : *S'Brent*. or "Our Village Is Afire".

This is how the Jews feel, and this is how they felt for centuries. They were always trying to pretend that all is fine while living among people who deep in their hearts considered them to be foreign and wicked. They tried to be oblivious to it and emphasized the more bearable aspects of their existence. They watched the spread of the flames of modern, well organized, anti- Semitism, but was there anything new there? It has been like that for at least two thousand years.

About 70 AD Jews were chased out of their land known as Judea. The Romans made a province out of Judea, renamed it Palestine, and from that time on Jews became wanderers.

In Christian Europe Jews were despised and isolated. Most were given permission to live in a country only when the given country could benefit from their residence. Disenfranchised, defenseless and dependent upon the good graces of their benefactors, they were frequently used as scapegoats.

Practically every significant change of, or challenges to, church doctrine resulted in persecution and/or murder of Jews. The Crusades, Spanish Inquisition, rise of Martin Luther, are but a few more prominent examples.

The spread of Islam was frequently accompanied by forceful conversion. At the very start many Jewish tribes were wiped out in Mecca for refusing to accept Mohammed as their prophet. As time progressed the Jews that settled in Africa or Asia, under predominantly Islam regimes were permitted to freely participate in the day-to-day life and cultural developments, even though Islam did not view other religions with favor

With the onset of the eighteenth century, years of autocratic and theocratic rule came slowly to an end. The end of this century saw significant internal upheavals in France, the North-East of America, and other smaller countries. The rights of the people to collectively manage their own destiny had gained general recognition, and frequent acceptance. Jews benefitted from this liberalization. In most European countries they were given equality in the face of the law, portending an end to their persecution.

The industrial revolution, which followed this temporary renaissance, brought about the development of new means of production that, in turn, also created new problems. New discoveries and inventions in science and engineering were quickly implemented, often at severe costs to human welfare. Autocracies, defeated not so long ago, began to re-emerge dressed in different cloaks.

One of the most important new powerful groups was that of industrial barons. In that group Jews, particularly Jewish bankers, occupied a prominent position. The useful qualities of this new class, such as organizational skills, and strong leadership, were quickly clouded over by greed, the foremost expression of which was the fierce exploitation of the less fortunate. This exploitation, with time, brought about the birth of new ideas and governing concepts, which alleviated the plight of the poor.

Wars, however, did not abate, nor did anti-Semitism. The presence of wealthy Jews among the industrialists fueled more hate. False accusations and smears kept the flame of anti-Semitism burning all over Europe. From Tsarist Russia to the North Sea, Jews were being blamed for all the maladies brought about by endemics, industrial development, political blunders, and wars. Vicious rumors spread by various sources helped to keep the flame of anti-Semitism burning.

The last big war fought on the European continent cost millions of lives. Historians called it "World War One, a war to end all wars." The twenty-one years following World War One were at first years of prosperity, but later turned into years of depression, and political unrest. At the end of that war, most newly written constitutions, or other legal precepts of governments on the continent of Europe, included the right to vote. This right, granting the underprivileged and persecuted a voice in the determination of their future, also became a potent tool in the hands of various political leaders who began to assert themselves and reach for power.

On the European political scene, socialist movements were particularly popular. Socialists stood for freedom of expression, equal distribution of wealth, freedom from hunger, and freedom of choice. On that platform socialists were elected to power in Great Britain, Germany, France, and Italy.

Russians also elected a socialist government following a brief revolution which overthrew the czar. This government was soon tumbled by the Bolsheviks, a group espousing communist gospel as preached by their leader Lenin. Communism stood for world revolution and dictatorship of the proletariat, ideas which most Europeans yearning for individual freedom viewed with suspicion. All of these movements attracted large numbers of Jews who saw in them an end to their plight.

As soon as the Russian revolution settled down, a man named Mussolini came to the fore in Italy. Impatient, and frustrated with the ineptness of the Italian government, and the slow evolutionary political credo of his own socialist party, he formed the Fascist party, overthrew the government, and granted himself absolute powers. Free elections were abolished, and the Italian Monarchy retained.

The problems of socialist, and generally democratic forms of government, became further magnified by the depression that struck all of Europe by the end of the 1920's. Unrest became the rule of the day. In France the depression brought about a government of the extreme left comprised of socialists and communists. In Germany strong leftist movements contended for power with the newly established German

Fascist Party, which, recognizing the general appeal of socialist thinking, named itself the National Socialist Workers Party (Nazi's for short). Strong fascist movements also sprung up in Spain, Portugal, Belgium, Norway and other European countries.

In 1933 a string of general elections in Germany produced no clear winner. The Nazis drew the most votes of all participating political parties, but were far from receiving a clear majority. After a series of behind-the-scene maneuvers and chicanery, Hitler, the leader of the Nazis, was asked by the aging and somewhat senile president Hindenburg to form a German Government. Once in power, Hitler quickly went on to eliminate his potential challengers. Many members of his own party, whom he distrusted, were shot. His political adversaries were either jailed in camps, which he called Concentration Camps, or executed. He proclaimed the Jews responsible for all ills facing society, and the current chaos in Europe in particular. He threatened to exterminate them. The average German could find work building roads and constructing a powerful war machine. Unemployment was eliminated. German Anti-Semitism reached new highs. Expulsion of Jews from Germany began.

Spain's reaction to the depression was similar to that of France. It elected a leftist government. No sooner was the government seated when a fascist general, named Franco, attacked with army divisions made up of the professional army and Berber units from Spanish Morocco. He quickly assumed power over one third of the country, surrounded Madrid, and a civil war began. Hitler, now allied with Mussolini, threw his support to Franco. German aircraft, tanks, Italian ships, and military personnel from both of these countries were promptly dispatched to the front. Spain became the test ground for Hitler's armaments. The Spanish republicans fought bravely. Volunteers from all over the world joined in the struggle. Help from the Soviet Union was no match for the mighty German tanks and planes. The Spanish government fell. Fascists took over. Hitler had won his first big test.

Wasting no time, Hitler was readying a second War. Under the slogan of *Lebensraum* (literally translated: *room to live*) he asserted his rights not only to territories he viewed as congenitally German, but also to those of his eastern neighbors. He considered Poland and the Ukraine, the breadbaskets of Europe, to be part of his lebensraum. At first, he cleaned up the Rheinland of foreign troops. Next, the Saar and Austria were annexed into the Reich to the applause of the majority of their inhabitants. Some influential European leaders attempted to appease him at a conference in Munich. As if to reward their naiveté, the Germans swallowed Czechoslovakia.

In August 1939, Hitler announced his determination to annex the Free City of Danzig, and demanded ground access to East Prussia via a Polish Corridor, which would endanger Poland's access to the Baltic Sea. His demands grew stronger by the day. War appeared imminent.

One of the pillars of Hitler's program is the destruction of Jews. Will he achieve this objective? It is a question that occupies the minds of frightened Jews throughout Europe. Among them is a 16 year old young man. He too is petrified, yet curious and anxious to witness and experience the War's impact should it break out. Like millions of other Jews he has no idea of what is about to happen.

The Cast Of Characters

My immediate family, the **Winokur**s, consist of my father Abraham, mother Esther *Radogowski*, myself and my sister Deborah.

On my mother side there are *the* **Boases, Diamants,** and **Schipfers**.

The Boases are comprised of six orphans: Bella and Sheindla (twins), Ita, David, Sara and Izaak (also twins). They are children of my mother's deceased sister Debra.

Haim Diamant is married to my mother's sister Hannah. They have three children: Itka, Izaak, and Julek. Izaak left the German occupied Poland for Vilnus, Lithuania.

My Mother's brother Chaim, went to the USA, where he changed his name to Schipfer. He is married and also has three children. Details regarding their names and that of his wife are lacking.

My maternal Grandparents Gershon Radogowski and Nacha Lieba Schipfer live with the Boases. Their nephews, Zajwel and Julek Radogowski live with their families in another section of town.

On my father's side David Winokur, my grandfather, died before I was born. He and his wife Tauba Kahane had four children: Abram (my father), Bajla, Leon, and Rose.

Bajla Winokur married Wolf **Wajsbrot.** They had three children: Heniek, Dworah, and Lajb(Leon).

Leon Winokur emigrated to Belgium in 1928. Rose Winokur married Dave *Rosenthal*. They had no children.

Mordecai *Chaim* **Rumkowski** -Mr.R, was the ghetto leader, appointed by the German Governor.

Other people appear, as they did in real life. Their true last names, in many instances, have not been mentioned mainly because the author either forgot or found no need to more closely identify them.

Chapter 1
THE VOYAGE

Life is full of surprises. After all, had life consisted of a series of foreseeable and predictable events, it probably would be dull, and boring. At this instant I am sick of the surprises the Nazis pull on us. I know that the game that is played by them is aimed at raising our hopes for staying alive while carrying out our extermination. We know that, and yet cannot give up our hope that perhaps this time they will do what they promise: Lead us into a place safe from bombings and conducive to survival. But, deep in our hearts we know that the Nazis never kept their promises. We expect a new surprise.

The train moves. After a while my eyes get used to the darkness. I notice some elongated cracks in the wall next to the door through which rays of light creep in. There is room there for a couple of people. I grab Debra by her hand, make my way towards the slivers of light, and we settle down leaning our backs against the wall. Our knapsacks are between us. The box car is full of people. After the tumult of boarding has settled down, there is hardly any space left on the floor. I try to relax. Strangely I feel no remorse or regret about leaving my hometown. The place we go to cannot be worse, it can only be better. Besides, it is August 1944. This damn war cannot last forever.

"Have you seen a toilet around here?" My sister Debra apparently has some urgent need.

"Yes." Answers a voice next to her "See those two buckets out there in the corner?"

"My God. What will happen when they fill up?"

"Don't worry, Debra, do what you need to do. We will worry later," I console her.

One bucket is already occupied. She gets to the second. Meanwhile I turn towards the wall. The cracks are wide enough to look out. All I see is trees and meadows rushing by as if they were in a hurry to get someplace.

A few hours have gone by. Cousin David comes over and squeezes in next to me. We share the look-out crack, not only to observe the landscape, but also to breathe in fresh air. By this time the air in the box is saturated with the smell of human sweat, and the stench emanating from the makeshift toilets.

Dusk has descended upon the landscape. Evening is here. The train stops in a small Polish town the name of which is totally unfamiliar to us. The doors slide open. A SS guard looks in and orders two men sitting by the open door to pick up the buckets, which by this time are overflowing. The men leave the car, and soon come back with empty buckets and a small barrel of water. This should help. The doors close. The train resumes its boring refrain: Rat-tat-tat., rat-tatta, rat-tat-ta.......

As I lie here contemplating our fate all kinds of questions fill my mind: Will we have enough food to last through the voyage? Where are we going? How long will we be trapped in this miserable box? Will we die on the way? Why are the trains so horrible? Too many questions begging for an answer.

After a while I grow too tired to keep my eyes open, but in the sleep-like trance that engulfs me, my mind enters a state of animated play-back. My life passes in front of me at a tremendous pace. Years become days, then hours... then seconds....soon time seems to have lost its meaning.

1939

Proclaim this among Nations:

Prepare for battle
Arouse the warriors
Let all the fighters come and draw near
Beat your plowshares into swords and your pruning hooks into spears
Let even the weakling say: I am strong
Rouse yourselves, and come!

Joel 4.9

Chapter 2

A Late Summer Morning

Sometimes sleep can be very rewarding. One wakes up invigorated, full of stamina and strength, ready to tackle whatever may come. At other times sleep can be exhausting, fearsome, and downright debilitating. You awake feeling as if the whole world had rested on your chest overnight. This is how I feel this morning.

Though my mind is still numb and my heart hardly beats, I begin to discern rings of the big clock on Freedom Square. Still groggy, I count them off: one, two, three… The seventh hour has struck. Time to get up! I open my eyes into the blinding daylight. It takes a while to get used to it. As if on order, my body automatically rises.

On my feet, I lean over the sill of the open window. Outside unfolds the morning of the first day in September 1939. The sun tries to break through the smog and early fog hanging over this eternally drab city. Scents of the approaching autumn combine with the stench of exhaust fumes that spew out of the countless high stacks burgeoning from the local textile factory buildings. The mix produces a strange aroma that saturates the cool morning air. It is beginning to feel like fall. Here and there, a few yellow leaves float in the air detached from misplaced and lonely trees.

The city is waking up. A few forgotten sparrows chirp merrily on the neighboring roof. Wagon drivers are heard urging their horses. Their shouts are mixed with bangs of window shutters being removed by store clerks, and the rattle of wagon wheels. Every few minutes another factory whistle blows. A new day is born, and with it my premonition that this day will be more important than any other day in my life. Before I fell asleep, father said that if war is to start, it will most likely start in September. This is the time when all crops are in, and food for the winter is safely stacked away in storage bins.

Our backyard is empty, only sounds of a radio receiver emanate from a neighbor's apartment. I turn away from the window. The stove is glowing hot, and a tea pot has just begun to burst its first puffs of steam, indicating that the water is coming to a boil and will be ready for tea brewing soon. My father's voice reaches me from the adjoining room:

"Lolek, Are you up? Come in here! Have you heard?" "Heard what, Dad? I was asleep!"

"This is no joke. The Germans claim that they were attacked by Polish military units. Another invention of Goebelsí propaganda machine. Their radio keeps on repeating that lie every ten minutes. They say that they were compelled to invade Poland to protect the fatherland. Eventually this will sound truthful to most German ears."

"Compelled, huh? What crap!" I reply in disgust. "Let me run down and see what's going on."

I slip into my pants, pull a shirt over my head, put on socks, shoes, and speedily descend three floors of steep stairs. The backyard slowly fills with neighbors. One puts his radio in the window and tunes it to a German radio station. A new transmission has just began. The voice of the announcer blares out:

"Achtung! Achtung! Hier ist Radio Gleiwitz und Goerlitz. Das Oberkommando der Wehrmacht gibt bekannt..."

The German language was not new to us. My father was forced into the German army, and the end of World War One found him in Brest-Litovsk with the newly formed Polish Legions. We were all multilingual, having been taught to speak at least two, sometimes three, languages. My maternal grandmother was very fluent in four, and saw to it that her children and grandchildren could converse in at least three tongues. At home we spoke Yiddish, German, Polish. Quite frequently, we conversed in a jargon that must have sounded very strange to outsiders.

A radio announcer went on to repeat in a slow, deliberate, tone what I had already heard from my father. He also declares that the advance of

German troops into Poland is proceeding smoothly, as planned. How ridiculous that sounds in light of the original announcement that the Poles planned the attack. How stupid. Who do they think they are dealing with, idiots? The radio boasts that Krakow is within reach of the German army as is the entire province of Polish Silesia. Poznan, another Polish city placed further north is being bypassed, but is expected to fall soon. The "citizens" of Danzig, meaning Nazis, have taken over the government and declared the city to be part of the Third Reich.

This news is truly disturbing. My anxiety increases with every fresh news item. We turn to radio Warsaw in the hope of hearing that the German radio announcements are a pack of lies, another example of Goebels' propaganda. What we hear instead is only patriotic music interrupted by military mobilization codes. Things are really bad! I am petrified. Where is the valiant and gallant Polish Army, the Air Force, and the Navy? Where are all the handsome officers in freshly pressed uniforms adorned with shining sabers on their sides I used to admire during national holiday parades? Where are the planes, the tanks, the cannons - the new Prime Minister bragged about only the other day?

I am not even sixteen years old. Yet, I managed to keep abreast of all major political developments over the past few years. My fondness for politics must have started in my mother's womb. I began to draw cartoons of politicians at a very early age. The faces of Blum, Laval, Pilsudski, Deladier, Smigly-Rydz, Mussolini, Chamberlain, Hitler, Stalin, Churchill, Eden, and so many more, are virtually engraved in my mind. It's a hobby that I genuinely enjoy, and hope to make use of in the near future.

We are living in very interesting times. All of those politicians running back and forth, as if their coat tails were on fire, look so ridiculous. The faces of the fascist dictators are a cartoonists dream. Drawings of politicians' heads literally swell my notebook.

Though often frightening, this year has also been terribly exciting. I frequently get a kick out of sports, movies, books, but nothing can be compared to the potential for a real live shootout on the stage of the world, and I am right in it! To follow the political moves on the European continent is like watching a good chess game. You may be kibitzing only, yet you try to anticipate the players' moves, and get excited when your intuition proves right.

The latest move on the political stage involves the Free City of Danzig. Germans living in that city have, at the prodding of the Fuehrer, become ever more persistent on joining with the fatherland. Just a couple of weeks ago the Polish Government issued orders to partly mobilize its armed forces. This came in response to Hitler's cancellation of the German-Polish non-aggression treaty. Poland signed this treaty only five years ago to protect their eastern borders. Following the cancellation, Ribbentrop, the German minister of foreign affairs, visited Moscow to sign a peace treaty with Stalin. Irony of ironies! Poland's non-aggression treaty with Hitler was primarily aimed at the USSR, and now Hitler signed one with Poland's foremost enemy - the very same Russian Bolsheviks the Poles aimed to protect themselves against. In light of these developments the Polish government began to freely encourage hostility toward the Germans. Sporadic demonstrations blossomed out in the streets like mushrooms after rain. Reason vanished. Irrational, chauvinistic, passions took over.

These gatherings quickly turned anti-Jewish, anti-Russian, anti-Czech, and anti-Lithuanian demonstrations. Ignorance and hate governed the day. The outraged cries of the mob still ring in my ears: Down with the Jews! Down with Hitler! Down with Stalin! Annex Zaolzie! March on Klajpeda!*

This past week, the demonstrations got real ugly. Some demonstrators turned against others accusing them of being German. Participating Jews, as well as Jews among the onlookers on the sidewalks, were pulled out, cursed at, and beaten.

Jews were easy targets. Most Jews somehow stood out in the crowd and could readily be recognized. Because of that they rarely dared to leave the predominantly Jewish neighborhoods of this city. That's where they felt safe. This time, though, we thought things would be different. After all, don't we face a common enemy? Isn't it time we forgot about hatred, and mobilized all the strength we could master?

Apparently not. The deeply rooted hatred prevails. The Jews are the people who crucified God's only Son, who use Christian kid's blood for their un-leaven bread, who are either communists or capitalist determined to exploit the poor Poles. To many a Pole the Jew is the common enemy, and Hitler's attitude toward Jews is justified. If only he could limit his appetite for conquest and subjugation and stick to his basic Jew-hatred, he might have been accepted by the broad Polish masses.

It is not easy to erase prejudice that has been implanted and nourished over centuries. In this Polish society anti-Semitism was taught in schools, preached from the pulpits, and passed on from generation to generation. Most of us are not surprised that Jew-hatred has placed us in line with the enemies of the State.

Yet, the government has called upon its Jewish citizen to make their contribution to the defense of the country. A cousin of mine was called into the army just two weeks ago. He is a sergeant in the engineering reserves. Before he left to join his division, he dropped by in his woolen khaki uniform to bid us good-bye. I was proud, and envious, watching this tall, handsome, man in full military dress. I wished I was old enough to join him. What a thrill that would be. He left with tears in his eyes uttering only, "Till we meet again - *Do widzenia*.". We sure hope to see him back soon.

I run back to our apartment to update my family on the latest developments. Some relatives and friends arrive. All of us are distressed, concerned, and feel the need to meet in groups. Other people may know more. Who knows? They may even have direct information from the front. Together we head for the street.

Groups of people have gathered here and there. One can tell by the excited loud conversations, accentuated by hand gestures that these are mostly Jews. I approach one of the larger assemblies. The topic is the war and what to do about it. Some insist that the proper thing to do is to help defend the capital of Poland -- that means we should march toward Warsaw. This argument is supported by the fact that Polish soldiers are nowhere to be seen. Should the Germans break through; our city will not be defended. The next line of defense will be around Warsaw.

Others find it unreasonable to leave home at this time. They argue that an exodus from the city will only clog the main roads. Our empty homes will attract all kinds of thieves and looters. We may not have a place to come back to. Still others try to assure themselves that the situation isn't really that bleak. The Polish army has had a history of valor and heroism and can stop the Germans and teach them a lesson they will never forget- let's wait. These discussions go on and on. Frustrated, I break away. A visit to my maternal grandmother's place may provide some reassurance. She always knows what is right to do under any circumstances.

My grandparents live only one block away from our house. The fog is slowly dissipating, disclosing an azure blue sky interspersed with puffy white clouds which lazily sail along the vast, heavenly emporium that stretches way above the low, lingering smog. The sun rises, and on its way spreads its warm, soothing rays over the murky streets which seem to come alive, encouraged by the warm light. On the corner, horse-drawn taxis, called Dorozkas, stand in a row, vainly waiting for a customer. The smell of fresh horse manure is in the air. A driver feeds his horse with water from a tin bucket. Every so often the horse pulls its nose out of the bucket, shakes his head, and whinnies merrily. On the sidewalk, a man pushes a wagon ahead of him filled with grinding and sharpening tools. He loudly announces his presence: "Come, get your scissors and knives sharpened! Here today may not be here tomorrow

Chapter 3
GRANDPARENTS' HOME

My grandparents' walk-up flat is on the fourth floor of a crowded and large, for the existing standards, stucco building. They share a three-room apartment with six of my cousins -- children of their oldest daughter Debra. The cousins became orphaned following their father's death of blood poisoning, and shortly thereafter, their mother's lost fight with tuberculosis. My grandparents, took in all six orphans, and raised them as their own. My mother, who at her sister's death bed promised to help out, did her share by teaching the girls her trade, that of a seamstress. These were not grandparents' first adoptions. At the end of the last century they also adopted two orphaned nieces, one of whom left for London, and the other for New York.

The oldest of Debra's children were twin girls, Bella and Sheina. Bella commenced work as an apprentice in my mother's atelier. After roughly five years she was ready to establish an atelier of her own, in which her two sisters, Ita and Sara, in turn, went through the learning process. Sara and her brother Izaak were also twins. They were the youngest of the batch. Another brother, David, became a tailor and after having finished his apprenticeship with a well-known local ladies coat maker, joined his sister Bella's enterprise. Sheina seemed to be bored most of the time. She neither had the taste for nor the desire to learn a trade. She wound up as grandmother's helper, cleaning the apartment, shopping, and helping to prepare meals.

About two years ago, Sheina decided to move to Palestine to join her paternal aunt who was married, but childless, and lived in Tel-Aviv. A year ago we learned that Sheina married. Shortly afterward, she had a son whom she named David.

Izaak also exhibited signs of unhappiness and refused to get himself a steady job. He was now twenty-two years old, and did not appear to mind being supported by his siblings. His major preoccupation was hanging around the sports club Maccabee, and chasing women, rather indiscriminately. He didn't care what the female looked like, how old she was, or of what religion. As long as she wore a skirt, she presented a target for his desires.

In addition to Debra, grandmother had two other daughters, Hannah and Esther, as well as two sons: Izaak and Chaim. Hannah was once a very beautiful woman. Toward the end of World War I, she met and married a man named Haim D. She bore him three children; two sons named Icek and Julek, and a daughter Itka. Haim was rich at the time. He made his money in the fresh fruit wholesale business and in real estate. The end of the war found him gambling his fortune away in Monte Carlo. Huge losses forced him to move the gambling closer to home to a resort by the Baltic Sea named Zoppot. The Zoppot casinos were his hangouts until he lost his entire fortune. He finished penniless, then borrowed enough cash to open a retail fruit store.

As kids, we loved to visit the store. There were always aged bananas, pears, plums, or peaches around which could not be sold to customers, and had to be eaten or thrown out. Besides, there was also a movie house -- the *Corso* -around the corner that showed mostly American cowboy pictures, and we loved cowboys. Tom Mix, Ken Maynard and William Desmond were the screen heroes of my early childhood.

With time, the fruit business had to be closed for lack of credit. Haim tried different things to support his family. At last he became a tobacco and condom salesman. In spite of his financial setbacks, gambling remained in his blood. He was constantly ready to drop whatever he was doing for a poker or blackjack game. He wore pince-nez rather than framed glasses. They made him look, somehow, more prosperous, and, possibly brought on a reminder of the good old times. In reality, he was a very sick, and prematurely aged, man. I would frequently meet him in the street dragging a suitcase full of merchandise, and coughing profusely. He was a chain smoker and the spit- soaked cigar or cigarette never left his mouth. Some said he even chewed on them in his sleep.

Icek, Haim's eldest son, was a tall, handsome fellow, with dark eyes, pitch-black hair, and a dimple in his chin. At twenty-two, he was getting more attention from the weaker sex than he could or, for that matter, was willing to handle. He, too, was a tailor. He worked at one of the most exquisite women's coat ateliers in town. His brother Julek was, in contrast, short, but also good-looking like his older brother. We used to call them Pat and Patachon, after the famous comic duo, where Pat was a thin, tall fellow and Patachon a corpulent short one. My Father got Julek into the textile business and taught him weaving. Their sister Itka, an attractive teenager, caused more than one sleepless night for her parents. She frequently attended "Five o'clock" dances that lasted deep into the night. That she was intimate with boys was no secret. Grandmother, angered by her independence and defiance, called her "the tramp." Itka worked in Bella's seamstress atelier.

Grandmother's favorite child, my maternal uncle Izaak, was taken into the Russian czarist army before the outbreak of World War I. This was when the city was still occupied by Russians. He served as an interpreter and was discharged right before the war's end with the rank of lieutenant, and an advanced case of tuberculosis. He died shortly thereafter. Chaim, grandmother's youngest son, failed to meet her expectations. He turned into a bum, refused to work, and, two years before the start of World War I, was given a one-way ticket to America.

The older of my grandparents' two daughters, Esther, is my mother.

My maternal grandmother is of short stature, but tall in wisdom and understanding. She wears a wig, as befits a righteous and religious orthodox Jewess. The wig hides a pair of carefully combed out and plaited gray braids. Judging from old family portraits she was once an attractive woman. But by the time I knew her, age had begun to take its toll. Her eyes are now covered with cataracts, and lost their original sparkle and color. Her face, always adorned with a glowing maternal smile, became deformed by a stroke, and the smile turned into a strange, twisted grimace. Heavy wrinkles cover her forehead, cheeks, and eyes. She suffers from osteoporosis and walks stooped with her shoulders above the neck. We, her grandchildren, called her "Bubbe".

My grandfather is an unusually quiet, reserved man. He is tall and erect in stature. His head is bald and shiny. A prominent nose protrudes from an otherwise wrinkled face adorned with a trimmed, rounded gray beard. The nose supports his wire-rimmed glasses, which cover a pair of sentimental dark eyes. His eyes are separated by a sizeable boil that protrudes like the horn of a rhinoceros. Grandfather is an orthodox Jew, and as such always wears the orthodox garb consisting of a long black coat, white shirt, black pants, and shoes. A black cap known as the "Jewish Cap" always covers his head.

When grandfather was still a boy, he learned the weaving trade, bought a weaving loom with a shuttle, and earned a living producing material for smaller textile enterprises. He retired about ten years ago. Now, a good deal of his time is spent praying in the synagogue three times a day and filling in the rest of the day helping Bubbe. We call him Zaide. At family gatherings he mostly stays aside. His primary function on these occasions is to prepare a little shot of vodka diluted with sweetened water, into which a piece of lemon rind is squeezed for good taste. This hospitality is extended to everyone, including his grandchildren, who are permitted to taste it starting at the age of about five. We like this brew. It warms us up and makes us feel good.

Bubbe's place is open to all of her children and grandchildren. Her house is our oasis. Bubbe is always ready and eager to shield, reach out, and provide help in soothing an injured leg or ego. It is, therefore, not unusual that at a time like this I would seek shelter and consolation in Bubbe's home. Even in normal times I somehow always felt more comfortable discussing my problems, whatever they might be, with Bubbe, rather than with my own parents. They were too busy eking out a living.

As I near my grandmother's house I can see a group of familiar faces approaching from the opposite side. There is Izaak D., his brother Julek, and their sister Itka. They, apparently had the same idea, or urge to be together, when they heard of the latest developments.

We meet at the gate, exchange the traditional "servus" greeting and proceed up to the fourth floor along a set of old wooden stairs. I am the youngest of this group, and mainly to show-off, run skipping two or three steps at a time. On the fourth floor I enter the apartment. My cousins aren't far behind. Only Julek D. is held back by a friend he met at the house gate.

The apartment, in which Bubbe, Zaide and my six cousins live, consists of a huge room partitioned into one large and one small room, and an adjacent tiny windowless room. A single large window faces the backyard. The larger room serves as a bedroom, a client fitting room, and partly also as a working room for Bella's and David's atelier. The smaller partitioned room provides storage and additional sleeping and working space. The clients, who come to try on their clothing, are shielded by a folding screen. Only two beds remain standing during the day. The others are folded away and placed in the working room. Bubbe and Zaide live in the adjacent, windowless, small room which serves as a kitchen, and bedroom. This has become my second home.

Following my graduation from elementary school, two years ago, I enrolled in night high school, and began working for my cousin David. At first I would carry out the simpler tasks like delivery, basting, or finish stitching of coat linings. With time, I was permitted to do more advanced work such as machine sewing of sleeves and finish machining of other coat parts which enter into the assembly. Much of the time, I would sit by the large window, stitching and singing, or whistle in harmony with the other cousins who worked there.

We frequently sang to the music of yard bands which seemed to drop by every hour or two for a backyard performance. A few coins wrapped in paper were always ready to be tossed down through the open window for the traveling concert makers. After a while we became very good at group singing of the latest pop songs and in whistling tunes we picked up from the latest Fred Astaire, Deanna Durbin and Shirley Temple movies we saw at the Capitol movie theater on the corner of our block. We were ardent movie goers. American movies created fantasy worlds in which we could lose ourselves and dream of a better future. We all entertained the hope that the world would offer us a better and brighter future than our drab present. In the meantime, we must be satisfied with our film-inspired dreams and other illusions sometimes provided by horoscopes and card readings.

Chapter 4
THE GYPSY

There were many Gypsies, always traveling from place to place. They camped at the city's outskirts with their crated wagons, skinny horses, and multitudes of children. It was a colorful lot, seemingly poor but happy. They went from door- to-door, yard-to-yard, earning their pay by dancing, singing, playing the violin, fortune-telling and, yes, sometimes stealing. Each gypsy "pack" had a king, who ran the show and collected the earnings or bounty off his subjects.

One day, I recall, a gypsy woman dressed in colorful garb came to the door of Bubbe's apartment. Long pitch-black shiny braids matched the color of her eyes. A red rose-imprinted babushka with a gold rim covered her head. Her, black, bushy eyebrows appeared to be in concert with the slight fuzzy mustache on her crimson upper lip.

The Gypsy woman was insistent, and cousin Bella decided to invite her in for a card séance. That day Bella was particularly curious what the future had in store for her. She had just broken off with a neighbor whom she had dated over the past eight years. Bella was of medium height, with a sparkling personality. A bright, friendly smile almost always adorned her face. She was twenty-nine and anxious to get married. Her twin sister had married in Palestine, and already had a baby.

Not long ago, Bella had been introduced by an adoring married neighbor to his brother Yakov. He had just returned from four years in Palestine, where he had worked on a kibbutz. He was looking to get married, and return with his wife to the kibbutz. The other day, they had their first date. She liked Yakov, and was curious whether he liked her enough to, perhaps, even marry her.

After a small bargaining prelude, Bella agreed to pay the price the gypsy demanded, providing that she also read her sister's, Ita's, and my future. The gypsy woman agreed. She spread her wide skirt, and sat down at the cutting table which we quickly cleared of work. She reached into her skirt pocket and produced a much-used dirty, old, strangely deformed deck of cards. As if to provide the proper background, she took a wide, colorful scarf off her hips, spread it on the table, shuffled the cards, carefully squared off the deck, and placed them in front of Bella, asking her to cut. Slowly, and with apparent premeditation, the Gypsy posted on the table the first seven cards, face up. Having carefully scanned them, and examined her subject with piercing eyes, the Gypsy proceeded to talk.

"Madam, I see good things happening to you in the very near future" she said, stopped for a while, closed her eyes, and sighed, as if to gain inspiration.

"Go on!" my cousin urged, anxious to find out what fate had in store.

"Madam mustn't be so anxious. I have to read my cards as they appear. Madam is looking for the truth. No? "

After a while she continued: Madam will have luck in love, I see a gentleman entering madam's life" She again paused for a while and continued, emphasizing every word. "This gentleman has serious intentions."

By now Bella, full of expectations and curiosity, had obvious trouble holding herself back. "Where will he come from?" she asked.

"Madam must be patient. He is a tall man and comes from overseas. He wants to marry Madam and take her back home".

At this point all of us onlookers gasped almost simultaneously. The Gypsy woman, sensing that she was onto something real, continued:

"Madam will marry this man and bear him a child."

I watched my cousin's face turning red. She began to tap with her fingers on the tabletop as if to release the pent-up curiosity.

"Madam will travel, but not very far," the Gypsy said as she pulled her next series of cards.

Suddenly her face saddened. She paused for a while, then said:

"Madam must be careful to avoid men in uniform", but quickly continued as if to get away from the subject, "Madam will have a good marriage. There will be lots of love in this family".

Bella, now very excited asked, "How about life? Health?"

The gypsy stretched out her hand and asked Bella to rest her palm on hers.

She examined the myriad of lines running in all directions, carefully looked at the fingertips, and then said, "Madam. I see tougher times ahead, but I cannot tell what this means. I don't like to speculate." She stopped, and declared the session over.

The next in line was Ita. She was single, and had no immediate prospects for marriage. She didn't have male friends, nor can I remember her ever going out on a date. Ita was a tall, thin girl with dark blond hair and grayish blue eyes. Her face was elongated and always serious. She hardly ever smiled, and when she did the smile seemed to be forced. She worked in Bella's atelier and in addition to sewing was entrusted with the financial aspects of the operation. In very few words she was the family accountant and banker.

The Gypsy shuffled the deck and placed it in front of Ita, asking her to cut. Ita hesitated at first then cut the deck with an obviously trembling hand. A deuce of spades came up followed by six other cards. The Gypsy appeared confused, thought for a while and said:

"Madam, I see money in your past and present. You are surrounded by it. It is in your pockets, and in your mind. That is all I can say."

Ita grimaced: "What happens to the money?" she asked in an uncertain voice.

The gypsy looked up, coughed, as if to prolong the answer, and quietly said, "I see money now, but the future is not clear," and quickly added, "Madam has no reason to be concerned at this time."

"Do you see any change in my status? Any men?" inquired Ita.

"Madam has not been lucky with men, and this may continue for the next year or two. After that I see madam's luck changing." The Gypsy woman's voice dropped to the point where it was almost inaudible, "Hopefully for the better."

Ita's face turned red, her eyes bulging from their sockets. She shouted, "You are a thief, a faker, a liar! Were it not for my sister, I would have never let you over this threshold."

Obviously boiling mad, Ita stood up and left the table with an expression of disgust and disbelief on her face. The Gypsy didn't utter a word. She just sat there motionless for a while and then nodded to me to come closer to the table. I was next.

I cut the cards the Gypsy handed me, and she proceeded to lay them out.

"The young master has a bright future in front of him, but he will have to struggle to get there. I see sickness and sorrow, but after a while I see the sun shining again." She appeared to be very enthused as she continued: "Master will travel far -- beyond wide oceans -- I see a wedding and children. The words seemed to be pouring out of her uninhibitedly. "I see a long life, not very rich, but comfortable."

She took my palm and kept on reading: "Master's long life will be disrupted by illness many times, but Master will come out of it all right."

After a while, she stated, "Now, I have spent enough time here. Please let me have my pay." With these words she declared the séance finished, stood up, gathered her belongings, collected the agreed upon reward, and swiftly left the flat saying *"Blogoslaw Boze"*. I didn't like the tone of her voice. "What the hell did she mean by that?" I wondered. She asked God to bless us. Was she just trying to be nice, or did she know more than she told us? In the end it wasn't really that important. The whole thing was a joke. Why did Bella invite her in the first place?

The entire Gypsy fortune-telling episode was soon forgotten.

Chapter 5
THE SMELL OF WAR

The large room of my grandparents' apartment buzzes with excitement. Finally, after all those long years of useless negotiations, the shameful appeasement of the Nazis has stopped. The war is on! Most of us are elated. No more Munich's. No more Chamberlains!

Julek enters the room, "Have you heard the latest?" Julek's voice is full of excitement "They say that France and England will soon declare war on Germany."

"Hurray! Vivat!

The discussions become more lively and animated. A sort of happiness bordering on jubilation fills the room. Hitler will finally be taken care of! Why France will probably attack at any moment now. They have the Maginot line and have no reason to fear German attacks. Can you imagine an impenetrable line like this? Too bad Poland did not think of that! Boy, Poles will never learn how to take care of themselves! England cannot remain far behind, you see Poland has friendship treaties with France and England, they must act quickly to meet their terms. Now, the U.S.A, Canada, Australia, and all the British colonies will also join in soon. So here you are, in a couple of months the whole thing will be over.

What about the Russians? They don't like the Poles. They still remember the defeats in the wake of World War I. But aren't the communists Hitler's worst enemies? Why, can't you see? It is in the Soviets' interest to postpone war with Germany. They will come in later after the antagonists have bled themselves to death. Stalin has tanks that are three stories high. Can you imagine? All that power will now be patiently waiting to enter as a final arbiter. Do you really believe that the Soviets are strong? They will never be able to muster an army to defeat even a weakened Germany, never mind the Allies. But what if France and England were to make peace with Hitler? God forgive! They cannot do that! He will swallow them piece by piece as he swallowed the smaller countries. Italy? Italians are lovers, not soldiers. They couldn't handle Negus in Abyssinia. These and other opinions are being tossed around, examined, and interpreted with incredible passion in the heat of our discourse.

Suddenly, the shrieking sound of sirens. Simultaneously the radio announces that foreign aircraft have been spotted in the skies. The sound of exploding bombs fills the air. Panic strikes.

"Wet your kerchiefs and place them against your nose," someone shouts.

I feel faint. Do I smell gas? Can it be that the Germans are resorting to its use so early in the war? Why, it's barely begun! All the stories about the use of chemical warfare suddenly flash before me. Will I die or become permanently disabled and hoarse like that man I once was introduced to by my father? He fought on the Western front in World War I, and was stuck for months at Verdun. At last the sirens stop their hounding squeal. A few minutes pass which seem to stretch into hours. Then quiet.

No more explosions. I am alive, and so is everybody else. The clear alarm sounds. The bombing is over. "The enemy planes are gone," the radio announcer proclaims. Bubbe, as we would expect, has kept her cool. Now on her way into the room with a pile of wet towels to be used as the poor man's gas masks, she stops and unloads her burden.

"Kids," she says. "It is not good for you to be away from your parents at times like these. The clear has sounded. Go home quickly."

There are no objections. We make our way to the door. One by one we kiss Bubbe good-bye, and descend into the street. The ringing of fire engine bells can be heard coming from every direction. The shiny new trucks speed past fully manned with firemen dressed in their long black coats and helmets. Not too long ago these engines were driven by huge Belgian horses. The improvements were instituted by our mayor whose objective was to have the best fire department in Europe. Walking down the street and watching the engines pass, I feel assured by this competent force responding in such timely fashion to the emergency calls. How I hope the Army were that way too, I mumble to myself, as I near the grey stucco apartment house -- my home.

Chapter 6
Our Place

The house I live in is located on a narrow street paved with round stones the size of a cat's head; hence the name cat-head stones. The concrete sidewalks are cracked and full of potholes. We live only one block away from the city's main drag, and two blocks from the centrally located Freedom Square.

The Freedom Square is surrounded by commercial buildings, the City Hall, and a church. At the center of it is a four story tall obelisk-like monument with a statue of the Polish freedom fighter Tadeusz Kosciuszko standing tall and proud on the very top of it. Copper cast murals, depicting various episodes from his life, surround the elevated base. One mural shows his victory over the Russians in the battle for independence, a victory that was soon followed by defeat and banishment. Others portray his experiences in the American Revolution. He was one of the more prominent generals there, and was given credit for his contributions to victories in a number of battles against the English. There is even one mural showing him shaking hands with George Washington. Poor Tad died in exile in Switzerland. Never saw a free Poland.

A large house gate terminates the passage connecting the street to our backyard. By law the gate is closed and locked every evening at 11 p.m. Only the house superintendent keeps the keys and anyone returning after 11 p.m. must ring a bell and properly identify himself before the superintendent unlocks the gates to let him. On both sides of the entry hall are staircases leading to individual apartments. Our apartment is located on the third floor.

A red painted and lacquered door exhibits a small copper sign engraved with our name and right under it "Ladies Atelier". This is my mother's business - she designs and makes ladies dresses, to order. The handle of a manually actuated bell sticks out just below the sign. Inside, the apartment consists of a small entry hall, a reception room, which also serves as a fitting room for my mothers customers, and a combination bedroom, work room, and kitchen.

The reception room is small but clean and rather elegantly furnished. The floors are red, waxed and shiny. A furniture set, purchased from a Polish nobleman and given to my parents as a wedding gift, provides the main garnish. The antique set consists of a small table with four chairs, a commode, and two large paintings. The table top is chiseled with a beautiful and intricate oak leaf pattern. Its legs are also carved with oak leaves. The same pattern is present on the high backs of the green upholstered chairs. The commode with Corinthian columns on each side, ostensibly supporting the top on which crystal vases and bowls are displayed, is decorated throughout with the same leaf motif, as are its doors, and the frames of two huge pictures which complete this set.

The pictures are entitled "D*ie Goldene Hochzeit*" and "Die *Silberne Hochzeit*", which stand for The Gold and Silver Anniversary. These are rare engravings. A very limited edition, both signed by the same artist. The entire set is made of black mahogany. Next to the large picture window, covered with many types of perennial plants and flowers, is a mirror with two drawer sets on each side. The mirror has two movable wings and a full body-sized center. It is placed there specifically for my mother's clients to view themselves during dress fittings. The walls are painted with a light green texture decorated with tiny red leaves; so is a door which leads into what we call the living room.

The "living room" is the center of all activity. This is where we live. Two large beds, moved against one wall, partition the room into two sections. A large window covers one wall. The section next to the window is the work station. Here, three girls sew dresses under my mother's direction. There is one heavy and one lighter sewing machine. A small table serves as the cutting table on which my mother cuts the materials which eventually turn into beautiful, chic dresses. An ironing board with a perpetually heated charcoal iron, that I frequently tend to, complete the work station.

On the other side of the beds is a couch, a small dining table with four chairs, a large commode, and a cast iron coal stove for cooking and baking. A round steel duct with two adjustment elbows connects the stove to a hole in the wall. This arrangement, in addition to making a vent, also helps to distribute the heat in the winter. The long extended pipe is an excellent heat distributor. A wooden bench supports the wash bowl, water pitcher, and a large water bucket. Our tap water is of very poor quality, and drinking water has to be carried in from the fountain on Liberty Square. The double window, covered with white lace curtains, faces the street. Another window, located in the dressing room, faces the backyard.

The yard is well cordoned-off on three sides by the rear walls of the neighboring houses. A picket fence girds the yard on the fourth side.

Part of the backyard serves as a dump for lead slugs produced by linotype machines belonging to a nearby printing shop. Another part is occupied by a winter fuel dealer. Big trucks or, more frequently, horse drawn wagons, regularly unload or pick up wood and coal for distribution. This activity leaves an almost continual cloud of fine coal dust in the air.

A couple of years ago things were even worse. The recently installed sewage system did not yet exist. In its place a huge outhouse occupied a good portion of the backyard. It was always filthy. Even the small cubicles, with access restricted to building inhabitants, could not be kept clean. In fear of catching some venereal diseases people preferred to stand on the seat, and judging by the results, their aim left a lot to be desired.

Beside the outhouse was the garbage dump. A wooden platform with a centrally located small gate made for a cover. The platform was old and rotten, leaving most of the garbage exposed. Rats, the size of hares, played joyfully in this stinking mess. With time, we learned to recognize them and gave them names taken from cartoons which preceded the main features in our local movie theaters. Every second week or so, a large horse-drawn wagon arrived and cleaned the garbage dump. Another barrel-like wagon would show up with a huge pump to empty the outhouse slime at the beginning of every month. I was told by my father that this refuse turns into an excellent fertilizer when sprayed onto farmer's fields. The fact that the produce thus grown found its way to our kitchen table never bothered me, although at times, when perched on the seat in our outhouse, I would marvel at this heavenly transition.

In the yard stood a water pump with a large, double-rimmed inertia wheel. To pump the water a bucket was placed underneath, or hung on the protruding sprout. The wheel was then turned until the water began to appear and the bucket was filled up. As children, we would use the wheel handles as seats and hang on to them as the wheels rims were moved by other kids. This was our Ferris wheel. True, it was a dangerous way of relieving our energies, but in lieu of better playing facilities it had to do.

Chapter 7
GOOD NEIGHBORS?

The house we live in has recently changed. Before that change it was kind of unique. The most amusing part of it was its backyard outhouse. At night this outhouse turned into a whorehouse. The two compartments, left open intentionally for public use, served as working holes for a few local prostitutes. Their business soon became the basis of a game that we, the local children, invented. We tried to guess during the "negotiations", which were taking place on the street in front of our gate, whether the John would buy or not. Each right guess earned a point. The score was further expanded by guessing the duration of the stay in the outhouse.

Some of the Johns looked like university professors, others like poor blue collar workers. As for the latter, Friday evening was their prime time. Pay checks in their pockets, they would first stop in a local tavern, have a few for the road, then visit a whore before wobbling home on their, by now, highly insecure legs. Sometimes, Jews dressed in the Chassidic garb, with long beards and side-locks, dropped by hiding their faces behind a newspaper. It seemed they wanted to taste the forbidden fruit, before heading home after a long and exhausting business day.

The installation of modern sewage systems and running water in each apartment deprived us of a lot, but by no means all, of this fun. The old outhouse was replaced by a new, sewer connected and water equipped, brick house tastefully ornamented on the outside with small figures made of cement. A large white painted door with a strong lock limited entrance to the tenants only. Inside, clean partitioned cubicles, also locked, provided restricted access for specific tenant key holders. Each cubicle was shared by four tenants. The place was maintained by the superintendent in excellent shape. This modernization had an obvious adverse effect on the prostitution business, and the girls were compelled to find a new working spot.

Soon, a vacancy sign appeared on the gate of our house. An apartment, located on the first floor, with easy access from the street, was for rent. Before long it was rented by a very distinguished and prosperous looking couple. They renovated it, and moved in. All tenants were elated. The old tenant who occupied this place never took care of it. The rooms were run-down. The windows dirty. A foul smell emanated from the place. At last we would have clean and decent tenants. Our new neighbors apparently had no children. That, too, was a blessing. Our apartment house was overcrowded with kids. They constantly played in the stairways or backyard. They became a nuisance blocking the way for the older people. All that noise and commotion deprived our neighbors, who worked on the second shift, of much needed sleep. So, for a while, all tenants were happy with this turn of events.

One evening, a couple of weeks after our new tenants moved in, my father came home from work visibly annoyed. He whispered something into my mother's ear. She immediately responded with: "and I thought they were such nice and decent people!" The exchange that followed left little doubt in my mind that he was solicited by our new lady-tenant, a couple of blocks away, on his way home from work.

This was big news! I quickly ran down the stairs into the backyard and on the way notified all kids I met of the new discovery.

From that day on our old games came to life again.

About a month after this discovery, petitions were passed around asking the landlord to evict the little bordello. It took about a year to do it but at the end of August it happened. One day, clerks from the housing authority arrived, and accompanied by local policemen, carried out the eviction. The policemen were not happy. They stood there with sad, elongated faces, probably mourning the loss of their weekly payoff. Bribery was a good part of the cop's income. In this society almost everyone could be bought.

Chapter 8

LAST CALM DAY

Sounds of fire engines always invoked in me a combination of fear and excitement. I relax as the fire engines pass, and the street becomes eerily quiet following the bombing attack. Queues of people which formed at the food, clothing, and fuel stores to purchase whatever might have been left over, have disappeared. Merchants are gradually closing their stores. Shutters are going up, and locks are installed over the steel cross-bars. The city shuts down. The first Sabbath of the war will soon arrive.

In our apartment, father is busy cutting long strips of paper. A big jar of glue is on the table. Apparently, the radio has just given instructions to paste long, end-to-end strips on window panes. The strips should prevent the pane from being blown out. Instructions also call for keeping the windows covered with a blanket or heavy paper to make the city less visible at night to enemy bombers. Mother sends the girls home. There will be no more work today, nor tomorrow. Now she is busy digging out the blankets from the cupboard. My sister, Deborah, helps her.

Deborah, Debra for short, is the youngest of Bubbe's grandchildren. She was named after my mother's sister, who died prematurely after having brought the six siblings into this world. She is a bright, intelligent, and a pretty twelve year old. She has a slightly oval face of very white complexion, straight light brown hair, brown eyes, and a perked-up little nose. Next year she will finish public school, and should times improve, may go on to high school.

This past summer Debra spent in a village not far from the city. The whole family, from my maternal grandparents down, rented a cottage for the summer, and we alternated taking one or two weeks of vacation each. Only Debra stayed for the whole summer season. This gave her frail body a chance to convalesce in fresh country air. She returned just about a week ago with a deep tan and healthy appearance. After the long, harsh Polish winters, we all can use a nice vacation. But, now that the summer is almost over it is of no use to dream about junkets in the sun. More urgent things remain to be done.

Before the depression life was entirely different. The whole family would rent a large villa for the summer. Mother's business was prospering. She had one of the finest ateliers in town. Her customers used to arrive in chauffeur-driven cars. Father had a good job as a textile engineer. We lived in a huge, elegantly adorned stone building, right across the street from Bubbe's place. The apartment was large and comfortable. There was hot water, a bathtub, toilet, sinks, a gas kitchen, and lots of play space. The building was well kept up. The tenants were mostly professional people: businessmen, doctors, teachers, lawyers. The place was ideal for my parents, but we, their children, were not exactly enthused by it. I recall that the slightest noise created by us, while playing in the circular, red-tiled backyard, was cause for immediate complaints by one or more of the tenants. Within minutes the superintendent was there, chasing us off the yard into our apartments.

The depression had a dreadful impact on the family. Mother's business declined. Father lost his job and had to settle for a weaver's job in one of the big textile factories. We could not carry the rent. My parents struggled for some time trying to hang onto their home, but eventually had to move. Over the past eight years we have been squeezed into two rooms, and must make the best of it.

I help father with the window stripes. When this is done we try out the blankets. It looks all right. We are ready for the German planes. Let them come and they will only find the pitch black night. That is if the moon will cooperate. Mother starts cooking the traditional Sabbath dinner. There will be sweet carp in gelatin sauce, chicken soup with rice, brisket of beef with sweet, red cabbage, sweet carrots, mashed potatoes, followed by apple cake and tea. This has been a tough day for all of us. Mother, in particular, worked hard to keep the house in order, do the work, and prepare dinner. Now, she looks tired and complains of a severe headache.

Chapter 9
HEADACHES AND CANDLES

Mother has been having migraine headaches for a long time. I once overheard my cousin Bella tell her friend a story about how mother's headaches began. She was not aware I was nearby, listening behind a partition. Apparently, a few months after the wedding, my father began to return from work very late at night. When asked by mother where he had been, he would say that he was busy working at the party's headquarters. As a member of the social- democratic Bund, he must contribute two to three hours a night. Every member does it and he cannot be different. This answer did not fully satisfy mother. She complained to my Bubbe who, in her wisdom, suggested that mother use Bella, who at that time worked for her, as a detective.

One day Bella, dressed in a long coat with a hood over her head, waited in front of father's work place. Finally, the doors opened and the employees began to file out. There was father rushing through the gates. Bella followed him to a house located within a five minute walk from the factory. She saw him climb two sets of stairs and disappear behind a door. Bella sneaked up to the same floor and knocked at the neighbor's door. A little old lady cracked the door open and asked Bella what she wanted. "Does this apartment belong to the "Bund"? Bella asked pointing at the door behind which father disappeared. The lady laughed. "You must have the wrong address. There is no "Bund" here, besides I don't like those social-democrats, I am a Zionist". "Then would you mind telling me who lives here? I may have been given this address because the tenants are party members". "You are correct", said the old woman, "the tenant is a young lady who does belong to the "Bund". "Well, I am sorry," said Bella "That explains it. It was my mistake".

As soon as the old lady closed the door, Bella noted the apartment number and left in a hurry. Mother, when informed of this, decided to face father that very evening. Bella stayed on as a witness to the scene. As soon as he came home, instead of putting the warmed up dinner in front of him, mother, in a trembling and emotional voice, suggested that he go back to his lover if he wanted to eat. There would be no dinner tonight!

Father got mad, screamed some irrational excuses, and left the house. The next eve he was back home, begging for forgiveness and promising, from now on, to be true. Mother accepted his pleas, but as time went by there were a few other meetings with the same girl. Mother got tired of fighting and for my, and her own, sake (my sister was yet to be conceived) decided to give it time.

Meanwhile, mother suffered from these infidelity junkets. She worked hard, running the atelier, cleaning house, cooking, and taking care of me. Bella adored her, and helped mother as much as she could. Still, this way of living took its toll, and mother developed acute migraine headaches which continuously pestered her. The birth of my sister and the renewed fidelity of my father should have brought on some relief, but her workload increased considerably, and the headaches persisted.

The dinner is ready, the table set. Today, Friday, the meal is at a later hour. Normally we would eat dinner at one or two p.m. On Fridays, we had dinner in the evening, as tradition would have it. This, in spite of father's agnostic convictions.

Mother lights two candles nestled in a tall, nicely decorated, silver candelabra. She covers her face with her hands. Remains there for a while, murmuring the prayers and sobbing, while we watch with halted breaths, and grouching stomachs. Finally, she uncovers her face, and utters the Friday night blessings circling her arms about the lit flames.

I love to watch the candle blessing ceremony. This custom is part of my heritage and upbringing. I get excited, and my heart speeds up a bit, as I see the flame of the match take hold of the wick and produce a beautiful collage of colors in which tiny fire crackers jump merrily around. The wick's pointed flame reaches upward towards the ceiling, and flickers at the suggestion of the slightest air movement. The smell of the burning wax fills the air. I watch and wonder. Here, right before my eyes, the processes of creation, consumption, and final extinction, appear in the lit candles. Later a cloud of smoke emanating from the empty holder will confirm the end. The candle will be gone, but the gas it creates will linger on. "Will it be dissipated all over the globe? What will it turn into?, For how long, and then what?", I wonder gazing at the candles' flames.

This evening dinner is consumed in silence. I can feel the heavy shadow of uncertainty hanging over our table. As soon as the meal is finished and the table cleared, we turn to the radio. The Polish stations continue to play solemn marches, interspersed, now and then, with mobilization codes. The Germans keep on announcing new successes. And so it goes for the entire evening. I lie down on the couch and reach for the latest book I have borrowed from the library. It is Remarque's *"Im Western Nichts Neues"*. I look at the title and grin. It isn't really all quiet on the western front. To the contrary, there is war, just like twenty five years ago. Mr. Remarque, you must have hoped, writing this book, that wars would end with the Great One. Alas, history does repeat itself.

I lift my head from the book - my parents and sister must have long gone to sleep. My father's snoring is getting louder. I undress and join my father in the already warmed up bed. As I undress I wonder what the future has in store for us.

Chapter 10
MY EDUCATION

Book reading was my passion. From early childhood on I was encouraged by my parents to read books. I was taught to read at the age of four. One day my Zaide took me to a religious school for youngsters known as a *'cheder'*. He registered me and introduced me to the teacher, a 'Rebbe', with a long beard and solemn face. He was dressed in a white shirt covered with a shawl-like garment in which a hole for head penetration was the only opening. Knotted fringes with tassel-like ends hung down from each of the garment's corners. His baggy black pants reached over the shoes touching the floor, and seemed to be sweeping it with his every step. A loose tie, never properly tacked under the shirt collar, hung around his neck. A small head covering, a Kapl, was seated on the apex of his semi-bald head. He carried a leather striped whip in his hand and his entire posture seemed to say "behave yourselves, or else".

Reading of the Holy Books was never done without *nigun,* or chant. Starting with the book of "Genesis", he taught me how to read, or rather, chant, in Hebrew. His whip was very persuasive; I learned to read in no time. My Zaide checked on my progress almost every day. I could tell that each little bit of my newly acquired knowledge filled him with pride. Though I learned to read Hebrew very fast, I never understood well what I was reading, nor did I really care.

My parents started at about the same time to teach me Polish and German. Their approach was more relaxed. Although not void of threats, i.e., "There will be no play today unless you finish", it was more successful. At the age of seven I began elementary school. At that time

I was already pretty proficient in reading Polish and Yiddish. One day, I remember, my father took me to the library. The place was run by the "Bund". It had large wooden shelves, all filled with books which appeared to have entered a second stage of revival. Most of the books were old, moldy, with worn covers, and in some, one had to turn to the first page to discern a title. The books were printed in Yiddish and Polish, although some German and Russian could also be found. I read whatever I could get my hands on.

At first was Defoe's "Robinson Crusoe". I got so absorbed that I truly began to feel stranded on this little island with Robinson Crusoe and his girl Friday. As years went by, the adventures of Tom Sawyer left me spellbound. I loved Marc Twain. In my early boyhood Jules Verne fascinated me with his fantastic and mind-boggling escapades. Max Brandt kept my adrenal fluids flowing with the ever present battles between cowboys and Indians.

I felt depressed for days when I finished J. F. Cooper's "The Last of The Mohicans". In my fantasies I tried to picture what it must have felt like to be the very last of a group, tribe or nation on this earth. The very last Mohican, Jew, or Pole, never to reappear again. Later on I fancied into the world of medieval times. H. Sienkiewicz's "Quo Vadis" took me into the world of early Christianity, and introduced me to the details of life in the Roman Empire.

The chivalry and haughtiness of Alexander Dumas' "Three Musketeers" kept me spellbound, as did R.L. Stevenson's "Treasure Island". As I slowly matured, I began to venture into love relationships between man and woman. Flaubert and Maupassant fed my thirst with their short stories and novels. "The Pearl Necklace" left me circumspect of pretty but empty and frivolous women. Never will I marry a woman like that! I read the biography of Leo Tolstoy, and found it interesting. Just imagine: a gambler, womanizer, sometime thief turning into a deeply religious, righteous man. His "War and Peace" was long, tedious, and too rich for me to digest.

Dostoyevsky, Tschechov, Turgeniev were depressing, distant and as cold as the long Russian winters. I found it arduous to follow psychological novels or plays. Later I turned to Hugo. "Les Miserables" left me sorry for the underprivileged fighting masses, and Jean Val Jean grew tall in my imagination. He was, without doubt, a true hero.

The French revolution and its aftermath were by now deeply engraved in my mind. Freedom and the end of slavery were goals worth giving one's life for, but why did most of its heroes turn into villains? I could not comprehend Robespiere's, Danton's or Marat's actions. Was it greed, power, ideology, that drove them to their miserable ends? Dickens' "Tale of Two Cities", although interesting, did not enlighten me further on this subject.

I turned to the Russian revolution, and there, too, I found very similar patterns. Fifteen years after the revolution most of its leaders were either dead, executed, exiled to foreign lands or in Siberia. Why do revolutions devour their leaders? I wondered. Novels by Zola, Gorki, Sinclair, Lewis, Koestner and others, that I consumed, created a lot of sympathy and understanding for the underdogs, the deprived, the persecuted and the oppressed. I could easily identify myself with their heroes. After all, our life was not exactly a bed of roses.

Henry Sienkiewicz chose "Quo Vadis Domine?" for the title of his book. "Where Goest Thou, Lord?" Where am I going? Where will I wind up?

Now, I read Eric Maria Remarque's *"All Quiet on the Western Front",* and deeply sympathize with the plight of the poor soldiers stuck in an ugly war they never asked for, that seems to be lasting forever. There sure is a lot of misery in this world. A nagging fear and uncertainty get a hold of me, before I fall asleep.

Chapter 11

OUR GENTILE NEIGHBOR

Another day has dawned. Mother wakes me up by pulling off the blanket.

"Get up and bring some wood from the cellar. I will soon be out of it. My God, it is Saturday, why didn't I think of it yesterday. What will the neighbors say?"

Mother always worried about what the neighbors might say. We live in a house that is over ninety percent Jewish. This is the Sabbath, a day when people must rest. Gathering kindling, chopping wood, even turning the lights on is considered work and is strictly forbidden. One is supposed to relax, pray, and enjoy the holy spirit of the Sabbath. I am not concerned with the neighbors' opinions of us. By now everybody knows that we are not too religious, and that we kindle our own fires on the Sabbath without the help of a Gentile.

"O.K., O.K. Don't worry about the neighbors, mother," I respond sleepily, "give me a couple of minutes to wash my face".

I fill the wash-bowl with water, soap my face and neck, rinse, dry off, and change into a pair of old slacks, shirt and sweater. The axe, which I need, rests near the door in the entry hall. I grab it and run down the stairs into the cellar.

The cellar is a place with small subdivisions, each having its own door and lock. The cubicles belong to individual tenants. Each cubicle is connected via a chute to the yard. This is a place where everything that cannot be placed in the apartment is stored. Here is coal, wood, potatoes, carrots and cabbage. It is much cheaper, and also prudent, to buy these commodities in the fall and store them in the cellar for the oncoming winter. Father has already started his purchases, perhaps a little earlier this year because of the unstable times.

On top of the coal and wood he got a couple of bags of flour and sugar. These were our basic staples. Father also bought some salted butter. Mother was storing in jars all the chicken and goose fat she could save in her daily cooking chores throughout summer. A number of jars of jam, prepared this summer, were also lined up on a shelf, as were sour pickles, and bottles of rhubarb wine. The latter expertly bottled by grandfather, sealed with special self-venting corks, and identified with Yiddish labels, were placed in the coolest and darkest spot.

I begin to wonder how long all that food and fuel will last. Will it last to the end of the war? The Germans, should they come, may take it all away. They probably have little or no butter and other staples since Hitler, to build up his army, converted it all into steel - at least so say the papers. I pick up a chunk of wood, place it on the chopping stump, and chop it into smaller pieces. A couple of more pieces, and I gather the wood in a bucket, close the cellar door behind me, making certain that the lock is firmly in place, and start climbing upstairs.

"Good morning." The dark belly of the cellar corridor suddenly comes alive with the sound of a girl's voice.

"Good morning," I reply looking in the direction of the emerging figure of a pretty, but lean and pale girl - and quickly add "Servus Krysia" having recognized the daughter of tenants who live in the cellar.

She smiles and nods her head: "Servus."

Krysia lives with her parents, an older brother, younger sister and a smaller brother in an apartment carved out of one of the cellar cubicles. Since we have lived in this house I visited the place only once. It was a dark, dingy grotto. The smell of cooked cabbage seems to have permanently embedded itself in its walls. A chute converted into a window stingingly permitted some rays of light to enter the area. There was a mattress on the floor and a divan on which all of them slept. The father of Krysia worked twelve hours a day, six days a week to support his clan. He was an alcoholic. Particularly on Fridays he would come home drunk, mean and angry. Many, too many, Poles lived that way.

As kids, we often watched him tumble down the stairs singing some weird, undistinguishable song at the top of his voice. As soon as he'd disappear into the dark guts of the cellar corridor, vile cursing would begin, as well as the sounds of crashing dishes, and the screams of the rest of the family. In no time, the girls would come running out, followed by their mother with a small boy in her arms, all screaming at the top of their lungs. More frequently than not blood would be visible on their exposed limbs or faces. Mr. K would not follow. He would remain in his misery until, totally exhausted, he collapsed into sleep. This is when the family would quietly sneak back into the apartment. What he did to his family was, usually, more visible the day after, when some of the kids, and frequently his wife, displayed shiners on one or both eyes, and blue finger-like marks on their limbs.

This family and the one of our superintendent were the only Catholics in our apartment house. Krysia's older brother, Wladek, started working in a coal distribution center after dropping out of public school at the age of eleven. Soon, he began emulating his father. Drunk almost every day, and particularly vicious on pay-day, he would show up in the backyard, throwing rocks and chasing the playing kids, screaming "Filthy Jew bastards, go to Palestine!" Once, he pulled a knife at a boy who dared to stop him. Since that time the children learned to get out of his way. He is about my age. We played often together, and I am the only one of his Jewish neighbors he listens to. Once, when he was in a rare sober and reflective mood, I gave him a little lecture about filth, dirt, Jews, Poles, etc. This lecture never really penetrated his demented mind. He was in no condition to absorb reason, or for that matter, question things that were out of the realm of his comprehension.

Krysia picks up a couple of wood pieces I dropped and follows me up the stairs into the backyard.

"Look," she points towards the superintendent's window, "Do you see what I see?"

Right in front of the window of her first floor apartment stands the superintendent's wife, bare chested, milking her breast into a baby bottle.

"I have seen that before," I reply, "My mother told me she sells the milk to women who have no milk of their own. I think this is called wet-nursing."

Krysia, embarrassed, hands me the wood and runs into the street.

Back in the apartment, I pile the wood neatly near the stove, and sit down at the table where mother is ready with scrambled eggs, bread and tea.

"Anything new?" I ask father

"Not much. Apparently the English are still trying to get Hitler to reverse his actions. Chamberlain and Halifax still think there is a chance. One never knows, or should I say the ever optimistic Chamberlain never knows," Father adds with a bit of sarcasm in his voice.

"And at the front...?"

"Not much. Apparently the Germans are still advancing. The Polish radio talks about a vicious fight at Westerplatte on the Baltic Sea. It doesn't look good." Father's face displays a discouraging grimace. "Come on, get ready, let's visit grandmother. I wonder how she feels today."

Chapter 12
My Father's Family

Father's mother we call "Bobe" to differentiate her from my maternal grandmother, "Bubbe." This name fits her well, since my father's family hailed from the Ukraine where the local Yiddish had a different dialect - the vowel U (pronounced OO) in this part of Poland, turned into O in Russia and the Ukraine. Her husband, my paternal grandfather, died of a heart attack about a year after my birth. I do not remember him, but from the description of others, he was a tall, red haired man who, like my maternal grandfather, Zaide, was also Orthodox. He lived, with his family, in a small town in the Ukraine. It was a picturesque place, nestled at the foot of the Carpathian Mountains. Czarist pogroms before World War One caused him to give up his small business, a watering hole for the local peasants, and leave for the big city. He selected our city because it was bustling with new building activity. Textile factories were popping up practically overnight. It seemed that the city was quickly developing into a strong competitor of Manchester, the largest textile center in Europe.

Grandmother has been sick for the last six months. Father and I are on our way to visit her. She lives downtown in the old city quarter where the buildings are in a terrible state of disrepair, and the blessings of centralized sewage systems still remain hopelessly distant. Streets, with sidewalks so narrow that only one person can negotiate them without falling onto the cobblestone drives, are typical of this neighborhood. This section is inhabited mainly by Jews. Gentiles are here in a minority. It takes about twenty minutes to reach grandmother's place.

On the way we pass different houses of Jewish prayer. There are the single prayer rooms belonging to one Chasidic sect or another, and there is the huge Old Synagogue with its beautiful front facades, rising stairs and two lions of Judah guarding the entrance doors. A multitude of all types of synagogues, large and small, is dispersed over this entire city. Most Jews do believe in God and pray, often three times a day. Particularly now, when we find ourselves in war with a vicious enemy, the synagogues are more crowded than usual.

As we walk these narrow streets, all stores are closed. A Sabbath aura seems to be enveloping everything. It is so restful and quiet. The smell of cooked *Tcholent* lingers on in the air. Juices fill my mouth. To bypass the religious restrictions for cooking on the Sabbath, religious Jews have their wives prepare pots with meat, potatoes, various vegetables and spices. The pots are delivered to the bakery before sundown, Friday, where they are placed in an oven and cooked about fifteen hours. Now, we pass small boys and girls, dressed in their best for the holiday, retrieving the pots with *Tcholen*t, and rushing home for lunch.

Although the services in the synagogues have been over for some time, men dressed in long, black garb, similar to that of my grandfather's, are still slowly filing out quietly discussing the latest events. Women dressed in their best holiday attire, holding their kids by the hands, or carrying them in their arms, rush home to set the Sabbath table.

We are negotiating the hill leading to the house my Bobe lives in. She moved here about a year ago.

Before that she lived with her then-single daughter, Rose. Father found for Bobe this very inexpensive flat after Rose got, finally, married. The rent is shared by him, Rose, the oldest sister Balcia, and her youngest son Leon. Leon left for Belgium after the first World War, married an Argentinean woman, and now lives in Brussels.

Rose married at the age of thirty three. My Bobe, always afraid that she would remain an old maid, helped to arrange the marriage through a marriage broker. Her husband David R., a tall, bald and muscular man, had been widowed for a couple of years. He lived at the edge of the old city, in a small two-room flat. One room was converted into a combination bed, kitchen, and living room. The other room was filled with two hand operated knitting machines for the manufacture of socks. Huge rolls of wool, cotton, and synthetic yarn, of many thicknesses and colors, filled the floor.

My uncle was a sock-maker. I used to visit him frequently on my way home from Bobe, and watch him swing the machine handle back and forth generating the tube first, and then switching over to another machine which made the sole and heel. The sock tips were sewed in by hand to form the final product. Different weaves required different machine heads with different needles and needle set-ups.

Every Friday afternoon a boy from the wholesaler would show up, pack and carry away the week's production leaving a signed slip with the types of socks and number of pairs taken. My aunt Rose was usually not home. She worked as a bookkeeper in a wholesale coat business, twelve hours a day, including six hours on Sunday. Saturdays were days off. I felt that their cohabitation was not exactly harmonious. It was more a marriage of convenience. She had to get married. He welcomed the marriage because his business was highly competitive, and subject to lots of ups and downs. My aunt's salary filled the low spots. Besides, my aunt had substantial savings.

David R. liked to live like a big spender. Before long, he spent all of my aunt's dowry, claiming that he had fallen on bad times, and owed lots of money which he was forced to pay off. Things got worse when Aunt Rose one day returned from work earlier than usual, and found her husband in bed with their next door neighbor. I knew that reasonably attractive woman, because she seemed to be always around when I visited them. What followed were long and loud family conferences, threats of divorce from both sides, aggravation and worries, which even touched me. I felt deeply sorry for Aunt Rose. After a couple of months of this fracas, both sides finally agreed to consult a Rabbi. The Rabbi, a wise man experienced in family matters, convinced my aunt and uncle to resume a normal life. It was agreed that she would not ask for the money he spent, and in turn he would break off his affair with the neighbor. This settlement did not require much of a sacrifice on uncle's part since the object of his attention has, meanwhile, found another lover.

My aunt Balcia W. was the oldest of Bobe's children. She was tall, had a head of pitch black dark hair and blue eyes. Her olive-pigmented skin added a Mid-Eastern flavor to her appearance. She must have once been very attractive, but missed the boat waiting for her prince to arrive on a white horse and pluck her out from the misery of her daily existence. This never happened. She had to compromise, settling for a short, bald and lame man whom we called Uncle Wolf. He was a cheerful character, and as if to spite his physical fault, he always jumped around in a very energetic way.

Uncle Wolf owned a small furniture factory, in partnership with his brother, Jake. The son of Wolf's brother also worked there. He was a corporal in the military reserves, and was recently mobilized. I remember frequently visiting the place, which was crammed with wood lathes, drills, saws and other assorted tools. Whenever I got a special project assignment in school involving making something out of wood, like a bird-feeder, or cane, I would drop by and within a couple of hours walk out with a professionally looking gadget. Sometimes, it appeared to be too well made, and I had to twist, turn, or punch a few "missed" holes into it to make it look amateurish. It was certain to give me an A in Arts and Crafts.

Wolf and Balcia had three children. Heniek, the oldest, was my age and we played together every so often. He was bright, an excellent student, and the pride of Bobe; after all he was her oldest daughter's son! Dvorah, a pretty girl, looking very much like her mother, was the age of my sister Debra. Leib, the youngest son was a bit of a bully, skipping school and frequently getting into fights with neighbors' kids. The whole family lived in a flat a couple of blocks away from Bobe's.

We knock at Bobes's door, and her weak and hoarse voice invites us to enter. The room is rather small and dark. The only window faces a windowless side of the adjacent building. The air in the room is thick. We greet Aunt Rose, who is sitting on Bobes's bed, and open slightly the window to let in some fresh air. Bobe has been sick for the past year, and this week she became incapable of leaving her bed. Consequently, a rotating watch was set up, and it was my father's turn to relieve Aunt Rose.

"Anything new, out there?" asks Rose.

"The same old story," says Father. "It doesn't look good. I am afraid that the Germans may be here sooner than we think."

"You have always been a pessimist. Things cannot be as bad as you see them. Don't worry. There is a God up there. He will keep them out!" Aunt Rose had enough of bad news.

"You are saying foolish things, Rose. We may as well face up to the facts, no matter how bad they might be," Father retorts.

"Haven't I heard that before? Then why did you wait until now to face up to your facts? God knows - you had a chance to leave this God-forsaken continent and go to Argentina, yet you stayed."

Rose is getting impatient and looks at her watch. "It is time to leave. Dave is waiting for his lunch."

She picks up her bag, and the empty pots in which she brought grandmother some hot food, and leaves, patting me on my head:

"I heard you have made a lot of progress. Soon I will order a coat from you," she smiles. "I have left a couple of pots full with food, Mother will not be able to eat it and it will get spoiled. Why don't you have dinner here," she says.

"Thank you, Aunt Rose."

Aunt Rose was right. I remember a number of years ago father talking of leaving Poland for Argentina. He argued that there he would be able to get a job as a textile engineer and live infinitely better than here. Since that time, this topic was brought up at least once every couple of months. Some of his friends left and wrote him about the higher standard of living, the good pay, and the abundance of work. After every letter he would get excited, but soon the excuses would come up: "I have no money for tickets for all of us", " My mother is sick and I could not leave her", "I am too old to learn a new language", "They probably have the latest in weaving machinery, which I might not understand" etc., etc., etc.

Mother was not very supportive either. She was concerned about leaving her parents behind, perhaps never to see them again. She also was skeptical of all the good things Father's friends wrote about...and by God, Argentina is so far away: "It is like going to the other side of the world." And so it went, on and on.

A few hours have passed. We ate. Bobe couldn't sleep but kept her eyes closed while muttering something to herself. We tried to make conversation but she seemed to be too weak to care. Aunt Balcia showed up and relieved us of duty. She would stay until midnight and give Bobe a couple of pills to induce the sleep which she needs so much. "Poor Bobe," I think as I kiss her goodbye. She opens up her glazed-over eyes and manages to squeeze out a faint smile, as if to say "I know you care, my child".

On the way home we reach the Freedom Square. The place is almost empty. Walking towards us are two tall men dressed in black shirts, black riding britches and shiny black boots. Small army-like caps adorn their blond heads. As we come closer we note shields with the symbol of lightning on their right arms and caps. From a distance of about ten feet they begin to examine us closely. They seem tough and mean. First they gaze closely at my father, who looks fairly Aryan with his crew cut hair, steel blue eyes, and a square cut mustache under his straight nose. Then they look at me.

"Get off the sidewalk Jew," one shouts, "Or we will kick your pants in. Go to Palestine."

I run across the street.

"Is this your boy?" They ask father.

"No," he replies, "he just happened to be walking here".

They pass father, and keep on walking in the opposite direction. Neither father, nor I, dares to turn around. These are Polish Fascists who try to ape Hitler. We know the penalty that awaits us were we to start an argument. I am used to these insults, and have been beaten quite frequently in neighborhoods not densely populated by Jews. That is why one had to be able to defend himself. Yet, I am somewhat frail, pale, skinny, and of average height, and all my life I paid more attention to reading and learning than to sports.

Before I started working I spent some time on our school soccer team. I did not like to run so I always played right or left back on defense. As a small boy I tried swimming. Once, when we were vacationing in our leased villa close to a lake, I went swimming with my cousins Izaak D. and his brother Julek. I was eager to learn. They showed me a couple of strokes and swam away leaving me behind in relatively shallow waters. There were other kids with me. Some were just splashing and playing with the water, others were attempting head stands. Before long I was standing on my head in the water. During one of these maneuvers I suddenly slipped, tipped over, and started to take on water. In panic I tried to get up, slipped again, and finally managed to stand up. This experience shook me up. I never tried to learn to swim again.

To be able to protect myself I acquired a keen interest in boxing. While in school we would form teams, and fight for three real rounds. Soon this sport turned into my hobby. I would follow all world championships. There was Sharkey, Dempsey, Tunney, the brothers Baer, and others too numerous to mention. Max Baer became my early hero after he beat Primo Carnera. Primo was a giant of a man. I remember how little Max, fighting in shorts decorated with the Star of David, knocked out the Italian Goliath. I saw that fight in the movies at least three times. Marcel Cerdan was another one of my boxing heroes. The latest was Joe Lewis, who not long ago knocked the wind out of Max Schmelling in the first round. Schmelling, a German, had apparently an order from the Fuehrer to win at any price. Good for Joe. I created a scrapbook with all the pictures of interesting fights I could clip from the local newspapers. The mere thought of strong men getting beaten up frequently by weaker ones raised my self-confidence by a small notch or two. Sport though is not my forte.

Chapter 13

RETREAT

This is Sunday morning, the third day of the war.

I read a lot about wars. Eric Maria Remarque introduced me to what could be called modern warfare. When this war broke out I expected to see casualties. Perhaps lots of them. Wounded, maybe even dead, as depicted in *All Quiet on the Western Front*. But nothing prepared me for the atrocious scenes unfolding right before me.

I am in the street watching, pathetic, mud covered, hay lined, horse-drawn, crooked wagons bringing wounded soldiers from the battlefield. The scene reminds me of a painting of the Napoleonic Army retreating from Moscow, a copy of which I once saw in the local museum. At the time it impressed me as a nice realistic painting. Almost like a photograph. It showed wounded, bleeding, soldiers stumbling across the snow covered steppes. I was impressed but not really moved. It was, after all, only a painting. Now, to see the result of war with my own eyes is awesome and shocking. I feel like crying.

Up to this moment we have lived under the illusion that the war is still distant, and that there is still a chance that the German armies shall be repelled. The retreating Polish soldiers bring us back to reality. I see soldiers full of pain. Bloody bandages cover their limbs and heads. Fear is in their faces. Most scream to attract our attention. The cobblestone paved street makes for a rough ride that shakes the vehicles, and causes some of the wounded to slide out through the wagon's rear onto the street. I run over and help one climb back onto the wagon.

"Where are you coming from?" I ask.

"From Czestochowa," utters the soldier. "Please. Get me some water."

Now I can see white, dried out saliva collecting in the corners of his mouth. His visibly stiff tongue seems to be sticking to his lips that are cracked, blue, and bleeding is spots. He begs in a shaky, barely audible voice:

"water… please".

"Help! Stop!" I scream. "Get some water! These soldiers are dying of thirst!" Within a minutes a few men appear with water buckets and glasses. Some even manage to produce a couple of bales of hay which we try to spread to make the soldiers more comfortable. A number of women from the tenements have shown up with hot tea, milk, candy and bread. We wash the soldiers' faces. They thank us, and implore Jesus to bless us as they cross themselves.

"How is it on the front?" someone shouts.

"Bad. A disaster!" Cries out a soldier. "The Germans broke through, and there is no front. Chaos everywhere. Our generals and most officers fled as soon as there appeared to be a possibility for an engagement with the enemy. We were leaderless yet attacked the German tanks with our horse cavalry. What a calamity!" The soldier mumbles, "We were told to march towards Warsaw. You cannot stop tanks with horses. Where is Warsaw? It's a disaster!"

"How far is it to Warsaw?" asks another soldier.

"Oh! A hundred kilometers or so. It may take you three days to get there", someone volunteers.

"Let's go! " Shouts the leader of the convoy, a young Sargent whose muddy, torn uniform has seen better times.

We all stand there petrified in total silence as the wagons begin to slowly move away. Doubt permeates my mind and turns quickly into fear. I tremble. Is it all over? My throat tightens, and tears come to my eyes. Another convoy approaches. The same disarray. The same misery. The same calamity. I am petrified by the dazed faces, the torn clothing, the mud, the scarcely covered wounds. That scenery is too much for me. I run home.

"What is going on?" Father asks as he opens the door and sees my sad face. "Have you seen what's happening outside?" I cry out trembling with fear. "The wounded soldiers say that there is no front anymore. No resistance! Finished! Kaput!"

"Don't over dramatize," Father tries to console me. "The Polish radio just gave an account of the fighting. Apparently they are still holding out at *Westerplatte*, and giving the Germans stiff resistance near Poznan and Krakow. The war isn't lost. Not yet."

We turn on the news broadcast. The British have issued an ultimatum. Hitler must vacate the Polish territories he took by 11 a.m. If not war will be declared. The French ambassador also handed over an ultimatum in Berlin. No news from the Soviet side, but rumors abound that Ribbentrop, the German foreign minister, is again visiting Moscow.

"How can that be?" I ask father.

"This is politics, my son. First they sign a treaty with Poland, then they break it. Now they signed a treaty with the Soviets. Eventually, they will stab each other in the back. Let's wait and see what will come of it." Father is trying to analyze the desperate situation we are in.

The eleventh hour has passed. There is no German response. "The British people are at war with Germany!" declares the Polish radio announcer. Soon, the French government issues a similar declaration. At last! We are not alone anymore in this struggle. From now on things will be different. The Germans will forever regret what they started. I feel the adrenalin rising in my body. We'll whack those Germans till they are lifeless. Soon the whole affair will be nothing but a short memory. What a day this is! "We are winning," I scream, as I fall into my father's embrace. Even he, the eternal skeptic, is clearly moved. His eyes glisten with tears, "Maybe, just maybe, it is still time to reverse the action, and stop that madness." World War One made a pacifist out of him, so particularly now his hopes, which until this moment were in open conflict with the harsh facts, begin to rise. I have rarely seen him this elated.

The sudden sound of sirens interrupts that happy interlude, reminding us that war is still on. We rush to wet our hankies, and together with mother, Debra, and two of mother's seamstresses, descend into the cellar. Although it is Sunday the girls are at work helping mother to finish a number of dresses for her wealthier clients, who are getting ready to leave for either Britain, France, or the New York World's Fair.

Someone pulls out a little crystal radio set, tunes in the needle, and the city station appears clear enough over earphones. Some of us can hear, "The German Armies have bypassed Poznan, and are advancing along all fronts. Some units of the Polish army, once bypassed, have reassembled and hit the enemy from the rear. There ensued a big battle with lots of casualties on both sides." We are all excited. At last, finally, there are some signs of honest-to-goodness resistance. The announcer goes on to say that our city has been declared an "open city", which means that there is an agreement between the opposing sides not to fight over it. Almost at the same time the sirens sound the "all clear" signal. We fear that the "open city" announcement probably implies that the city will soon fall into German hands. I know, too well, that the Germans are obsessed by another, this time politically motivated, religion called "Nazism." It preaches the superiority of the Aryan (whatever that means) race, and the belief in one ultimate leader of the German people. Hitler, their God, has vowed to destroy the Jewish people. I have read about book burnings, beatings, and destruction of Jewish houses of prayer, businesses, and concentration camps for those who oppose the Nazi regime. Who knows what the National Socialists have in store for us? Can they be worse than *Endek's,* the Poles of the viciously anti-Semitic National Democratic Party?

Chapter 14

A Bit Of History

Lodz. This city of 700,000 is almost equally divided between people of Polish, Jewish, and German origins. Poles are in charge of the governmental bureaucracy, the city departments, and police. The textile industry, which took hold over the past 120 years, was primarily built by Germans and Jews. The work force is composed of poor Poles and Jews. Jews also own many small businesses and stores, and are prominent in teaching and medical professions. The Germans are conspicuous in engineering, designing and factory supervision.

Germans, mostly Protestant, are treated with a good deal of respect. They have their own German schools which, in compliance with the law, use Polish as the prime language. Some of them are very nationalistically disposed, and despise their Polish "Landlords". Others have assimilated and pass as good Poles. The commander of our garrison is a Gen. Lange, obviously of German ancestry. There are very few cases of extreme poverty among the German citizen. Jews, too, have managed to preserve their customs and culture. They have their own schools, some of which are sponsored by the government.

The Jews, persecuted and expelled from many western-European countries, came to this land beginning with the tenth century. The real immigration, however began in the fifteenth century when a newly chosen Polish king, *Kasimir The Great*, invited the Jews to settle here. He offered them life in peace, in exchange for their help in building a stronger and more eminent Poland. After his death it was said that he found Poland in wood, but left it in concrete.

For centuries Jews in Poland lived in piece with their neighbors. At times they even had their own parliament and enjoyed their own autonomy. They were ground administrators, silversmiths, farmers, tradesmen, artisans, musicians, and money lenders. The money lending business was perpetuated by Polish nobility who used the Jew as a proxy in their financial dealings. Lending money for profit was strictly prohibited by the Church. With time some Jews became rich and used their capital and talents, as did Germans, to construct this city's industrial base. Yet, most of the city's Jews were poor, and barely squeezed out a living. They came here to escape pogroms in the unfriendly countryside, and to find work.

Following the Treaty of Versailles, Poland gained its independence, and Jews were given the same rights as gentiles. The public schools were divided, wherever possible, along religious lines. Jewish culture began to flourish. New - ethnic - political parties, Jewish classical theater, orchestras, newspapers, were created. On the surface, Jews had not had it so good for some time.

Unfortunately, the deep seated dislike of the Jew has also imposed limits on these freedoms. For instance, a Jew cannot become a clerk in the governmental bureaucracy; he cannot rise high in the military, or become a policeman. The number of Jews attending Polish institutes of higher learning is limited by law. Jewish students must occupy special seats assigned to them. When a Jewish child is born in our city, its first name is usually registered as a 'Yiddishized"

Old Testament name. So Moses becomes Moishe. There are no Peter's, Tadeusz's, or Pawel's on Jewish birth certificates. Careers are limited, but some Jews, particularly in the academic domain, bypass the limitations by converting to Catholicism. Yet, in spite of the quotas at universities, and other academic obstacles, wealthy Jews are getting well-educated and join the ranks of professionals. Often they travel abroad to get degrees, and then return to set up medical, dental, or law offices.

Like the majority of Jews, most of the Poles live in poor, frequently substandard, conditions. The Polish peasant is uneducated, ignorant of politics, and completely dominated by the parish priests and aristocratic land owners. The worker and farmer has been traditionally exploited and given little chance to become well-educated. Few can read or write. Education belongs to the aristocracy. The Polish middle class is small, and made up primarily of governmental bureaucrats, army, police officers, professionals, tradesmen, and small shop owners.

It may be said, without exaggeration, that Poland is a historically messed up place.

Even in times of its highest glory the Polish nobility did not trust one another, less so the King himself. This mistrust was responsible for the creation of a kind of democracy as early as the middle ages. When a King died, the nobility chose the new King. Because of mistrust among themselves, the Kings they finally agreed to most frequently turned out to be foreigners.

Poles knew of little peace in their often glorious past. There were times when the borders of Poland spread from the Baltic to the Black Sea. But most of the time, Poland suffered from invasions, either by the Swedes or Prussians from the North and West, Russians or Mongols from the East, Hungarians and Austrians from the South. Over the past two hundred years, and up to the Treaty of Versailles, Poland was frequently partitioned and occupied by others, or shrunk to the size of Warsaw and its environs.

The end of World War One found a partitioned and impoverished Poland with two, surprisingly, well organized Armies. One with Gen. Josef Pilsudski, an ex-socialist, at the helm, and the other under the leadership of a Gen. Jozef Haller, an avid nationalist and anti-Semite. Pilsudski built his Legions in German-occupied indigenously-Polish territory, originally with German approval. As it became apparent that the Central Powers (an alliance led by Germany) were about to lose the war, Pilsudski, taking advantage of the opportunity, turned his Legions against them. He was arrested, jailed in the famous Magdeburg prison near Berlin, and released after the armistice was signed. Haller, a high ranking officer in the Austria-Hungarian Army, was called upon by Polish emigrants in France to lead the freshly formed Blue Polish Legions there. In April 1919 he returned to Poland when asked to do so by Ignacy Pasderewski, a famed pianist, rabid nationalist, and then the newly named prime minister of the Polish Government.

Following the armistice, Pilsudski tried to gain as much territory for Poland as possible. In contrast to Haller's ideas, which were based on a land grab, Pilsudski's dream was to merge Poland, Lithuania, Bialorus, and the Ukraine into some form of federation. He tried to realize this dream with the aid of a leader of the Ukrainians who went under the name of Petlura. An excellent opportunity arose when the Bolsheviks came to power in Russia. The Alliance, now victorious over Germany, feared that the Russian revolution may link up with the Red uprisings in Germany, and was determined to do something about it.

After the official end of World War One, a plan to attack and quell the revolution was formed. Poland, and others, were to attack from the outside to help the Czarist White Russian Forces fighting from within. The newly formed Polish Army, reinforced with American "volunteer" fliers and planes, were assigned the role of attacking over the full width of the eastern front, while Allied troops attacked from the North attempting landings at the port of Murmansk.

Initially, the war against the Soviets progressed very smoothly. Polish Army units penetrated as far as Kiev. With time, the Poles found it difficult to maintain their extended supply lines. Continuous attacks by Ukrainians and Bielorussians, (who feared a reborn Poland more than the Bolsheviks) did finally make the situation untenable. The weakened army could not sustain the assaults of the reorganized Red Army under the capable leadership of a young Gen. Tuchatchevsky. The Reds went over to the offensive, and in a massive move, pushed the Poles back against the gates of Warsaw. Out of the ensuing chaos a huge force of volunteers was finally created. A surprise counter-offensive by the volunteer army led by Pilsudski, and aided by some Allied forces under the French General Weygand, managed to turn back the poorly supplied, and stretched Reds. The Polish victory was decisive. The Red Army retreated in chaos.

To flatter the clergy, this victory was officially designated as *Cod Nad Wisla* the "Miracle by the Vistula River". Eventually the Soviets sued for peace. They lost a sizable portion of Bialorus and the Ukraine, and Lithuania, which (at odds with the Polish plans) was forced to give up a chunk of its southern land to Poland. A new map was drawn.

Poland held its first nationwide elections. The elected Polish president was promptly assassinated by nationalists who were inspired by Haller. Insisting that the election was a national sham, Haller kept propagating hatred and disgust for democratic procedures. Following the assassination, Polish nationalist parties continued to brawl with the Socialists, while other assorted parties actively fought the left and right. The mess lasted about six years. Pandemonium, bordering on anarchy, caused Pilsudski who was the Polish Army's commander - to dissolve the parliament and call for new elections. The elections were rigged, and Pilsudski was virtually guaranteed dictatorial powers. Haller having declared himself against Pilsudski, moved to Switzerland, where he began to plan Pilsudski's downfall. His plan was never carried out. Pilsudski was a battle tested, shrewd, intelligent, and above all, benevolent man. He had a soft spot in his heart for Jewish citizens, many of whom served under him in his Legions, and took part in the anti-Soviet war. He helped the Jews to achieve the degree of freedom they now have.

The day Pilsudski died was a black day for the Jewish community. We cried our eyes out. We lost a friend and benefactor, and became deeply concerned and fearful about our future. His body was interned in the Wawel Castle where it rested for a while in the company of Polish Kings. Soon it became apparent that the Catholic Church, a certain Cardinal Sapieha in particular, did not like the idea of an agnostic commoner buried side by side with the Kings. The case went to the courts, and eventually the Cardinal ordered the exhumation and reburial of Pilsudski's body in a nearby cemetery. The Government did not dare to object.

The Church is a national institution here, and has tremendous powers. Particularly in the small villages, the Church's power is absolute. Most Poles are deeply religious. Portraits of Christ and Mary hang in every Catholic home. Christ is usually shown as a Slavic-looking blond man with blue eyes and a trimmed beard. Mary, the mother of God's Son, looks like a typical pretty Polish mother. These appearances are calculated to permit the people to closer identify themselves with the Godly Pair.

To the ignorant farmers, Jesus and Mary were Polish. Mary is known as the Holy Mother from Czestochowa, after she supposedly appeared to some peasants on a mountain called Jasna Gora near that city. The tacit Polish origin of the Mother and Son of God is important to the process of indoctrination. By denying Christ's origin, Poles can more closely identify themselves with hateful teachings that portray the Jews as killers of Christ. They can also see and understand the link between the death of Christ and the alleged Jewish death threats to Poles. The constant rumors of Jews using Christian children's blood for the Passover ritual are never denied.

The "Protocols of The Elders of Zion", an old Marist forgery, are often quoted by priests in their sermons.

It was, therefore, not at all surprising when soon after Pilsudski's death, a new wave of anti-Semitism broke out. Pogroms hit the small towns and villages where Jews lived. Even to this day most troublesome are the weekly markets where the local peasants and Jews meet to sell, buy, or simply barter goods. The newly appointed heir to Pilsudski, a certain Marshal Smigly-Rydz does not seem to be concerned by these developments. He seems to be lost in the awesome task of governing an unstable country, seriously threatened from within and without.

Lodz is now a particularly vulnerable city, with a good portion of its citizen is of German origin. It is located not very far from the German border.

Chapter 15

A Wedding

I climb out of the dark cellar into the gleaming noontime daylight. The blue sky and sun are assuring. Life goes on.

Back in the flat we eat dinner. Father leaves to take care of his sick mother. He inquired this morning about work. Apparently there won't be any work until the situation becomes clarified. My sister attempts to read a school book for the new grade she will be in this fall. I start reading a book that I got out of the Bund library. The girls and mother are busily working away to meet mother's obligations to those lucky customers who soon will be out of range of the conflict.

Mother's, favorite employee, and mine as well, is a pretty girl called Lola. She is a good worker, honest, talented, and endowed with a beautiful voice. When she sings arias from Carmen or Tosca, her favorites, we frequently drop what we are doing and just listen. Her singing creates a warm, tender atmosphere. My favorite is Grieg's Peer Gynt. I know every note by heart and quietly whistle the tune as she sings. Everyone who knows her knows also that Lola aspires to be an actress. She is an avid Kino Magazine reader and often talks of films and their stars. I think she probably dreams of replacing Jeanette McDonald in duets with Nelson Eddy, or starring with Tyrone Powell, Robert Taylor, or maybe a more chivalrous Errol Flynn. When she sings I can picture her leaving this grim place and rising high above the clouds. I see her drifting west towards the American mainland and landing in the Mecca of films, Hollywood, where life is so easy, and things almost always have a happy ending. My cousin David, who I work for, has a crush on her. David is a slim built man of average height. He has blonde, curly hair, blue eyes, and a pronounced nose. He took her out a couple of times, but nothing came of it. He is very shy. We frequently tease him about it, but he is still trying.

Lola is singing a haunting popular song about a girl who longingly, waits for her Love and when he does not appear, commits suicide. The other girls and mother are humming in. The song is known as The Last Sunday, and according to the papers is responsible for a number of suicides among young girls in Europe.

The pages of the book I try to read become fuzzy, gray, scrambled, and I slowly doze off. Suddenly, I feel someone pulling at my arm.

"Wake up! You have time to sleep the days away at your old age" It is Bella attempting to sit me up on the couch, "I have an important announcement for all of you."

I know" says mother "Poland won the war."

"This is no joke Aunt Esther" she turns to mother "I am getting married!"

"Let me guess. It is the fellow from Palestine, right?" Lola cuts into the conversation.

"Well, you are right. It is Yakov." Bella's face assumes a light pink color as she continues in excitement. "We are getting married tomorrow. Everything is arranged. We have been looking for some time, in secret, for an apartment and finally found one on the main drag. Yakov has already bought some furniture. We will move in right after the wedding."

"Why so soon? Where will the wedding take place? Who did you invite?" Inquires mother, now a bit alarmed over this sudden development.

"Aunt Esther, I kept on telling you that I like this fellow and that I was going to hook him. Well, I didn't have to work too hard. He was the one who proposed a week ago. We decided to keep it a secret until all was arranged. We do not want a large wedding ceremony, especially now. We want the Rabbi's blessings and the blessings of our closest relatives. As far as work is concerned, things will be very much the same. I have plenty of room in my apartment. Ita, Sara and Itka will be working with me. This will leave David in the old apartment with more room for expansion. He has been complaining lately that there is not enough room for the two of us in Bubbe's place. Yakov works all day as a salesman, and he will be out of our way most of the time. You see, this solves many problems."

"Well, all I can say *is Mazel Tov*," says mother as she embraces Bella and kisses her on both cheeks. I can see tears glistening in her eyes. Mother always felt responsible for the six orphans. Finally, they are on their own, and the oldest is getting married. One silent promise to her dead sister fulfilled. Bella is now fully independent and will soon be in a nest of her own.

"Mazel Tov," a chorus of all present responds. Lola's voice is the loudest. She would like to be at this point, but marriage would probably ruin her dreams of an artistic career.

"I have, already told the good news to Bubbe, Zajde, and my siblings. Now I have to run to Aunt Hannah." Bella excuses herself and departs in a hurry.

Time, indeed, is short. A war is on. Who knows what is in store for us in the future, I wonder, trying to digest the good news and its implications.

Now, I will be working alone with David. There will be no girls to kid around and sing with. All the fun will be gone. What a boring job this will turn into. The money certainly is not there. I make ten zlotys a week, seven of which goes to my parents. Ten zlotys!

Were it not for the war it was my mother's hidden wish that I become a designer and move to Paris or Vienna. In school I was pretty good in drawing. A boyfriend of hers, one that she met before my father, went to France, and is now a big dress manufacturer. She was preparing for the day when I would have mastered the art of sewing and then continue on to design school. I ducked, whenever she brought up that subject, because I hated to disappoint her.

My secret ambition was to become a political cartoonist. My father sensed this and tried to encourage me as best as he could. My caricatures of the political leaders of our time are pretty good. My friends and family like them. The technique I developed was based mainly on Law, a cartoonist for the Manchester Guardian, whom I admire. His pen is secure and concise. Not a single stroke is wasted. The sarcasm and ridicule of the "Establishment" is sharp and almost always hits the bull's eye. He is syndicated all over Europe, and his cartoons appear in the Workers Week, a magazine subscribed to by Father. Who knows when the time will arrive that will permit me to realize my dream, if ever. I always disliked being a tailor, and did it only to help the family to get over the hard times they have fallen into as a result of the depression.

I was glad I didn't have to work today because David did not feel well, and tomorrow David will probably again close shop because of his sister's wedding. This leaves me more time to do what I really like - read and draw.

It is now Monday, the fourth day of the war, and also the wedding day for Bella and Yakov. There was a lot of commotion this morning. Our neighbors' son had just returned from the road leading to Warsaw. His report is very dismal. He says he saw German soldiers driving towards Warsaw in trucks and motorcycles. The roads leading to the capitol were crowded with people trying to make their way to the city. There are plenty of dead and wounded among the marchers. Apparently, before advancing to their current positions, the Germans strafed the crowded roads with guns from low-flying aircraft. It is very messy. He implores anyone with ideas to march towards Warsaw to stay home.

Leaving home at this time is now out of question. The Germans are bombing Warsaw, and are about to complete their encirclement. The German Radio communiqués are in sharp disagreement with the Polish radio, which claims that the big western cities such as Lodz, Poznan and Krakow are still in Polish hands, and contends that the Polish troops are beating the Germans all over the eastern front. The Polish radio is only partially right. Apparently, the Germans have chosen to bypass the big cities and aim at the heart of Poland. As far as we are concerned, that is our family, the decision has been made. Our young people will stay home and wait until the situation in the field has clarified.

Meanwhile, we have a wedding to attend to. My father, mother, Debra and I dress in our finest. My shoes are polished and shine like mirrors. I spent a half hour getting them to that point. We march down the eerily empty streets to the house in which the wedding is to take place. Save for an occasional policeman, there are no troops, not even wounded, to be seen. The family of Aunt Hannah, with their "patriarch" Haim are already there. They are also dressed to the hilt. Bella and Yakov will pick up Bubbe and Zaide. The Rabbi has just arrived. He spreads a paper on a side table, and begins to fill it out with an Indian ink pen in fine calligraphic Hebrew print. Haim, father, and an older brother of Yakov are providing the necessary data. This is the wedding contract known as a *"Ksuba"*. It is an esthetic looking document engraved with floral ornaments and Hebrew words. A scroll-like outline defines the space into which all details shall be recorded for posterity. I watch the Rabbi filing in the empty spaces with a steady and, in a sense, artistic hand.

The room is beginning to fill up. The families of the bride and groom are all here. Bubbe and Zaide have just arrived with the bride and groom. As Bella promised, this will be more or less a formality, rather than a wedding in the style people are accustomed to. The civil wedding papers have already been obtained from the City clerk. The bride is dressed in a stylish gray suit, which complements the dark grey suit of the groom.

"They make a nice couple," says Mother to her sister Hannah.

"O! Yes. Only if Debra and Moishe could be here to witness the wedding of their daughter," Hannah replies holding back tears.

"Do not be so sad," mixes in Bubbe. "There is a God up there," she points to the ceiling. "He watches us and also permits them to watch. I am sure they have their blessings."

The male cousins, including myself, get busy stretching the canopy. It is made of purple cloth adorned with golden embossing and tassels. All four sides are covered with golden fringes. There are four poles to be held upright. Zaide makes the selection of pole holders: myself, my cousins Julek D, Izaak D, and a younger brother of Jakov. We stretch out the canopy so that it is almost fully flat at the top. The bride is led under the canopy by Zaide and Bubbe. My mother and her sister cry out loud and tears stream from their faces. The groom is brought under the canopy by his older brother. His parents died some time ago. He is over six feet tall, has short curly light brown hair, blue eyes, and a square cut face accented by a strong nose and bushy eyebrows.

The rabbi adjusts his yarmulke, strokes his beard with his left hand, and begins to read from the bible which he holds firmly with his right hand. He is brief. After a chapter from the book of Exodus, he starts the formal reading with the traditional *Har Hayad*. The groom takes out a wedding ring, places it on the finger of the bride and repeats after the rabbi the conventional vows. Someone hands him and the rabbi a glass of wine.

After the wine blessings are recited by the rabbi and repeated by the groom, who takes a sip from the glass, the groom hands his glass over to the bride. She repeats the vows, and tastes the wine. Finally, a glass is placed under the groom's foot. He steps on it. It crashes. It is supposed to remind those present of the destruction of the Temple in Jerusalem by the

Roman Emperor Titus. Everybody shouts "Mazel Tov". The women cry. We all wish the newly wedded couple lots of luck. The canopy is removed and the wedding is over. My mother's eyes are still red from crying as she and our family leaves the room.

We all walk towards the newly wedded couple's furnished apartment on the main drag. The tramways are still running, but are half-empty. We reach the indicated house number and the couple leads us up to a third floor apartment. The apartment is very roomy by our standards, and nicely furnished. Bella always had excellent taste in almost everything she did. The floors are freshly polished with red wax, and reflect the daylight. There is food on the table. A wedding cake, vodka, gefilte fish, and knishes. The bride's sisters, Ita and Sara, do not look very happy. They probably wish they had come that far too. They are quiet and sob as Yakov's brother raises a glass of vodka to toast the couple.

"May the newlyweds be blessed by the Almighty and may they be permitted to lead a comfortable, healthy, and happy life. Let us hope that their children will grow up in peaceful, better times, free of hatred and anti-Semitism. *Le Chaim.*"

We all respond with "Amen", and sip the strong tonic from our glasses. The conversation carries on. We taste some of the food. It is delicious.

The wedding party breaks up. We don't want to attract attention, and space our departure. We leave one by one. Back in our flat, mother returns to work. It is four in the afternoon. My sister and I decide to walk over to our schools to check for any new announcements.

Chapter 16

VISITING SCHOOL

My sister and I enjoyed attending school. First, it provided a refreshingly new, educational environment. Secondly, we made many school friends, and those acquaintances formed the pillars of our social life platforms, away from the dirty backyard of our house. The house friends were forced upon us. School friends we could choose.

Debra's school is about a block and a half away from where we live. It occupies three floors, and is part of a large apartment complex. This Elementary School is reserved for Jewish girls only. Boys attend separate schools.

We look for any new announcements but the board seems to be plastered with last spring's activity. We continue to my night school. It will take about fifteen minutes. The walk is pleasant as we pass through a couple of city parks. Soon, the large concrete buildings appear. This is an interfaith school, the Gymnasium. The school is free of tuition, and attended by students who desire further technical schooling but cannot afford full time high school. Courses are given by day and in the evening to suit the student's free time.

"How are you?" Someone's voice reaches us from the rear.

"Good afternoon" I reply, turning my head in the direction of the voice.

A familiar figure of a bearded man wearing a beret emerges from behind a tree. He walks briskly toward us holding cane in his right arm:

"Are you anxious to get started?" the man continues in an inquisitive, perhaps somewhat sarcastic tone.

"I know this guy," I whisper to Debra. "He is Professor K, my math teacher."

Turning towards Professor K, I say "I am in no hurry, not now. Hope this war will soon be over, so that I can continue with school."

Professor K was an excellent teacher of mathematics in the Technical Evening School I attended following my graduation from elementary school. In the algebra and trigonometry classes he taught I learned for the first time about mathematical logic. As far as I was concerned, Professor K had one problem. He was an old nationalist and Jew-hater. On one hand, it quite obviously hurt him when the only two Jewish boys, in a class of about twenty students, were usually among the first to comprehend any new theorem or proof he developed on the board. On the other hand, one could not help but sense the kind of self-satisfaction he apparently experienced when the material he taught was soaked up by a handful of inquisitive minds.

Most of the students had little interest in what was presented. They came from disenfranchised, poor, frequently alcoholic families, and attended school because of prerequisite requirements for their jobs. Often discouraged by the poor response of the students, Professor K would turn the lecture into a political attack on Jews.

According to the professor, all Jews were capitalists and aimed to rule the world. Here is a typical exchange between us, the Jewish students, and our professor:

"Look at the Rothchilds."

"Sir Professor," we replied, "have you heard of Morgan, Vanderbilt, Rockefeller, Getty, Hunt, Krupp, Nobel -- or do you need a longer list?"

"Yes," he had heard of them, "but the Rothschild's were money lenders and squeezed the last grosz out of the poor."

"Doesn't the Professor know that money lending was one of the few trades left for the Jews to pursue? Perhaps he ought to blame the Church for its unreasonable laws."

"Oh, no. The church was protecting the poor from the Jews, who are responsible for the low living standards of the Poles. Why? Because rich Jews exploited poor Poles."

"Aren't the overwhelming majority of the Jews poor? How about the rich Germans? There were more of them in our city. Don't they exploit the poor?"

"Well, the Germans are our traditional enemies. We don't talk about them doing us harm anymore. We hate them, and with time will get even with them. Besides they are Christians."

My explanation of this diatribe amounted to: The Germans are strong and you Jews are weak. We cannot do anything about them, but we can certainly keep you in line if we wish.

When the communist part of his argument was brought up, the other Jewish boy and I were personally touched. We were poor, yet very patriotic.

"The poor Jews are communists" he shouted.

"I've heard that tale before. It is the basic catechism of all Jew haters. I never met a Jewish communist in my life."

He laughed: "Don't you know that the organizer of the Red Army was Trotsky, a Jew?"

We did, "So what? If it were not him someone else would have done it. The time was ripe for an uprising against the Czar," we said.

He countered by smiling at the Catholic boys: "Isn't it a fact that Zinoviev, Kamieniev, Radek and many other leaders of that uprising were all Jews?"

"Where are they now?" We answered a question with a question. "They are dead. Killed by Stalin. Isn't this a fact?"

And so it would go, on and on. There was actual hatred between us, but, strangely enough, also mutual respect. Very few Catholic boys dared to engage him in political discourse.

"Well, there may not be any school this year." Professor K went on. "Things are not shaping up too well for you, nor for us, for that matter."

"Let us hope that Hitler gets defeated soon," I answer, "then we may get a chance to carry on our arguments, and keep on learning. I owe you a lot, sir."

"This time it will be different. When we win we will have things our way. Jews really belong where they came from. Let them go back to Palestine. They will be better off there." He begins to preach his old gospel "And by the way, is this pretty little girl your sister?"

"Yes, Mister Professor."

"What a pity. She does not look Jewish at all. Get your parents to convert.

Become good Catholics, and good Poles. As long as you cannot be distinguished from the rest of us I wouldn't mind it at all. By Jesus, talk to your parents about it. It may save your lives." The Professor's suggestion gets my blood boiling.

"I am afraid we were born Jewish and will die Jewish, and this fact does not make any worse Poles of us. We are as great "patriots" as many others I know. We have to run," I say. "It is getting late." *Do widzenia*, until we meet again, Mister Professor."

I grab Debra by the hand and we start walking at a fast pace, leaving the Professor standing and looking in our direction for a while. We check the school schedule, and there is no news. Debra is obviously unhappy about Professor K's attitude.

"Who does he think he is?"

"He is Catholic, a Polish aristocrat, a professor, and a...jerk," I reply, "and in spite of this, I respect him. At least he is no hypocrite. I know he respects me, too. He always gave me top grades. Let's go. It is beginning to get dark and we want to be home soon, otherwise Mother will worry."

We walk for a while in complete silence. Debra, it seems to me, is intensely contemplating something. Her head is bowed, and her eyes affixed onto the stones of the sidewalk.

"A penny for your thoughts," I jokingly interrupt her.

"Hmm. I was thinking about Bella's wedding." "

They looked happy, didn't they?"

"Yeah, but otherwise it was very sad. I am close to thirteen now, and I hope one day I, too, will get married. When I get married I would like to have a big wedding, with flowers, music, and to look pretty in a nice wedding gown. I would also like to have all of my friends and family there, not just a few."

"I agree with you. You still have a long way to go, though. By that time the war will be over and we will all be free. You will get your wish. Do not worry."

Dusk has begun to set in, Streets are getting empty, and we begin to hurry. As we reach our house we meet Yankl, a boy we used to play with, "Your mother has been looking for you all over," he shouts

Chapter 17

OUR AMERICAN CONNECTION

It is not with a great deal of exuberance that I check in for work this Tuesday morning. David tells me that many customers cancelled out. There may be no work soon. That bit of news doesn't disturb me. I expected it. I help David finish off a couple of coats, and drop by to say "Hello" to Bubbe.

A kettle of tea is boiling on the coal-fired cooking range. The steam is jetting out from its beak filling the room with a cloud of moisture.

"The water is ready. I felt like having some tea," Bubbe reaches for an empty, small brewing pot, shakes in a couple of teaspoons of dry tea leaves, and pours some hot water over them. "Would you like to join me in a cup of tea?" she says, closing the brewing pot and putting it on the table to permit the brew to darken. What a timely invitation. Outside there is nothing but fear and panic in the streets.

"Why not?" I answer. "You once promised to tell me about your family. Could you do it now?"

Bubbe is somewhat reluctant, but her dinner is all cooked. All she has to do is warm it up. Her little room is window-less, and a small light bulb dangling from a long cord is always lit. The light it sheds is not very bright. She pulls the bulb over to the bed, and fastens it onto a hook in the low hanging ceiling. We sit down close to each other. She puts my hand between her hands, and begins to talk.

Bubbe tells me of her childhood as a daughter of a land manager for a Polish prince. She was born in Czestochowa, where the miracle at Jasna

Gora took place. In her early childhood she lived practically in the center of a forest that her father administered. They had a roomy log cabin. She remembers a large fireplace giving off lots of heat, and herself sitting and studying in front of it, while the wolves howled outside around the house. During one cold, snowy winter night the wolves climbed up and looked into the window.

She had one brother, she tells me. He now lives in Bratislava, in the occupied Czechoslovak Republic. He has been there for forty years, and married a girl from an old Jewish aristocratic family. He teaches mathematics at the city's university. The last time she heard from him was three years ago. He sent her a picture of him.

"You must see it," she says, as she pulls out a large family album. She points to a picture of her brother. I see a slight man with a goatee, dressed in a finely fitted suit. He leans over what appears to be the side of a bridge. "This is the Danube River," she explains.

Bubbe rarely talked about her brother, nor did she keep up with him any regular correspondence. I, somehow, thought that Bubbe must have been considered an outcast by her relatives. A girl from a well-to-do family, well-educated, marrying a poor orthodox weaver. This must have been shocking in her time. Bubbe turns the page. A new set of photos appears. I see pictures of myself, as I was one and a half years old, pictures of Debra at the same age, my Bar-Mitzvah picture. We look at it. I have matured quite a bit since then. She tells me that copies of almost every picture of me and my sister were mailed to our cousin in America.

"What about Uncle Chaim, your son?" I ask.

"Well, that is a long story," she answers "I will tell it all to you sometime."

"Why not now?" I insist.

Bubbe reluctantly agrees. First she pulls out some pictures from the album. I have seen them before. One is of Uncle Chaim in a US Army uniform. The picture has a brown texture to it. It depicts the handsome head of a very young man, seated squarely on a pair of broad shoulders. A narrow collar separates the head from the torso. Small epaulets, two large pockets, and some military decoration give credence to his otherwise plain uniform. His face bears a faint, but seemingly proud, smile. He was the youngest of her children.

It all began right before the World War One. In contrast to her other children, Chaim simply refused to work after reaching the age of fourteen. When he was sixteen, and showed no inclination to get employment, Bubbe became fed-up with him. One day after a quarrel, she decided to let him float on his own. She wrote a letter asking her niece in the Bronx, New York, to offer him temporary shelter and help him find work in the new country. The letter was promptly mailed. That same day she visited the travel office and bought a one way boat ticket to America. In the evening, after the meal was over, she handed him the ticket and told him to start packing. In a week he was gone.

A couple of months passed. She began to get letters from her niece about his whereabouts. The first letter mentioned his safe arrival in America. After a couple of months of pointless job searching he decided to enlist. Following initial training, he came to say good-bye before being shipped off to England. That is when this picture was taken. Remembering his forced exile he swore to never, ever, write home. A few months passed. One day Bubbe got a letter from her niece in London. What a small world this is, she wrote. One day she was walking past some temporarily established military quarters not far from the street she lived on, when a soldier in an American Army uniform approached her. "Don't you recognize me?" He asked "I am your cousin Chaim. Now they call me Hyman, or Hymie, for short." She invited him for dinner a couple of times, until he was dispatched to the front in France.

The war ended and Chaim - by now Hyman - returned to the Bronx following an honorable discharge from the Army. After a couple of months he found a job and moved into a room of his own. For a while he seemed to have disappeared from view. One day, mother's cousin got a call from the Police in New Jersey. Would she accept a call from a fellow named Hymie? She did, and the full story of what happened was contained in bundle of letters that followed. Bubbe kept every one of them.

Apparently, one day, while lingering around Times Square, Hymie met a girl. She was a redhead with green eyes. He thought he liked her so they dated a number of times. On his last date he suggested they go to a burlesque show in Union City in the state of New Jersey. After the show they had a couple of drinks and wound up in a small hotel. The inevitable happened. They had intercourse. After the date they returned home, and everything seemed to be normal for a while, that is until she popped the question: "When will you marry me?"

He could not believe his ears. He told her that he really was not serious. Perhaps never. This was a little too much for the girl. She called the police and asked them to arrest him on the grounds that he crossed state lines to have sex with her. He was promptly arrested and incarcerated in a local small prison where he was held for trial. The girl paid him daily visits, each time carrying some goodies. "Will you agree to marry me?" The same question popped up at every visit. Finally, one day before the trial he succumbed, and said: "Yes".

She dropped the charges. They got married.

Years went by without hearing from Hymie. One day Bubbe gets a letter from her niece in the Bronx. I was there when the letter arrived. "You read it to me then", Bubbe reminds me. Indeed, I remember, it started like all letters from this niece: "Dear Aunt Nacha Lieba and Uncle Gershon. It was good to hear from you. We hope that this letter finds you in good health, etc., etc." The letter contained a picture of Uncle Hymie and his family. The picture showed Uncle Hymie standing with his wife, a very Irish looking girl. To the right and left were two boys with obviously freckled faces. Sitting on the floor was a cute little freckle-faced girl of about six years.

As we look at this picture I can see Bubbe's eyes filling with tears.

"These are my grandchildren. Like you. Yet I never met them, and probably never will," she is now openly sobbing.

"Bubbe," I try to console her, "the world hasn't come to an end. Not yet. You have long years left to live, and this war won't last forever. As soon as it is over I promise you, I'll find your son." I utter these words, but inwardly strongly doubt if this could ever happen.

"You are very nice, my boy. People do not live forever. I am eighty-five years old. My time is running short. The Almighty was very good to me, letting me live that long. I feel bad for your generation. Who knows what the maniac Hitler will do to you."

We keep on leafing through the pages full of photographs. Bubbe dries her eyes with a handkerchief, as Izaak D. appears in the door.

"What are we crying about?" he asks Bubbe in a soft, consoling voice. "Have no worries. The war will eventually end and everything will be as it was." At this stage I do not consider this to be a consolation, but Bubbe does. To maintain the status quo was all she lived for.

"I wish you were right," Bubbe has stopped crying and closes the photo album. "We were just looking through the pictures, and they brought back some sad memories."

"What's new," I ask Izaak.

"The news is not good. We are surrounded, and the Germans may enter any minute now," he continues. "I talked to some friends of mine. We are all thinking of leaving this city and joining up, somehow, with the Polish Fighting Forces. Warsaw cannot hold out very much longer. May be one week or two at the most. It makes no sense to march towards Warsaw. Besides, we would have to cross German lines. Our plans are to go southeast and then turn northward and cross the River Bug. The remnants of the Polish Army should try to reassemble there. We are sure that this river will form the next front line."

"When are you guys leaving? Can I join you?"

"You cannot!" Bubbe's voice is now strong and firm. "You must stay here with your parents, and besides, you are too young. They won't take you."

"Bubbe is right," says Izaak D. "Julek is also staying home to take care of our parents, and he is much older than you are. I did meet Izaak B., at the Maccabee club this morning. He, too, wants to join us."

"I do not like this, but if you have made up your minds to go, I respect your decision. When are you leaving?" Bubbe's eyes are again filling with tears.

"Tomorrow at dawn."

"May God bless you, and watch over you. Hopefully we will see you again someday. Your future has been written in Heaven and there is nothing we can do to change it." Bubbe is true to her fatalistic philosophy of life, "By the way, when is Rosh Hashana this year? It cannot be far away."

I look at the calendar. "The first day is a week from this Thursday."

"We must pray, especially hard this year, for the Almighty to grant us another year of life, health, and freedom."

Interesting, I think to myself. Here is a wise, worldly, well-educated woman who still believes in the power of prayer. To us young people who have grown up in the age of "enlightenment", and socialist "awakening", her orthodox beliefs seem to be full of superstition and mysticism, and defy all modern thought or logic.

Izaak and David show up. We have now a foursome. How about a game of Bellot. All agree. Bubbe serves tea with cookies. We play until dusk robs the day of its light.

Chapter 18

BUSINESS TALK

The two Izaaks left this morning. I went, with Julek, to the meeting place. There were quite a few young men there. All had back-packs and food. They didn't seem to be worried about the Germans. One of them, the apparent leader of this pack, seemed to be familiar with the area they would pass through. He was very confident they would make it. This made me feel better. After some embraces, they left.

Now we are on our way to the house of my Aunt Hannah. She cries when we tell her about Izaak D.'s departure. He was the apple of her eye. Uncle Haim coughs and curses, but does not show any outward emotions.

"Come here," he calls me over to the dining table, where he is having breakfast. "Has your father mentioned anything about what he intends to do when work and money have run out?"

"No. We have not discussed it yet. You know David is practically out of work. That means that I too will be free. Father has not worked since last Thursday. He has only one check due. Mother's work will also be finished in a week or so. I really don't know how we will manage."

"Tell your father to drop by. I have some ideas. People will smoke, no matter what, and the current inventories of cigarettes won't last forever. You know who makes cigarettes in Poland, the Government. It's a monopoly. No government, no cigarettes." Haim's words sound intriguing.

"What should I tell my father? Do you have anything specific in mind?" I inquire.

"Nothing spectacular or glamorous. I am thinking of setting up a little cigarette factory. I know where to get tobacco and empty cigarette cartridges. He can find some small plungers and we will be in business. A Zloty is a Zloty. We will surely need money to get by. These are bad times."

"This sounds good, Uncle. I will talk to father about it." I am already excited at the mere thought of doing something else, not tailoring, for a change.

"How is everybody?" Itka enters the room.

She has just returned from Bella's house. She worked till lunch. Half a day only. Things are slowing down there too. They had lots of cancellations.

"Mother, you won't have to worry. They called off the Five O'clock Dance today." A hint of sarcasm is apparent in Itka's voice.

"Thank God for that. You see, there is a good side to every scourge," Hannah responds.

Itka without the Five O'clock Dance on Wednesdays is like a fish without water, Bubbe used to say. It is also apparent now that despite the critical war situation Itka's thoughts are still at the dance floor where she can fox-trot, tango, shimmy, and do the Charleston to her heart's content. At work, all one had to do was whistle one of the latest tunes such as "Alexander's Ragtime Band", or "Catch the Tiger", and she would drop whatever she was doing, catch the rhythm and get into her ecstatic foot shuffling and hip wiggling. She was also a decent tap dancer. Sometimes on weekends, we would borrow a neighbor's RCA gramophone, and play the latest jazz records. Itka and a neighbor's cute redheaded daughter would tap dance until they fell to the floor totally exhausted.

"Who knows when the dances will be resumed," Itka worries.

"For my money they may stay closed forever. I won't miss them. At least you will be home on time. One less thing to worry about." Uncle Haim is genuinely relieved by this turn of events.

"I have to go now," I announce. I kiss Aunt Hannah and Uncle Haim, wave "*Servus*" to Itka and Julek, and depart. The railings of the three flights of stairs are tempting, so I descend sliding.

On the way back I pass the Liberty Square. Kosciuszko proudly stands there with his faithful saber in hand. Near the City Hall I see soldiers in uniform standing next to a motorcycle with a wheeled seat attachment. They look strange. The color of their uniforms is a bluish green, rather than the khaki I am used to. Can it be? I get closer. I can hear them talk German. Indeed, the Germans are here! Apparently a patrol has entered the city to check on its status. They knew exactly where to go to, straight to the City Hall. I do not dare to cross their path and take a different route to get home.

There are screams arising from our backyard as I approach our house. Soon, kids come running into the street followed by a bald, corpulent man. He wears a long, white, night gown which hangs over his black pants. He holds up the pants with his left hand, and wildly waves his tightly fisted right arm. His suspenders are off, and the pants keep on falling down and getting in his way as he chases the kids:

"You bastards. I will teach you a lesson. Your parents are no better. You son of a bitches, watch out, if I catch you, I will beat the shit out of you!" He screams at the top of his deep, hoarse, baritone voice.

I know him well, he is Mr. T., the baker. He has been chasing kids as long as I can remember. He works the night shift, and sleeps in the daytime. Unfortunately for him, his windows face the backyard. In the winter all windows are closed and very few kids frequent the backyard, but in the summer the screams of the children can keep a hibernating bear awake. Over the years he has developed a deep hatred not only toward the children, but also toward their parents. His two blonde, blue eyed daughters at times participated in the commotions, and were usually the first victims of his flaming ire. He never spared the whip. His fist left marks on the girls' faces. Ashamed of the outward signs of beating, the girls would frequently skip school. This led to more beatings. The vicious cycle never ended. Neither he nor his wife, a very ordinary woman, can read or write. Now, Mr. T. is, again, in a trance. I ignore him and walk up the stairs.

"The Germans are here," I loudly announce as I enter the apartment.

"I know," answers Mother. "The German radio made the announcement a couple of hours ago. The Polish radio has been silenced. According to the German communiqué, they will make a grandiose entrance on Friday before noon. All citizens of German ancestry are encouraged to line the route and welcome their liberators."

"I will be there. Cannot hurt to meet your new bosses," I venture adding somewhat sardonically, "Who knows? They may turn out to be better than many a Pole. The press dispatches we read over the past couple of years may have been sheer propaganda. And then again, they may be true."

"I have known Germans all my life," says Father, as if to support my conjecture. "They have always been decent people, and are an enlightened, honest, and hardworking bunch. They cannot be as bad as the press made them out to be. You will find Anti-Semites everywhere. Why should they be different?"

"Father, the anti-Semites I know don't intend to quash the Jews. They talk about kicking the Jews out. Hitler talks about extinction. There is a big difference." I am trying to be a bit more realistic.

Deep down in our hearts we know that the press was right, and if anything, under-reported the Jew hatred prevalent in Nazi Germany. Yet we find it necessary to engage in self-deception, perhaps if only to quiet our fears and justify our inaction.

"Father, I just came from Uncle Haim," I quickly try to change the topic. "He has good ideas about trying to generate some income during these uncertain times."

"Haim's ideas never work," Father exaggerates. "Had he ever had any good ideas he would not have been in as poor shape as he is in now. Is it about gambling?"

"No, I think this time you ought to listen to him. He wants to manufacture cigarettes by hand and sell them on the street. You know he has tobacco connections. He will get the tobacco, and we will get plungers and empty cigarette cartridges. Set up a little factory in our house. Anybody can fill cigarette tubes. And if business really takes off we may employ the entire family. Why not?" I am slowly convincing myself of the idea's worthiness.

Father is not fully convinced. He used to be a heavy smoker but quit after the doctor warned him that his heart and lungs are not in the best condition. He was also apprehensive about having cigarettes around the house because I have taken up smoking. I have been smoking for about three years now. It was a sign of manhood respected by my peers - boys and girls alike. At this time, though, the thought of an income during the approaching days of unfamiliar new orders appears attractive and overcomes other considerations.

"All right. I know where I can get plungers and cartridges. An old acquaintance of mine has a tobacco store, and he is certain to have stacked up on this stuff. Come to think of it he is of German ancestry. His first name is Karl. I will try to see him tomorrow."

Well, it looks like we may set up a little business.

Chapter 19

SURRENDER

Although for all practical purposes things are very much the same, the thought that life may soon undergo drastic changes keeps working my mind. Fear of the unknown can raise havoc with your imagination, that night I could not sleep. I am up early. Mother is already up preparing scrambled eggs for breakfast,

"Can you jump down to the grocer's and get some fresh rolls, a rye bread, and a deco of butter?"

"Yes," I reply. "How about milk?"

"I am short of it, too. Could you get a liter of milk and a half a kilogram of farmer's cheese from the cow barn?"

"It will take me about ten minutes. I'll be right back." I grab a milk can and run down first to the cow barn, then to the groceries.

The barn, which houses about thirty cows, is located in the backyard of the house that Bubbe lives in. The owners, the K's, a nice Jewish couple with three hefty and muscular sons and an equally endowed daughter, have been supplying milk and cheese for the entire neighborhood for as long as I can remember. Last year the family K was struck by tragedy.

One summer evening a group of drunken Poles invaded their cow barn. At the sound of falling beams the father and his three sons ran out to find the invaders ravaging the barn and tearing the walls apart. Being heavily outnumbered, one of the sons reached for a kitchen knife and in the heat of struggle stabbed one of the invaders to death. At the sight of reinforcements in the form of athletic looking men employed by the butchery and bakery located in the same apartment house, the drunkards run away.

The son who committed the murder disappeared, and has not been seen since. Needless to say the K family has been heavily hit by the son's absence. They are now broken-hearted and have been talking about moving to South America. Rumor has it that this is where their son ran to.

I walk in, hand the milk can to the daughter at the door. She fills it with one liter of fresh milk directly from a bucket that seemingly was removed from under the cow only a while ago. The milk is still warm. She weighs half a kilogram of fresh farmer's cheese and wraps it in wax paper.

"This will be 70 groszy," she puts out the open palm of her hand.

I give her a zloty, collect the change, and proceed to the grocer. The smell of freshly baked rolls and bread, just delivered from the neighboring bakery, practically sucks me into the store. What an aroma. I always loved the smell of baked goods. I collect the required items, pay and rush back home.

The radio is on. Our city station now broadcasts in German. Warsaw still transmits in Polish. We can hear the news from both sides while we eat breakfast. The news is, as usual, bad. It amazes me how quickly we got used to receiving constantly bad news. We somehow expect it. It feels as if we have never known good news before. Of course, what is bad for us may be great for others. I leave the apartment with father. Father will visit his old buddy Karl to see if he can get the required cigarette making tools. I am on my way to Bubbe's house.

There are many German soldiers to be seen today. They are everywhere. Cars and motorcycles filled with officers are crossing the city from one end to the other. They requisitioned the Hotel Savoy, now *Hotel Manteuffel* on the corner of the intersection nearest to our house. Across from a kino, where Chaplin's "Little Dictator" was shown only a week or so ago. Today all the posters are gone. The hotel is one of the finest in our city. It has its own nightclub. I remember when Josephine Baker came from Paris for a series of performances there. The place was packed every night. We had never seen so many cars and taxis parked up and down all streets leading to this hotel. For that matter we never saw a mulatto, aside, of course, in the movies. It was a time to remember.

At Bubbe's I learn that many of our friends and acquaintances have been caught and put to work to prepare the quarters for tomorrow's grand entry. The word is out - stay off the streets if you want to stay out of trouble. Poor Zajde didn't know it. Apparently he was standing in front of the house gate a couple of hours ago, when three soldiers, who seemed to have had one beer too many, grabbed him and put the flame of a cigarette lighter to his beard. When the beard would not easily ignite they laughed, pulled on it, and, before departing, kicked Zajde in the groin.

In pain, and understandably upset, Zajde sits on the edge of his bed, his head bent, his eyes closed, only a quiet grumble emanating from his throat. "What did I do to them to deserve this?" he keeps asking himself. "Nothing Zajde," I try to console him. "They are a bunch of hooligans. God will punish them! You'll see." I know that the mention of God would soothe his nerves. After all, God is his protector, his benefactor, his teacher, his avenger. After a while he quiets down "God will punish them," he utters, and stretches out on his bed. Bubbe feels sorry for him. She does not say much, but sits down by his side and moves her hand gently back and forth over his bald head. "Gershon," she sobs, "We have survived together worse things than that. We will survive them too".

"You are a good wife, Nacha Lieba," he replies, "but I feel that this will not happen in our times, anymore. Maybe, when Mesiah comes we'll get a chance to celebrate their demise."

A knock at the door, and Bella enters. We told her what happened. She is very upset. She has heard similar stories from her neighbors. "This is just the beginning. Imagine, they barely arrived and not even formally occupied the city. What will happen when they officially become our masters?" She asks, "Nothing good. That's certain." She answers her own question.

David and Ita arrive. They also try to comfort our grandparents. Bella mentions in passing that they may leave the city, and settle in a little village where, she thinks, it may be easier to survive. I excuse myself saying that it is getting late and Mother must have cooked dinner, wish everyone a good day, and depart.

Back home Father has just returned from seeing Karl.

"It is unbelievable how quickly people change," He complains. "Imagine, just a couple of days ago he was a good pal. Today, he asked me to leave after I hardly had a chance to greet him. It is dangerous for him to be seen with a Jew, he told me. He also asked me not to visit him anymore."

"Well, there goes the cigarette business," I say somewhat sarcastically.

"Not yet." Father has apparently thought about it in more detail. "I can contact Zygmunt, and ask him to talk to Karl. You see, Zygmunt, in spite of his Germanic sounding name, insists that he is Polish. He dislikes Germans, but knows Karl well. I am sure Karl will listen, when he knows that he can make a quick zloty."

"So, all is not lost," Mother puts an end to the subject. "Let us eat". We eat in silence, each submerged in his or her own thoughts.

Chapter 20
ARMY PARADE

Another Friday is here. The second since the start of the war. The sun is shining through scattered clouds of all shades of black and grey. I am up early in the morning. The German Army is supposed to officially enter the city today.

In the street people begin to gather along the marching route to gain positions up front by the curb. The first ones to arrive are our ethnic Germans. Most of them carry bouquets of flowers. Some wear red bands adorned with black swastikas in a white circle. The mood among them is jubilant. They seem to be of high spirits, both emotionally as well as physically. The smell of alcohol is in the air. I have never heard as much German spoken in this city as I hear this morning. Some begin to chant "Sieg, Heil!" There are not too many Jews to be seen. Nor are there many Poles. I meet Krysia and her sister Helena and together we walk toward the street along which the parade will take place. It is only half a block from our house. We take up positions close to a store front in a tall building. A set of protruding concrete steps offers a good elevated platform for better viewing.

At ten o'clock sharp the sounds of a band are heard. The melody is unknown to me, the tune is somewhat monotonous, but the waiting crowd picks it up readily:

"*Die Strassen frei, die Reien fest geschlossen...*"

Quietly I whisper to Krysia, "What song is this?" A man nearby overhears me. "This is the Horst Wessell song," he states proudly. "It is a song written by one of our martyrs." We thank him for the explanation and move to the next set of stairs in an adjacent building so as to take distance from our kindly source of information.

The band comes into view. More flags are unfurled from out of nowhere. They are so reminiscent of the red flags of the Polish Socialist Party which I frequently saw in the First of May parades. I was told then that the red stands for the blood of the workers spilled in their fight for freedom from exploitation. The Soviet flag is also red but has a hammer and sickle in its upper corner.

The Nazis replaced it with a swastika emblem, and located the logo right in the flag's center. After all, I remind myself, the word Nazi comes from the acronym NSDAP, which stand for *Nazional Sozialistische Deutche Arbeiter Partei*. This party also represents a Worker's Movement. How can the same blood-red symbol represent such a divergence of ideas? I am a bit perplexed.

The first mechanized contingents pass by. I am impressed by the armored vehicles driving by at a snail's pace. I examine the individual soldiers. They look neat and clean. Almost every third soldier wears glasses, something rare in the Polish Army. They also look more civilized. Their hair is cut short, but by no means totally shaved off as is required in the Polish forces. Some comb their hair. It seems they want to make a good impression on the onlookers. Unit after unit marches by to the exhilarating applause and shouts of their ethnic countrymen. Not all units are mechanized. There is a horse-mounted unit, horse drawn wagons, tanks and artillery pieces. The marches slow down to a practical crawl. Suddenly, I hear someone shouting. I turn, and so do some of the onlookers. They look at me!

"Hand von Tasche, Mensch" - screams an officer. It dawns on me that I am keeping both of my hands in my pants pockets. The officer finds that threatening. I quickly pull out my hands and fold them on my chest. This ought to keep him happy. It does.

The march goes on and on. One column of foot soldiers with rifles and ammunition belts filing by after another. I look into their faces. They are tired but seem to be happy and visibly impressed by the turnout and flowers handed to the officers by neatly dressed, smiling little blond girls. A song cuts through the air here and there. The melodies sound strange to me. They are dreary, forceful, and yet harmonious in some strange way. How different they sound from the traditional Polish marches which frequently originate from the Polonaise or Mazurka, and are lively and melodious. I can decipher some words: *"Schoen ist Soldat zu sein. Rose Marie..."* At least the average Hans sounds human. He misses his girl but loves being a soldier - it is nice to be one, he says in his song. How quickly one forgets. Didn't their parents tell them about Verdun?

"I am going home," says Krysia, "I have had enough of this". I agree, and together we slowly walk toward our house.

"Do you think we stand a chance?" Helena's eyes fill with tears. "Will our soldiers ever come back?"

"Ever is a big word," I say, "I am sure they will, as they have done so many times before. The question is shall we be here to welcome them?"

The smell of Friday's menu being prepared by Mother and Debra reaches me as I come close to the door of our apartment. It is mellowing, soothing, and so reassuring. We are still here in spite of all those ominous developments.

Father is home. He contacted Zygmunt who seemed to be willing to play the go-between. He will give Karl a few days to familiarize himself with his new role and will contact Father as soon as he has something concrete.

Mother lights the Sabbath candles. The first week of war has ended. The German occupation has officially commenced. We eat and briefly discuss the events of the day. I relay what I saw at the parade.

"They haven't changed much," says father. "I remember my days in the German Army. The songs we sang were very similar. Mostly about soldiers and girls - girls and soldiers."

"The songs may not have changed," interrupts Mother, "but when I listen to the diatribes of their Fuehrer I get goose-bumps. I am scared and worried to death."

We all agree, but what is there to do? The same rationale is constantly reiterated. We have to stay here because of our family and besides we don't have enough cold cash to set out on the road to friendlier places. We know that this is only partially true. We still believe that where there is a will there is a way, but have now convinced ourselves of the absolute validity of our excuses. This relieves us from taking action. We retire for the night.

Author's Maternal Grandparents ca, 1884

Author's mother in 1910

Author's parents in 1923

The author - one and one half years old

The author and his sister in 1929

The author's Bar Mitzvah Picture

The author and his sister in 1936
Picture taken at the Freedom Square, Lodz, Poland

Chapter 21

NEW MASTERS - NEW POLICIES

Two weeks have passed since the German entry into our city. Life has undergone a terrific metamorphosis. Jew hatred has advanced from unofficial brooding and cursing to National Policy. The Germans are fully in charge, in spite of the fact that fighting still continues. Nazi policies and teachings are zealously followed. The Jewish populace has become a source for free labor. I have been caught a number of times and forced to perform manual labor. Once I cleaned, all day, the quarters of German officers at the Hotel Savoy, now renamed *Manteuffel,* scrubbed floors, washed toilets, laundered shirts and underwear. Another time, I was sent to fill the ditches we so conscientiously and eagerly dug for civil defense shelters before the outbreak of the war.

Perhaps the most puzzling event occurred when I was caught and taken to a hastily set up Institute for Racial Studies. Here I spent the entire day being subjected to oral, written and physical tests. During the latter my body parts were measured and recorded. Specific attention was paid to my head. The nose was carefully photographed and its profile traced on paper. The circumference of my head was recorded. The spacing between the eyes noted. The outline of my mouth with the surrounding lip borders was drawn. All that time the two German "scientists" in charge were murmuring to each other, seemingly puzzled and unhappy with the results. They finally painted a blue Star of David on my head and, with a warning not to wash it off, released me. They gave me orders to report back in one week. When asked for my name and address I eagerly complied, giving them the wrong data. They never saw me again, and I certainly did not miss them.

The Jewish New Year and Day of Atonement came and quietly departed. Since we were barred from assembling there were no prayers in the synagogues. Only in one of the large synagogues did the German SS stage a prayer session with an audience that was rounded up from the street and forced to participate. The idea was, we thought, to film the prayers for their own propaganda apparatus. Zajde organized a m*inyan*, which is a forum comprised of minimum of ten men, prescribed by the Talmud for communal prayers.

Prayer meant everything to my Zajde, by now a stooped and wilted old man. Prayer also assumed a much more profound meaning for us. In the utter bleakness around us, we turned in despair to the one thing the Germans could not take away - faith in the power and justice of the Almighty. The sewing room was converted into a prayer house. Linens were suspended in the rear to form a division for the female worshippers. Only family members were admitted for fear of being discovered. Grandfather led the prayers, assisted by, of all people, my agnostic father who had apparently not yet forgotten the rituals.

Father's subdued and hushed chants added a special aura to this clandestine concourse. He had a good voice. We all cried, without exception, as we prayed for forgiveness of our sins. On the Day of Atonement we grieved as we chanted *Kol-Nidre,* a prayer, according to our tradition, written during the times of the grand inquisitor Torquemada. This prayer was supposedly chanted by Spanish Jews under somewhat similar circumstances. Given the choice between death on the flaming stakes and conversion to Christianity, some chose the latter, but carried on with their tradition during secret revival meetings. As they did five centuries ago, we have spent our High Holidays in quiet seclusion and secretive worship.

The anti-Jewish propaganda is rampant. The movie on the corner presents propaganda pictures loaded with hate and venom. Their current "hit" is Shylock. The streets are as treacherous as mouse-traps. We must move very cautiously not to be caught. Most Jews are readily recognized by the local Germans, now called *"Volksdeutchen"*, or Ethnic Germans, and beaten. Jewish stores are frequently plundered, if not by the Germans, by native Poles. Jews are being removed from food queues. My little sister has become the savior of the entire family. With her straight, long, braided hair, and the little hooked-up nose, she looks like any Polish kid. She procures the food not only for us, but also for Bubbe, Zajde and the orphaned cousins. The German Mark has replaced the Polish Zloty as the accepted currency. It is very highly valued.

Father did somehow get a hold of the plungers and cigarette cartridges. Uncle Haim got lots of dried tobacco leaves which we finely chopped. We are in business. The paper tipped cigarettes we produce aren't perfect yet. We found that with firmly stuffed plungers there is a lot of waste, since many paper blanks get sliced open during the tobacco insertion. Now our cigarettes are slightly soft, but not loose enough to spill out when tested with a snap of the finger against the filled end. Uncle Haim had plenty of empty cigar boxes at home. We filled them with our cigarettes and hit the street.

Business is good. We sell the cigarettes directly to the smoker. No middlemen! Debra and I do most of the retail selling in the street. We carry cigar boxes suspended from our necks by a piece of string, and cry out: "Cigarettes! The best Tobacco! Come and get it." Father and Uncle Haim concern themselves primarily with the procurement of tobacco and empty paper cartridges.

The war has ended, at least for us. After the third week of fighting the last Polish remnants, Warsaw surrendered, Poland has, again, been partitioned between two prime antagonists, Russia and Germany. They say that in the north-east, the River Bug will serve as the border, while in the south-east the Soviets will be given all of the indigenous Byelorussian and Ukrainian territories, including the city of Lvov. The valiant defenders of *Westerplatte* also finally gave up.

People are again leaving. This time to Soviet occupied Poland. The hopes are high that war will never reach these parts. Why, there is even talk of the Russians moving to the old Curzon line, which would also give them our city. Then why run? Unfortunately, Father has learned from his old buddies at the Bund that the Bolsheviks despise the social democrats more than they do the Nazis. Two of the leaders of the social-democratic Bund were supposedly interned by the Bolsheviks, accused of treason, and sentenced by a military court to die. The sentence was promptly carried out by the Bolshevik commissars. Well, perhaps we are better off under German rule.

There are other reasons for the majority of our people to stay put. We refuse to venture into new, unexplored, territories. In the first place, we believe that sooner or later there will be war between the two colossi. In the second place why run from one dictatorship to another? They say it is like running from rain onto a drain. We also expect soon to hear from the two Izaaks. Some of our neighbors have already received letters via the Red Cross. Many letters are written in code. For example, one of our neighbors brought in a letter from his son from the city of Vilnus in Russian occupied Lithuania. In the letter the man describes in code how "Our Uncle Ivan, the one born in our city, will soon be home. We take it to mean that soon the borders will change and our city will be handed over to the Bolsheviks. At this stage we are not too certain whether this is a Godsend or curse.

Time passes swiftly by. We slowly make the necessary adjustments and learn to survive in the new, hostile, climate. Financially, we are at least as well off as we were before the war. But every day brings new developments. We have been caught a number of times and our cigarettes confiscated, that is, they went directly into the pockets of the police. The situation is very fluid. It is hard to tell what the next day will bring, thus we slowly learn to live from day to day. In a way, this routine, if one may call it that, has its own plusses: We have stopped worrying about the future. What's the use! We figure, we cannot do a thing about it anyhow. We, all Jews, are now in the same boat. No academic distinctions. No financial differences. Many rich Jews have either departed or are making preparations for exit. To the ones that stay, financial differences are not, at least outwardly, apparent. Insecurity and instability are slowly being accepted as the "normal" way of life, and as to the harassment and denigrations, well, it is temporary and will disappear as soon as the war is over. We hope!

The month of November is upon us. Leaves have abandoned their feeding source, the trees, and are now lying helpless and dying in the streets, forgotten and exposed to the vagaries of nature. The naked trees, almost piously, stretch their bald, dark wooden arms to the sky, seemingly praying to be spared for the next spring when they may reappear crowned again in their full, green glory. Nights are getting colder. Winter is just around the corner. The time has come to stack up on wood and coal, but these commodities are very scarce. Today is the seventh day of the month. I got up early and began to work on the day's cigarette production.

Father was up already. He just came in from his, so far, fruitless attempts to secure the minimum heating provisions required to survive the oncoming winter.

"We have been formally annexed to the Reich." he announces as he enters with a German newspaper in hand. "We are now in the Warthegau, part and parcel of good, old Germany."

"Congratulations," I say with a note of sarcasm in my voice.

Mother seconds my words with the Hebrew equivalent: "Mazel Tov."

"What does all that mean?" inquires Debra.

"We don't know, but sometimes it is better to be in the lion's den than to face the uncertainties of the open jungle." Father attempts to throw some positive light on this fearful event.

He may be right. Who knows? But what a choice!

"I have met Zajvel R.," Father turns toward Mother, "Your cousin. We got to talking about the oncoming winter, and I mentioned our lack of heating material. He said that he knows someone who can get us all we need for some gold. Perhaps a few rings, earrings, or strings of pearls."

"How much would be needed to get enough for the winter?" inquires Mother. "I don't know," Father replies. "Perhaps what we should do is gather our jewels, I know it isn't much, meet the guy and try to get the best deal we can."

Mother does not wait for Father to finish. She is already pulling out her jewelry from an old box which is kept in the closet under a pile of old shoes. It isn't much. A ring with a couple of small diamonds. A string of pearls. She adds to it by pulling off her wedding and engagement rings. Debra has a little gold ring which she got from Bubbe. We add it all together. Hopefully it will suffice to procure the necessary winter fuel.

"Be careful in who you are dealing with." Mother is seriously worried. "They may take away the last bit of valuables we own and give us nothing for it. One of my clients told me lately that when they attempted to exchange some of their jewelry for food, the merchant brought in German police who confiscated all they had. They say that all jewelry must be given to the Government so it can pursue the war to a successful conclusion. God forbid! I am telling you it is extremely dangerous to deal with strangers nowadays."

"You know what?" Debra enters the conversation. "I have heard from some kids that one of our neighbors works for the Nazis. They say that he tells them where the rich Jews are so that they can take away their gold and diamonds."

"Well, I heard the other day that someone saw Mr. K., our neighbor the baker, who used to chase you kids around, enter the Gestapo headquarters."

Father expands on Debra's bit of news. "We really don't know whether this is true or not, so please, keep your mouths shut. It is easy to get in trouble nowadays. I will need a blind pocket in my coat to safely hide the jewels." He turns to mother, "You know the heavy winter coat I had made to measure last year?"

"I'll fix you up with one in one hour," Says mother. "But please be careful. Make sure that Zajvel knows well the people he deals with."

Father gathers the valuables, inserts them into a small paper box which he places in the closet. We are extremely conscious of our appearances lately. Father has taken to wearing a short crew cut, which together with his small squared mustache, steel gray eyes, and a perfectly smooth nose profile give him a pure Aryan look. Still he would not pretend to be one, even when it comes to the daily purchase of food. All his appearance does for him is to shield him from being caught to do forced labor. I often wonder why father has not a bit more gall or "chutzpah", perhaps we would all be better off.

A couple of days have passed. Father managed to get the wood and coal needed to survive the winter, but in the process we lost most of our valuables. We really do not care. What is important is survival.

"When you have your health, you have hope," Mother says, and she is right. Without health, the chances of survival are very poor. Last night after the final delivery of coal was made, and shoveled into our cellar, Father took out a bottle of vodka. We rarely drink vodka in our house. That bottle was kept on the shelf, together with the jams and jellies that mother prepared for the winter. He opened it, and we all drank to health: "*L'Chai*m".

Chapter 22

GETTING TO KNOW DEATH

Today is Friday, the tenth day of the month. We run out of tobacco and I set out to pick up some from Uncle Haim's house.

"Hallo!" A friendly voice reaches me from across the street.

"How are you, Romek," I answer, recognizing a distant relative of mine. "Where are you running to so early in the morning?"

"I have to organize some raw material for our business," I answer.

"Take your time," suggests Romek. "Did you see this morning's papers?" "No." "Did anything of earthshaking importance happen?" I inquire, knowing well that had something happened affecting our status we would have noticed it by now.

"Nothing earthshaking happened, but there is an announcement in today's paper advising the city's inhabitants to visit the Old Market Square. Apparently our gracious benefactors, the Germans, have hung three people whom they call criminals. The city's population is advised to visit the place and see for themselves what may happen if, or when, someone gets caught performing unlawful deeds. I will be going there later this morning. Would you like to join me?" asks Romek.

"Yeah. I have never seen a dead body. Never mind one that is strung up in the air. I will stop by at about 11, when I have discharged my current duty. OK?"

"OK. It's a date. See you later."

It may be weird, but I am excited to see the corpses. Never in my life have I seen a cadaver. None of my relatives had died, at least within the span of my memory, and only once did I come upon a dead corpse. I remember that day well. I was returning from a summer camp vacation to our large apartment, the one that the depression chased us out of, when I noticed a commotion at the main house gate. Outside the gate, on the sidewalk, lay a bundle, covered with a heavy blanket.

The Police were there, so was our neighbor Mr. G. He was sobbing. I later learned from my parents that Mrs. G. was despondent after an "operation", and was playing around with the idea of committing suicide. She managed to realize that, jumping out her fourth story window. I also subsequently learned that the operation was an unsuccessful abortion which left Mrs. R sick for the rest of her life. This, so far, was my closest encounter with death.

It takes some time to reach Uncle Haim's place. Inside the apartment a couple of boxes are neatly stacked up in the corner, by the door, awaiting transport to the "factory". The D family is already up and about. Yes, they have heard about the grisly display on the Old Market Square. No, they do not have any intention of going there. I somehow feel as if I am being pulled there by some unknown force. Guess it must be sheer curiosity. I have read about people being hanged. Here is an opportunity to see a "real" display.

As soon as the paper cartridges are packed, I set out to deliver them to our house. On the way I meet Wladek, our neighbor, who is also heading towards the execution place. I drop off the boxes, and both of us head to Romek K.'s house. Romek K. is a first cousin of Julek, Izaak, and Itka. His mother is Uncle Haim's sister. She is a very active businesswoman. Together with her husband, she has managed to build up a nice tobacco business. They live around the corner from us, in an apartment in the rear of their store. He has a sister, a very pretty girl, whose looks have not escaped my attention.

The Old Market Square is located in the old section of town, about twenty minutes walking distance from our house. The streets become narrow as we enter the old city. This part of the city is inhabited mainly by destitute families desperate to eke out a living. Even in the best of times, this place reminded me of the sewers of Paris I read about in Hugo's novels. Dirty children with their noses in a chronic state of discharge litter the narrow, cobble stone faced streets. Raw sewage flows along the side channels formed by erosion. The place literally stinks. It is inhabited by poor Polish and Jewish families.

Slowly we make our way through the crowded streets onto the Market Square. As the market vista opens before us we notice only a few people in the square. Our citizenry does not seem to be interested in this horror show. The ones in the square are, like us, curious young spectators. At first glance, everything appears rather normal.

As we near the center of the square we notice the quickly improvised gallows and three fully dressed men dangling from the gallows' crossbar. I feel a strange sensation in my stomach. As I approach the hanged I notice their rather grotesquely deformed faces. The stiffened bodies rotate ever so slowly, propelled by the wind hitting the big cardboard signs placed about their necks. They lazily wind and unwind on the ropes around their necks. The signs remind the populace that these men have been punished for racketeering and black market activities. One sign indicates that the carrier is Jewish, the other two are Poles.

My stomach begins to grumble. I feel sick and turn away from this horrible spectacle. My companions also do not have stomachs for it. "Let's get out of here," I shout. We do not walk but run, first as fast as we can and then slowing down only at the entry into the street that leads uptown to our home.

At home I learn that Bobe is very sick. It is Friday eve, and all stores are closed. We cannot even get a prescription filled. Father decides to stay at her bedside all night. I join him, and together we watch her fade away. It is hard to witness the last hours on this earth of someone dear to you. She continuously struggles, gasping for breath as she lies there, depleted of her strength by age and disease.

I open the window fully, hoping that fresh air will make it easier for her to breathe. It is still relatively warm outside for this time of the year. The sky is dark but clear. Stars cover the entire firmament in every direction, as far as I can see. Bright moonlight illuminates the shabby buildings and narrow streets, creating strange figures of the falling shadows. I try to relax in my swivel chair by slowly rolling back and forth. As I doze off, time seems to have taken on a new pace, It creeps ever so slowly rather than moving at its normal clock-set rate.

Suddenly, a terrific explosion shakes the house, and makes the window panes resonate in loud vibrations. I wake up from the shallow nap that managed to consume me for a while. I look around. The clock on the wall above Bobe's head indicates midnight. Father jumps up from the chair in which he slumbered. For an instant he is disoriented, but soon regains his balance, "What is going on?" he cries. Both of us lean out the window. To the north we see a white cloud rising in the moonlit night. It seems to be coming from Freedom Square. Within seconds, other windows open up and peoples' heads appear. "What happened?" inquire some voices. Others panic and shout, "We are being bombed! Take cover!"

To us, it is apparent that some kind of an explosion took place in the vicinity of the Freedom Square. People in their night clothing trickle down into the street and begin to gather in groups discussing the enormous blast which so suddenly disrupted their nightly peace. Soon the police appear. The orders are clear. Disappear into your homes - or else! The streets quickly become deserted. Windows slowly close and people return to their beds, probably contemplating, as we were, various possibilities.

Bubbe lies motionless. Her breathing gets heavier. Suddenly a loud noise clears her throat, and then...silence. It is about an hour after the explosion. Father checks her breath with a mirror, and tries to get a pulse, without success. We lift her off the bed, place the body on the floor, and cover it with her own sheets. We locate her two cherished, silver candle holders. Affix one at the foot and the other at the head, insert candles and light them.

Father says "Kaddish", the prayer for the dead, and we talk for a while. As I fall asleep in my chair I wonder how within one day I managed to meet death, face to face, more frequently than I have in my entire life. I used to be frightened of death and all phenomena associated with post mortem existence, such as evils, ghosts, and other specters. Now that I have come eye-to-eye with its manifestations, I feel kind of absolved, cleansed of the fears, and strengthened. After all, death seems nothing more than the termination of life. A dead body is a lifeless body. Death is final, irreversible. Bubbe is no more. Only a bundle of skin, bones and associated materials which once gave life to her body still remain as proof that she once was.

The morning light pierces through the window curtains. We quickly straighten out our clothing and leave, locking the door behind us. We wash our faces and rinse our mouths with water at the backyard pump. Dry off with our handkerchiefs and set out to inform Bobe's daughters Bajla and Rose.

Bobe's death comes as no surprise. We all expected her to die soon. On the way home we notice a commotion as we approach Freedom Square. People come running crying and screaming:

"The bastards blew up Kosciuszko!"

"What do you mean?" we ask.

"The monument. It is all in pieces. Pulverized. Go and see for yourselves."

We do not need any further explanations. So that's what the explosion was all about. It is clear. The Germans decided to blow up the monument to shame and disgrace the Polish nation.

We buried Bobe on Sunday, according to the Jewish ritual which calls for a quick burial, but never on the Sabbath. The Sunday papers announced that Kosciuszko's statue was destroyed by Jews. So that is what they meant by the Big Lie. I have read about it before. It is supposed to be the forte of the master propagandist Goebels. I have listened to some of his radio speeches. The venom and lies which constituted the basis of every one of his orations were shrewdly shrouded in half-truths. The fact that these lies can be believed by others escaped me. Now those lies, and the allegations that can be drawn from them, are directly addressed to me, and my co-religionists. I tremble at the thought of possible retribution, and keep on hoping that the Poles will not believe them.

Chapter 23

THE BURNING ALTARS

Explosions and smoke drive us out of our beds. In the street, we can see black vortices of smoke rising all around us. No sounds of fire engines are to be heard. How strange. It is eerie. A policeman comes running down the street and urges us to retreat into our homes. "The synagogues are on fire," murmurs a Polish passer-by. Others confirm it. After a while, it becomes quite apparent to us that all synagogues in town have been almost simultaneously set afire, and permitted to burn out. We are terrified and sad. There is nothing we can do but retreat to the safety of our homes.

In the afternoon rumors sweep the town's Jewish population that we will be forced to abandon our homes. They say that some form of resettlement to the Polish Occupied Territories is planned. Mother cries, "First they destroy our houses of prayer, then they plan to resettle us. God only knows what their true intentions are."

"I don't believe in the resettlement rumor," says Father. "You just cannot re-settle a quarter of a million people so fast."

"Maybe not," I reply, "but let's not take any chances. I feel we should get the hell out of here."

"Where to?" shouts Father. "To Russia? Don't you know what happened to our party leaders once they got caught there? I would just as soon die here."

Once father raises his voice, I know it is of no use to start a big argument. I shut up. Pick up my box with cigarettes and leave to resume my morning peddling.

The streets, under the cover of the gray, obnoxious, smoke appear even grayer than usual. It is cold. I tighten the scarf around my neck, and button up my coat. The trees are bare, but some sparrows still chirp amidst their branches. Loose, yellow leaves swirl around in circles, propelled by the morning breeze. A group of people surround an announcement freshly pasted on the wall of our house. The paste is still running and the paper wrinkled in spots as if it were placed there in a great hurry. I move closer and begin to read:

"Beginning Thursday, the fourteenth of November, all Jews of this town are required to wear yellow armbands..."

The placard further proclaims that this is being done solely for the purpose of identification, and that any breaches of this new regulation will be subject to severe punishment.

"They must have lost faith in their ability to recognize Jews by their appearance. Maybe their measurement theories have fallen flat on their faces," I think out loud, as a bystander calls me over.

"Cigarettes, sir? The best in town. Firm and freshly packed!"

On Monday, a curfew is imposed on all Jews. We may roam the streets only between 5 a.m. and 8 p.m. This isn't really that bothersome. We are afraid to walk the streets in the daylight, never mind the hours of darkness. By this time, we have grown accustomed to rushing home at dusk. "If this is the worst they have in store for us, I'll buy it," says Mother. Nobody knows what "they" really plan. New rumors that all Jews will be concentrated in a ghetto in the old part of town have swept the city. We prefer not to listen to rumors. After all, they are only unverified figments of somebody's imagination. Yet, we know very well that so far most rumors have come true, especially the bad ones. November passed without further disturbances of crushing proportions. Thursday morning the second week of December, snow is falling, but we must prepare our daily production of cigarettes for sale, and sell them. Neither Debra nor I are anxious to hit the street. We'd sooner hang around the cooking stove which glows, and emits splendid heat. This night was very cold, and the coal in the stove burned out quicker than anticipated. Snow and ice deposits are forming in the north-eastern corner of our room right above my bed. In daylight they sparkle and shine like a million diamonds, and remain there in spite of the heat emanating from the stove. Instead of melting, new layers seem to be forming on top of the old ones taking on a hair-like texture that enhances their brilliance.

Mother is preparing breakfast. She managed to buy some eggs off a farmer who stopped his horse-drawn wagon right in front of our house. He appeared to be hauling hay, but hidden deep in the hay stack were eggs and cheese for sale. Most of our food is bought this way - on the black market.

The smell of chicory fills the air. The coffee we drink is mostly made of roots. Real coffee is hard to get, and is very expensive. Mother serves breakfast: rolls, scrambled eggs and coffee, when the ring of the door-bell brings all of us onto our feet.

"Who is it?" Mother's voice reaches a high pitch. "It is me, Haim."

We all breathe with relief. Mother opens the door and a frozen, aged, and puffing Uncle Haim enters the room. His face has not been shaved for a while and is covered with gray bristles. His gray hair is in disarray. His mustache carries tiny icicles that begin to rapidly melt in the warmth of the room. His glasses, barely supported by the tip of his nose, get fogged up by the moisture in the warm room. His shoes and coat have seen better days. He tumbles forward, reaches the hot stove and he begins to rub his frozen-blue hands over the hot oven plates.

"I came to make certain that you have enough material for this week's production. Don't know whether we'll manage to keep up with the necessary stuff. By the way, have you heard about the new decree?" Haim coughs for a while, then continues. "From now on we are required to wear yellow Stars of David with the word *Jude* inscribed in its center instead of the yellow armband."

"Are the Nazis trying to make Zionists out of us?" Father is obviously amused with the idea of Jews being forced to wear Stars of David.

"We must wear the yellow stars on the right front and back. The stars can be obtained from the Jewish Community Offices. I am sure we'll have to pay for them," responds uncle Haim.

"It seems the yellow bands do not serve their purpose. My God, what will they think of next to humiliate us with?" Mother is obviously dismayed.

"This is not all. I heard that they are planning to move us all into a ghetto. They say that by next spring we'll have to live there," adds Haim.

"Those rumors are not new, Zygmund mentioned that a couple of weeks ago. Apparently, he heard it from a highly placed Gestapo man. He also thought that the ghetto would be located in the old section of town," adds Father. "That's where my sisters Bajla and Rose live. They may not have to move at all."

"Lucky" says Debra.

The move into the old section of town is not something I am looking forward to. This section has no central sewage and no running water in the homes. More importantly, where shall we live? My Aunts Bajla and Rose have tiny apartments and could not accommodate even a cat. "Have you thought of trying to secure an apartment for us?" I ask my Father. "Not really. It is still unofficial, so why worry about it prematurely?" Father does not seem to be too concerned.

"The boy is right," Uncle Haim butts in. "When it becomes official, you will not be able to find anything decent."

Father turns the conversation back to business. This is now more important. We are running out of tobacco. Uncle Haim knows where to get more. Father puts on his coat and leaves with uncle Haim.

"Where shall we go to if a ghetto is formed?" I ask Mother.

"Only God knows," she replies in a hopeless tone of voice. "Your father still doesn't believe that the Germans are capable of doing that."

I am afraid she is right. Father still remembers the army and the First World War. To him, the Germans are cultured people who have given the world the Nietsches, Schoppenhauers, Haendels, Bachs, Beethovens, and all those other great thinkers, poets, philosophers, writers and musicians. How can they possibly be capable of atrocities against other people? This is beyond his comprehension, and he acts accordingly.

It is time to hit the streets and make some money. I flip the suspension cord of my "store-case" around my neck. Fill the case with cigarettes and walk into the street. It's colder than usual and time to wrap my shawl more tightly. The clouds above threaten to break out into snow. Some dispersed flakes are dancing in the freezing air. My nose is the first to feel the frost. I pull the shawl over it and leave only openings for my eyes. The feet will be next, but mother forced me to put on two pairs of woolen socks. The streets are filled with briskly running people, and my business picks up very quickly. Slowly I make my way to the corner. In the distance I see some people leaning over a bundle lying on the sidewalk.

"What's going on?" I ask a man rushing from the scene that I recognize as one of our neighbors.

"It's Sarah," he responds in haste. "She had one of her attacks, and as she was lying on the ground a passing *Volksdeutche* with a Nazi armband kicked her in the head. I think she's dead."

Our neighborhood had its share of "village idiots". They hang around within an area of about ten blocks. We all knew and made fun of them. There was Yankel, a homeless man, who could recite all the patrol men's names in every police precinct in town. He also performed the function of a local telephone book. He knew all telephone numbers of everyone who had a phone, including all state and government offices.

Then there was Czeslaw, an Old Pole who was habitually drunk. The man could drink vodka like no one I have ever seen. It was water to him. In absence of legitimate vodka, made by the Governmental Cartel, he would drink anything containing alcohol, including rubbing alcohol which was readily available in the local apothecaries. He derived his "income" from delivering pales of drinking water from the fountain at the Liberty Square.

Then there was Sarah. She had an elongated face adorned with two glowing, deeply recessed, dark eyes. Her black hair was thinning on her otherwise meticulously combed head. Her clothing was rumpled, but usually clean. Sarah has been roaming the streets of our neighborhood for as long as I can remember. She never begged for anything, but always found a sympathetic soul to hand her some food, enough for a day's nutrition.

Sarah was an epileptic. I had seen her many a time lying on the sidewalk in spasms, her extremities in involuntary convulsions, with foam forming around her mouth. Most of the people thought she was crazy, and treated her as such. Kids would spit on her, throw rocks, or simply curse her. Sarah took it all in her quiet, defensive way. Apparently, she is now dead. She is better off that way, I think. The *Volksdeutche* have done her a favor. Under these circumstances she would have died anyhow. That reminded me that I hadn't seen Yankl in a long time. Perhaps he is dead too.

My thoughts are interrupted by a customer: "Ten cigarettes, how much?" This will be one mark. We are taking only German currency. The Polish zloty is not considered to have any real value.

A few hours have passed. My hands and legs are stiff from the cold and the fingers and toes begin to itch. it is time to call it quits. I have sold more than three quarters of my wares.

Back home there is more talk about the formation of the Ghetto.

Father returned from his tobacco acquisition with two of mothers cousins, Zajvel R. and Julek R. Zajvel helped us get the coal for this winter. Their sister Rachel was one of the nieces adopted by my grandmother. She moved to London where she married into an English-Jewish family, the F's. They say that the F.'s have extensive land holdings in Palestine. They apparently own large orange groves, and also grow grapes for wine there.

Our family relationship here gets a little complicated. It so happened that Mother's cousin, and also Haim's wife's cousin, Julek R. married Uncle Haim's sister Meita. They have four lovely children, three boys and a girl. Julek's brother Zajvel is married to a woman named Rajzl. They have two sons. Rajzl's longing for a daughter resulted in her adopting a pretty girl in the early thirties. The girl was seven years old then.

Mother welcomes her cousins with an invitation to tea and cookies. They readily agree.

"I have not seen you in ages. What's new? How's Rajzl? How's Meita? How are the children?" Mother's questions pour out like water from a leaking pail.

"On my end everything is all right, you might say. Of course, this terrible situation we have found ourselves in has got us all worried," says Julek R.

Worried is not the right expression" adds his brother Zajvel R. "We are literally sick. Rajzl misses her sons. You know, they left home a couple of months ago. They are now in the Russian-held territories. Were it not for the presence of Sara, the girl we adopted, I don't know what we would have done. She is our patron angel. She takes care of us. Cleans the house. Shops for food, and generally keeps our spirits up."

Zajvel is a man of average height, but his body has been deformed due to a combination of a glandular disorder, which made him incredibly corpulent, and a short right leg which helped to disfigure his posture over time. To make things worse, his head was abnormally large for his stature. All these things, combined, resulted in a tragic, yet to some, comic, figure. He was a kind, wise, and soft spoken individual.

In contrast, his wife Rajzl is tall, domineering in stature, tough, outspoken, and very opinionated. His brother Julek, a handsome man about ten years younger that Zajvel, also suffers from a deformed and shortened leg. It was a "family fault", Mother explained to us. I could not understand this since all of their children were extremely well postured. Only Ruben, a son of Julek, seemed to always be out of breath. His lips were blue most of the time. In mother's opinion he had a "heart problem".

"What will you do if, or should I say when, a ghetto is formed," asks Zajvel.

"We really haven't given it too much thought," Mother turns to Father. "Perhaps this is a good time to consider the rumors more seriously."

"Do you have any plans?" Father turns to the two guests. "I, frankly, do not think this is a possibility, but in any case it won't hurt to give it some thought."

"Abram," Julek now moves closer to Father and looks him straight in the eyes. "I am certain of what I heard, and who I heard it from, that come next spring we -- all of us, without any exception -- will be confined in a ghetto."

"Well, let me assume you are right," Father seems now a bit more reasonable. "Where do we go? What do we do?"

"At this very moment there is not much we can do, but to keep our eyes open. When the order is officially given, there will be many houses completely evacuated by their Gentile occupants. This will be the time to step in and get a hold of some flats. I wish we could all live in the same house." Apparently, Zajvel has given this problem some thought.

"That is a wonderful idea," adds Mother, "Maybe we could also try to accommodate my sister with her family and my parents."

"As a matter of fact, Meita discussed that already with her brother Haim D. He will help to find quarters for all of us, in the same house, if at all possible." Julek's voice is somewhat garbled by the piece of domino sugar in his mouth, which he uses to sweeten the tea after the cookies have been consumed.

"We talked about the ghetto rumor with Haim just today, but did not get into details. Perhaps because it is too early to worry about it." Father still tries to push the bleak possibility of us being interned in a ghetto out of his mind.

At this point, I excuse myself, leave the table, and stretch out on the sofa with my book. It is a popular mystery story. Most of our libraries have been either burned or closed by now. I picked up this book a couple of weeks ago, in the park seemingly waiting for an eager reader. I took it home.

1940

He stalked among the lions
He was a great beast He learned to hunt prey He devoured men
He ravished their widows
Laid waste their cities
The land, and all in it were appalled.
At the sound of his roaring...
Nations from the countries roundabout arrayed themselves against him.
He was caught in their snare.

Ezekiel 19.7

Chapter 24

A NEW HOME

Early 1940 the ghetto rumors have become a reality. How we hoped that they were only hearsay, a figment of somebody's sick imagination. Unfortunately, they are true. We are getting ready to move. We are told that the movement into the ghetto is required to guarantee our own safety. We shall be given a town of our own, surrounded by high wire fences. We shall be safe there since German Army guards will be watching out for our well-being day and night. We shall have a government of our own. Our own schools. Our own food distribution centers. Huge signs are being put up on the ghetto borders, they read:

Wohngebiet der Juden - Eintrit verboten.

"Start packing!" Father directs us in an authoritative voice.

"I don't know where to begin", Mother seems helpless faced with the horrible prospect of leaving our flat.

The winter is almost over. It was a cold and cruel one. Yet we thank the Almighty for allowing us to survive. The more unbearable and ambiguous our existence becomes the more religious we get. My father has lately been talking to God more frequently than at any other time I remember. So do all of us.

Could this terrible weather, I wonder, have come from God? Why does he do that to us? It is warming up today, and the icy roads are beginning to melt but March has in the past been full of surprises, and the frosty weather may yet return at any time, hopefully not for too long. We are almost out of coal, and although it is already the beginning of March we use it very sparingly.

As the rumors had it, the ghetto will indeed be located in the old section of town. Since the order for Jews to vacate the city and concentrate in the old town section was not quickly adhered to, German police began to encircle city blocks and forcefully evacuate Jews. This process was, apparently, still too slow for the Germans' timetable, because just yesterday a great many houses on the main street were surrounded, its Jewish occupants beaten, and some say, hundreds of people killed.

My cousin Bella and Yakov live in one of these houses, but just as luck would have it, they were visiting Yakov's brother at the time. A month ago uncle Haim and Julek R. managed to secure a portion of a house that could accommodate, not without a lot of strain, most of our family. My Father's sisters were lucky. They didn't have to move since they already lived in the old city. So now we are packing in a hurry.

Outside, the streets are covered with a hard layer of packed snow which has been made tougher by intermittent, but infrequent, thaws. Sleds have replaced the wheel equipped taxi-carriages.

"I'll have to build a sled to move all the things we are capable of taking with us. Come with me down to the cellar. There is a lot of wood there. You can help me construct one." Father turns to me, rolling up the sleeves of his sweater.

"We have to make it big enough to drag the biggest load, and yet small enough to fit our strength. It is a long haul down to the old section." I am trying to size up the requirements.

"Let us pray that the weather stays cold, otherwise we won't be able to pull anything!" Father is obviously concerned with the prospects of a sudden meltdown.

"If the pulling gets rough we'll have to take smaller loads and make more frequent trips." I try to inject some logic into the otherwise senseless and hopeless situation.

In the cellar, we have no trouble locating two long beams, and a thick sheet of plywood. We strip some iron bands off an old crate. These will be used as the shoes of the sled to reduce friction. Three hours go by and we carry out a strong, hefty sled. Outside, we drill a hole at the center, reinforce it with a piece of sheet metal, and pull through a thick rope. The rope ends in two loops which can be thrown across the chest of two people. To the rear we affix two cross- reinforced vertical poles. They have a dual purpose: they prevent the stuff we carry from sliding off the sled, and they provide means for pushing the sled, thus somewhat relieving those pulling from carrying the full load.

"I know where we are going to, but exactly what kind of arrangement do you have?" I ask Father while carrying the sled out of the cellar.

"I discussed it with Mother. We shall all live in the same house. But we were a little too late, and will have to share one room with Zajvel. Still, we will be living closer to our relatives than before. We won't have to run blocks to see your cousins." Father attempts to put a ray of hope into a pretty grim situation.

"Well, I could have told you so. As usual, we waited too long."

I preferred to stop right at this point. What's the use fighting now when all is kind of settled? "What about Bella and Yakov?"

"They are leaving town. Yakov has a distant cousin in a small town in the occupied Polish territories. They intend to settle there. He believes that eventually Jews will not be permitted to live in the Third Reich. Perhaps he is right. I think we are safer here. At least in the ghetto we'll be protected by the Germans from Polish Anti-Semites." Father's explanations now border on the ridiculous, but I prefer not to engage him in further discourse on that subject. After all, there isn't a hell of a lot we can do now.

We drag out the sled, and place it close to the stairs.

"Let's take a load of the smaller things first so that we get a feel for the labor involved in shleping the sled." Father tries to perform an engineering test first.

I run up the stairs, gather some clothing, cooking utensils, loose smaller items, and drag them down to the sled. In the meantime, Father has also brought down a few chairs and the small black mahogany table. These are a few things that we will not need immediately, so why not use them for the first test trip?

We dress in our warm winter clothing, put on galoshes to keep the feet dry, belt on the harness across our chests and pull.

At first the sled won't move, but after a few coordinated shouts-and-pulls, off we go down the path which has already been hardened by thousands before us. The streets are full and the going isn't easy. Here and there exhausted or sick people stop and block the passage. It is like jumping over hurdles. We too have to stop very frequently to take a sip from the thermos bottle mother put in a bag on top of the sled. The tea tastes like a good wine. I never before appreciated its aroma and the sweetness of the dissolved sugar as much as I do now. Although it is still below freezing I begin to get warm. Slowly I discard the heavy shawl and remove my overcoat.

"You'll catch cold!" I hear Father's voice. "Don't worry, I'll be all right," I shout back.

After three hours of sled dragging we reach our destination. Under normal circumstances this would have been a fifteen minute brisk walk. The house we will live in is located on an abandoned street from which its old inhabitants, Poles, have been evacuated about a week ago. We are about one block away from the old city square on which the hangings took place in November.

The room is not as big as we thought. It is about 30 by 30 feet. The outside walls consist of a single layer of logs covered with painted plywood. Two windows provide daylight. In the center of the floor is a deep hole covered with wooden planks. According to father this hole is used as a refrigerator. In the summertime vegetables, butter and eggs can be safely kept there for a couple of days without getting spoiled. A small bulb suspended by an electric cord dangles from the center of the ceiling.

We unload our sled contents into a corner. It is apparent that Zajvel has already been here. A bunch of clothing and some paper bags full of a variety of small items cover the place under one of the windows.

"It seems that Zajvel is attempting to stake out his territory," I utter, looking around this pitiful place in sheer amazement, wondering how all of us will squeeze into it.

"You are right." Father keeps on sizing up Zajvel's bundles. "He picked the window next to the wall which forms a partition between this room and the flat on the other side. On our side all three walls are exposed to the outside. Oh well! Hopefully we won't stay here too long".

"Amen," I say out loud, but quietly wish I could agree with Father's conjecture. "Let's return home." Father is apparently upset. "We'll have a bite and return with another load. They say the weather may warm up. This means that the snow will melt, and we may not be able to use the sled."

On the way back to the house the streets are more crowded than a few hours ago. We raise the sled sideways and carry it. This way we can maneuver through the crowds with greater ease.

At home, Mother, with Debra's help, keeps on emptying the closets, cupboards, and all the drawers. What a mess. Mother and Debra are crying. I find it difficult to hold back my tears. Somehow, we intuitively feel that we have been overcome by a huge and terrible metamorphosis. Will the world ever be the same? I wonder. There is a certain sensation of irreversibility, impermanence, awe, fear, and helplessness in our actions.

"Do you think we will ever come back to this place?" I ask Father.

"With God's help we will. We cannot lose hope." I am amazed at Father's continuous reference to the Almighty. He must be pretty desperate, I think.

We have a quick bite consisting of a hard roll, butter and farmer's cheese which mother procured from street wagons. It seems that the next trip should be with furniture. We examine the framed mirror assembly and decide that we can live without it. Mother, most probably, will not have any more work. Hence no customers, and no need for a mirror to examine the fit of a customer's dress. We also decide against taking the huge pictures. Who needs them? There is hardly any room for a table. The large kitchen table is also abandoned. Sewing machines must be delivered to a central collection base according to an order of the authorities, and our cast iron stove is too heavy to be dragged along. So is the large cupboard in which we stored our clothing and worldly possessions. The things that we decide are absolutely needed are the beds, mattresses, and the fancy commode. To be sure these are also very heavy, but they represent value or potential comfort, and are worth the effort. In addition, we take our couch, assorted clothing and kitchen utensils. Another four trips and we will have all moved into our new quarters.

The sun begins to set over the street chaos, and the buildings cast elongated shadows as we start our second trip. The sled is heavy, loaded with the commode, table and chairs. Icy surfaces are gradually wearing off, and we hit many bare spots. It takes the four of us to slowly and painfully proceed to our destination. Father and I are harnessed up front. Mother and Debra push from the rear. Dark and depressing thoughts enter my mind. Is this how the Hebrews worked in Egypt? Are we embarking upon a new era of slavery? Will it last a hundred years, or maybe a thousand as promised by the Fuehrer? Who knows?

Chapter 25
THE GHETTO

Spring has arrived, but the buds on the trees lining our street seem to shy away from developing into full leaves. As a matter of fact, all of nature is still in deep winter slumber, as if it didn't want to wake up and face the "new order". At least, so it seems to me. The birds are late arriving. Or is it my imagination? I do not hear their cheerful songs the way I used to.

The usual refreshing and exhilarating smell of spring is overwhelmed by the smell of human waste which has soaked into the walls and clothing we wear. Our flat is very small, too small for seven people. The outhouse is about a hundred yards from our door, and too far to walk to in the freezing cold of winter. Our overnight needs, be it what they may, are discharged into one bucket placed as far away from our beds as possible. It is my and Sala W.'s job to empty the bucket whenever it fills up.

Food is still available, but the supply which we brought with us to the ghetto is rapidly being depleted. Luckily, Sala W., the niece of Zajvel and his wife, who took up residence with them, is also an attractive girl who knows how to make use of her charms. She is well developed and uses a lot of make up to further enhance her feminine charms. Her cologne provides some relief from the usual stench. A couple of weeks ago she met the son of a bakery owner. The bakery is only a couple of buildings down the street from our house. A quick relationship developed which brought us some distinctive advantages. We do not have to stand in lines, and the bread we get is fresh and uniform, not as crooked and distorted as that generally sold. She boasts that the bread she gets for herself and her uncle and aunt is free. Some deal. I have been wondering lately whether my parents would have tolerated this kind of behavior on the part of my sister. I doubt it. At any rate, Debra is thirteen, and Sala eighteen, so why speculate?

In marked contrast to our habitat, my Uncle Haim managed to get two and a half rooms for himself. His apartment is located on the first floor just across the yard from our flat. Zajvel's brother, Julek P., also got a couple of rooms for his family on the second floor above that of Uncle Haim. My orphaned cousins have a one room flat on the second floor. My grandparents settled on the third floor in a room smaller than the one they had in the city. Zajde cannot walk anymore and remains in bed most of the time. Bubbe keeps him company, but frequently ventures downstairs to visit her children and grandchildren. Their daily subsistence is provided jointly by all of us.

The other day I complained, in Bubbe's presence, about the terribly small place we have to live in. Seven people pressed into a small room! Bubbe looked at me with her wise eyes, smiled and pointed to the floor space next to the chair she was sitting in.

"Sit down, and I'll tell you a story"

I followed her order, as did Debra, who also supported me in my complaints. "Once upon a time" Bubbe started her story, "there was a very wise, knowledgeable, and astute Rabbi. His fame spread throughout the country and people came from afar to benefit from his advice."

"Bubbe," Debra interrupted, "we have outgrown children's' tales."

"This is not the usual tale." responded Bubbe "It is very apropos of the questions you are raising."

"Getting back to our Rabbi," she continued. "One day, a poor peasant, who had a terrible problem, heard of the rabbi's wisdom, and set out to get his advice." Once in the Rabbi's presence he stated his complaint. Rabbi, he said, I live in a small, poor village, in a tiny house which I built with my own hands as soon as I married. My wife has blessed me with five children. Our little home has since become very cramped. There is hardly any room to turn around. Now, to top it all, my wife's parents have been evicted by their landlord and ask to live with us. What should I do?

"Do you have a goat?" asked the Rabbi. "Yes," replied the farmer, "he is our only provider of the milk we drink". "Go home" says the Rabbi, "and take your in-laws as well as the goat into your home and come back in two weeks."

Two weeks passed and the peasant is back at the Rabbi's court. "Rabbi," he cries. "This is terrible! There is hardly any room to stand." "Do you have a dog?" asked the Rabbi. "Yes, Rabbi, I keep him outside in a little dog house I built for him." "Take him into your house," said the Rabbi, "and keep him there." "But Rabbi..." starts the peasant. "No but..." "Go home and come back in two weeks."

Every visit to the Rabbi resulted in further instructions to take in the chicken, a goose, and finally a calf. Another two weeks passed and the peasant faces the Rabbi again. He is totally distraught. "Help me Rabbi" he screams. "I cannot take it any longer." "Well," says the Rabbi, "go home and remove all your animals but not your in-laws and come back in two weeks."

Two weeks passed. The peasant is in the presence of the Rabbi again. "O Rabbi. Life is wonderful. Now we can move. My place has become livable again. Thank you Rabbi, for your wise advice and help." "Go home and give my blessings to your entire family," responded the Rabbi."

Bubbe ended her story and looked at us: "Do you get the moral of this story?"

O well! We get it all right. It sure could be worse. I guess this is the only thing we can count on. If things seem bad now, they will get worse tomorrow.

Chapter 26
OUR MR. R.

The official leader of our ghetto is Mr.R. He is an intriguing figure. The story goes that when the Germans took our city they called the Jewish Community leaders to a meeting. At this meeting the Germans asked for the *Aeltester,* which in German implies "head of" the Jews. Since the same word also means "the oldest" Mr.R, who was the oldest member of the leadership circle, raised his hand. He became the leader of the ghetto Jews. Before the war, Mr. R., a confirmed bachelor, was the head of a large Jewish Orphanage. His love for his orphans knew no boundaries. Some claimed it went too far. He always fought for more funding to keep the orphanage going. Now, he is our leader. As soon as the ghetto was formed in December of last year, he was the only person officially charged with the formation of a ghetto administration.

At first he attempted to run a democratic ghetto by inviting all political parties to participate in its government. The Germans named it the *Judenrat.* Among the parties laying claim to be representative of the populace were the social democratic Bund, the Zionist *Poalei Zion* (left and right factions), The orthodox *Mizrachi* and *Aguda* parties, the centrist Zionists, and the brown shirted rightist Revisionists. The communists were not officially represented but had some agitators dispersed among the populace. His government was made up of various divisions such as food, work, security, services, and a few other minor ones. There even was an education and entertainment division at the start.

In the last few weeks, however, Mr. R. began to exhibit signs of self-aggrandizement, and intolerance for others. We are afraid that this might bring about full dictatorship. After all, this is what the Germans had in mind. Their system isn't democratic either.

The Ghetto Police, which the Germans authorized a few months ago, has taken on the look of storm troopers. Although their uniforms are civilian, the caps, armbands, britches, and high riding boots attest to their full authority. Firearms are obviously taboo - they have been confiscated a long time ago. Instead the police carry wooden clubs which they have certainly learned how to use. Many of us experienced the efficacy of these clubs while standing in line for food. Mr. R. rides around the ghetto in a horse drawn *dorozka*. He occupies the back seat and waves at people crowding the streets as if to say: "Look here, I am your leader. The only leader you have. The only one you'll ever get!" He seems to enjoy his role.

Street singers call him The King. They sing new songs which they compose in his honor. The songs go something like this: Mr. R. gives us food, gives us drink, gives us manna. In the olden days manna was sent from heaven for the stranded tribes of Israel, today Mr. R. provides it on earth.

Mr. R.'s stature grows from day to day. He organizes schools, a theater, puts together bands and a classical orchestra. There is a ghetto newspaper, the primary function of which is to provide the latest notices and announcements. We also have a small scale night club in which, to the amusement of the listeners, stand-up comedians provide their interpretation of life in the ghetto. No criticism of Mr. R. or the German authorities is permitted. Sometime this summer Mr. R. began to seriously "industrialize" the ghetto. His main objective being to demonstrate to the Germans that we, the ghetto inhabitants, can do useful work in support of the German war effort and as such deserve to be kept alive. Factories opened up all over the place. The ghetto is proving itself to be capable of producing almost anything that might be of value to the Germans. The German in charge of this effort is a certain Mr. B., who acts as if he owned the entire ghetto and talks only to Mr. R. The people who work, do earn extra rations of food for their efforts. People who don't work are condemned to starvation- the rations they get are not sufficient to keep them alive.

With time, we- the ghetto inhabitants- have developed only one goal: Survival. This goal seems to become more distant with each passing day. As the work gets harder the rations become leaner. As the food intake drops so does production. And, as production decreases, so do the food rations supplied by Mr. B. It is a vicious, deadly, cycle we are in.

Mr. R must know all that. All he has to do is look at the rising daily burials. I often wonder what makes him tick. How he feels about the role he was dealt to play in this disastrous tragedy. Does he care, at all, how history will treat him? Time will tell, though I ponder how many of us will be around to give witness when the whole thing is over. Will Mr. R be around to give his account? As it looks now, he is very well fed and may be among the few who will survive.

Chapter 27

FIRST DEATH IN THE FAMILY

Spring has finally arrived. It is a beautiful April morning. The sun is shining, birds are busily building their nests. The lonely tree in our backyard sprang buds a couple of weeks ago. Now the buds are slowly opening up permitting the restrained leaves to develop while drinking from the well of the golden sunshine. We had breakfast as we got out of bed. Mother prepared bread, cheese and coffee. Butter is hard to get. Many of our ghetto inhabitants are not so lucky. They ran out of food a long time ago. Some people did not bother to bring any food with them, either because they felt that the war would soon end, or because they did not have enough money to buy the food with. Our meager supplies are also coming close to exhaustion. According to Mother they might last another four weeks.

After breakfast I join my cousins in the backyard. David seems depressed.

"I hate to be the bearer of bad tidings," David starts up the conversation, "but last night Zajde seemed to be in terrible pain. He moaned all night long. Bubbe, who spent the night at his bedside, called me about two o'clock in the morning. I went up, but did not know what to do to help him. I am afraid he is coming to the end of his struggles."

"How old is Zajde?" asked Debra.

"He is eighty four years old," volunteers Ita. "Watching him struggle in pain without being able do anything about it is very frustrating. I hate to say it, but he may be better off in the Other World."

"If there is one," adds Julek D.

"Life is like children's diapers; Short and full of shit," intrudes Sarah with a philosophical touch. I think I have heard it somewhere before.

"How can you say that?" I feel I have to enter this discussion before it deteriorates into a self-pitying feast. "Life may be short, but it can also be long. It depends on your own state of mind and the environment you live in. What is short to you may be eternity to others. People in India or Africa live a short life by our standards. Zajde is eighty four. God, if there is one, has been gracious to him and very generous. Under the best of conditions how many people live to this ripe old age?"

"Should he die would we know what to do?" inquires Debra.

"I think we will have to notify the cemetery crew," David is not too sure." Let's ask uncle Abram."

"The old Jewish cemetery is still within the confines of the ghetto. I know that because I went to register for summer school yesterday, and we passed it. It has a big black iron gate in front. Mother told me that her brother Izaak, her sister Debra, and uncle Moishe are buried there."

"What about the ghetto schools?" Julek wants to change the topic.

"Well, you know old man Mr. R. got permission from the Germans to open up a Hebrew school in the fields at the ghetto's edge. I was there yesterday to register. Apparently there will be an elementary, and high school in one big place. They told us that an effort will be made to also serve some food during the day," explains Debra.

Debra has reached the age of thirteen last February. She has grown up in a hurry during the last eight months, mentally, that is, not physically. Although she is taller than mother her physical female attributes still remain to be developed. The school, if it materializes, will give her an opportunity to finish the seventh grade of public school and continue on to high school. New factories are speedily constructed. The clothing factories are an immediate success. The reason for that is rather obvious. Our city was one of the largest producers of clothing materials before the war began, and a substantial tailoring activity developed around the locally produced textile materials. This activity was almost exclusively run by Jews even before the war.

As we stand there in the courtyard of our house suddenly we hear cries emanating from the open window of my grandparents room. We all turn pale. Could it be? We all rush upstairs. The door to my grandparents' room is wide open. On the bed lies grandfather fully clothed in his normal dark attire. His grey beard points towards the ceiling. His eyes are open, so is his mouth. The sunken cheeks appear to greatly exaggerate his normally prominent nose. His face is ashen grey.

"He is dead!" screams mother

Bubbe just stands there motionless, gazing at the face of her beloved husband. Quietly, she mutters "He is gone. Gone forever." Her eyes, it seems, have lost their capability to cry. She looks stoic and brave beyond anyone's expectations. Perhaps this is simply a disguised attempt to cover up her feelings of abandonment and infallibility of death. Who knows?

Within minutes the room fills up. Everyone is there. Father with a yarmulke covering the bald spot on the rear of his head, Uncle Haim in his old worn hat, nephews Zajvel and Julek, and all grandchildren. There is no room to turn around.

"Everybody out, except his children," proclaims Father as he lowers the body onto the floor with the assistance of Uncle Haim and Julek R.

We leave the room and assemble in the yard. Someone has to go to the Burial Squad to inform them that there is a body to be picked up. Simultaneously, the cemetery officials must also be quickly notified to prepare an open grave. Hopefully, we can bury him today, according to the laws of our religion.

Four long hours have passed. The burial detail arrived not long ago. They are in the process of cleaning the body. Once cleaned, it is smeared with the juice of a lemon and wrapped up in white linen. We have also managed to find a couple of boards which will be placed on the bottom and top of the body when it is lowered into the grave. No caskets allowed. This is traditional.

By the evening, we are all assembled at the open grave. A friend of Father's who was a cantor before the war and is now working at the cemetery, performs a heart-tearing rendition of *El Moleh Rachamim* which ends with the Hebrew words. "O Lord, lift up thy countenance upon us and give us peace, now and evermore. Amen."

All women are crying. The cantor's chant with its fine modulations adds drama to this tragic moment. It is now time to recite *Kaddish*, the prayer for the departed. Father has been chosen because there is no son present. Normally, this duty falls to the oldest son. The prayer for the dead begins with *"Yiskadal v'yiskadash shmei raba."*

"Your memory, dearly beloved, who during this past year left our congregation and returned to the Father's house, to eternal repose - ye, who walked with us to the house of the Lord, who lived and hoped, prayed and trusted with us in the one and only God of Israel - ye, whose places are vacant in this holy temple, and whose loss is still visible in the garb of deep morning which covers your bereft friends, whose hearts and wounds which your departure inflicted, are still bleeding - all ye brethren beloved in the Lord, Gershon R., your memory lives in this congregation and in this holy temple. We feel your presence and bless the hours you spent with us before God. O, be ye a messenger of peace to us, that even the most sorely tried and severely afflicted shall be the recipients of solace and consolation from the unfailing source of hope and comfort, the All merciful Father...Amen."

It is a long way back to the house. Bubbe walks very slowly, held under her arms by her two daughters. We hurry to break up the assembly lest it be interpreted as an unlawful gathering. That night as I lay down to sleep I wonder how many times we may still have to perform this ceremony, before the war and our internment - is over. I draw close to my Father and fall asleep.

On the world scene, the winter of 1939 - 1940 was not quiet. The Russians declared war on Finland. The Finnish government, it seemed to us, was sympathetic to Germany, but the Germans stayed aside, not wanting to aggravate the Russians. Despite the sympathy the Finns had for the Germans, their leader, a General Mannheim, caught our imagination. Here was a small country fighting off the advances of a huge Soviet army and doing it quite successfully. The war dragged on through the entire winter, and finally ended a few weeks ago, at the beginning of March. The Finns were defeated but not after a number of close battles that cost the Russians a lot of men, and equipment.

Shortly after the Russian victory over Finland the German Armies set out to conquer Norway and Denmark. Denmark was easily overrun. The papers smuggled into the ghetto talked about new "engagements" on Norwegian territory and in the fjords. Names like Narvik and Bergen have become part of our vocabulary. Whatever happened, it seemed for a while that the German Army has finally reached some serious resistance.

Although it was not clear whether the Norwegian Army was joining the battle, it was nevertheless obvious to us that British troops had managed to land in Norway, and were putting up a hell of a fight. Unfortunately, four weeks later the campaign was over. The Germans occupied Denmark and Norway. We heard that a Norwegian named Quisling is now in charge in Norway. The Norwegian King Haakon fled to London. The British are organizing their forces for an onslaught on Germany.

On the French front there is no news.

Chapter 28
HITTING THE STREETS

The spring and early summer passed quickly by. Our great expectations and hopes turned sour as soon as we began receiving news from the western front. In an attempt to break through the western front as quickly as possible and maintain the *"Blitzktrieg"* image, the Germans attacked by the middle of May. The feared, and by us admired, Maginot line was bypassed in no time. The Dutch put up some resistance which cost them dearly. The large port city of Rotterdam was flattened to the ground by the German Luftwaffe. Using what was described in the press as, "new and secret techniques", the German Armies managed to take all Dutch bridges and establish a clear route for the conquest of France.

The new French prime minister, Reynaud, and his General Gamelin have all but given up, says the local German newspaper, which is still being smuggled into the ghetto. England, too, has a new prime minister, his name is Churchill. He too will soon recognize the error of his ways and give in, says the German press. By this time, we have become experts at reading between the lines of the latest war reports. Alas, there is no indication there that the progress on the western front is being impeded. New German heroes arise. In addition to such better known names as Halder and Jodl one hears now of the heroic acts of other Generals with names such as Reinhardt, Reichenau, Guderian, and even once about the grand exploits of a young panzer group Commanding General named Rommel.

By the end of May our hopes were just about fully exhausted. Holland and then Belgium were defeated and the German armies penetrated deep into France. We read about Allied soldiers being trapped at Dunkirk. The start of June found the French Army at the threshold of total defeat. As the month progressed it became clear that the war in France was over. On June 21st, Hitler accepted the surrender of the French at Compiegne in a railroad car which was the scene of the German surrender to the victorious allies of World War One. What a humiliation, we thought. What revenge. Pictures in the paper showed Herr Hitler rubbing his hands out of pure joy experienced by the defeat of his long-time enemies. With the defeat of the Allied armies in Europe, our self-esteem hit rock bottom.

The pessimists among us see nothing but a dreadful end. "He will kill us all," they say. Why give him this pleasure? Not all of us are pessimists. There are also optimists who can see a ray of sunshine in the darkest sky. These people, my cousins and I among them, see a future which is not necessarily hopeless. After all, the Russians are still there. There is a German-Russian pact and Hitler will probably reach some kind of a territorial settlement with them. Our mail that we still receive from the Russian occupied territories keeps on hinting that soon our city will become part of the Soviet Union. From postcards we learn that Izaak D. married a local girl in Lida, near Vilnus, and just had a little son in July. A strange story reached us from our cousin Izaak B. He was in the city of Lvov and in his latest letter told us that he is homesick and decided to come back into the ghetto. The next postcard came from the city of Czeliabinsk in the Urals. His brother David thought that he was expatriated to do hard work because of his desire to leave the Soviet paradise. Maybe so, but let's face it: the Russians appear to be the only ones who can possibly help us.

Some noises coming from the street attract my attention as I am finishing breakfast. It sounds as if a demonstration was about to commence. I throw everything aside, grab a wooden stick and run out. People are beginning to converge on the Old Market Square. They march in groups, something that is strictly verboten, and carry placards which appear to have been made on the spot with inscriptions, "Give Us Bread", "Give us Work", "We are starving, we are dying". I join the demonstration as it proceeds to the Square. The crowd grows thicker as more and more hungry people join in. The screams can be heard beyond the ghetto confines. As we reach the Square the German military guards appear puzzled and scared. An officer soon grabs a field Phone, within minutes a number of trucks carrying soldiers in full field gear arrive. The soldiers quickly disembark, form a line, and at the order of their officer, begin to fire.

Havoc breaks out among the demonstrators. Panic. People attempt to retreat but the streets are still packed. Many people get run over, trampled to death. The soldiers keep on firing. As I turn to run I notice an open house gate. I quickly sneak in, find an exit to a practically empty parallel street, and rush home.

At the entrance to our house I notice mother standing with tears in her eyes. Father and Debra are not far behind. They heard the shots, looked for me, couldn't find me, and assumed the worst had happened.

That very evening our Leader, Mr. R., issues an announcement which definitely prohibits any gathering of more than four people, and warns that any attempt at future demonstrations represents a danger to all ghetto inhabitants.

Some people got killed today. Lots were wounded. I cannot even try to estimate how many. Who cares? Death is now so frequent that it does not surprise nor hurt anymore. The dead are envied, yet most of us wish to live, while those who don't commit suicide.

Chapter 29

BUBBE'S WISH

A beautiful August day has dawned. I am up early in the morning, although we have taken to sleeping late so as to conserve food. "When you sleep the body utilizes very little energy and your intake requirements are greatly reduced," says Father. He is probably right. I am nevertheless up and about. Mother, seeing me get out of bed, also rises and kindles a fire in the oven to prepare some ersatz coffee. Our supply of chicoree has been exhausted a long time ago. From now on it is ersatz, a cheap substitute. The word "ersatz" has assumed a high place in our vocabulary. We have ersatz wool, shoes, coffee, sugar, butter, cheese. I am beginning to feel that my entire life has now a certain ersatz connotation to it. We live in a world of cheap substitutes.

"Bubbe wants talk to us," Debra is calling out. "Come, let's go."

Bubbe has not been feeling well lately. Ever since her husband's death she has not been the same. The smile which adorned her lips has totally disappeared. She has practically stopped eating. The food she consumes is mostly liquid interspersed heavily with ersatz coffee. She seems deeply depressed and doesn't leave the tiny room which she now shares in Hannah's place with cousin Itka.

As we enter Bubbe sits on her bed. On her lap is a sheet of paper covered with writing. Her stroke-deformed face attempts to smile at us.

"How are you kids?" she asks. "Sit down next to me."

We dutifully oblige. She is now our patriarch, and the oldest in our family. As we sit down I have a chance to more closely examine the sheet of paper on her lap. It seemed to be a list of some kind.

"Kids," Bubbe continues. "My time on this earth is very limited. Shortly, I may have to leave to be with your Grandfather."

"Don't talk like that," interrupts Debra. "You have still a long time left on this earth."

"No, my children," she sighs. "I know what I am talking about. I am old, frail, and feel that I am beginning to lose my mind. The situation is bad. Food is scarce. Why hang around anymore?"

She looks at our sad faces. I see tears reaching her eyes. As the tears come streaming down she raises her eyes, looks on me and my sister and continues.

"I have lived a long time and been through an awful lot, but never in my life have I seen anything resembling our current situation. A terrible fate has befallen our people. I have a feeling that very few will survive this calamity and live to tell about it. This is no ordinary war. I had two sons in World War One. They were the only ones exposed to real danger. Although we, behind the lines, never had it easy, our fate was intertwined with that of the rest of the world. In this war it is different. We have been selected as targets, I am afraid, destined for extinction."

"Bubbe! You may be right, but why eat ourselves and mourn about it?" I interrupt. "The war will not last forever, and we will survive. You will see."

"This is exactly what our conversation is about. I am certain that some of you will survive. I also feel that the two of you have the best chance since you are my youngest grandchildren."

She stops crying and looks deeply into our eyes. You know that we have family which is out of harm's way. Some live in England, the USA, Belgium, France and Russia. I have compiled a list of all the addresses. Here it is."

Bubbe handles me the sheet of paper that she held in her lap." Read, and memorize it. I will test you on it in a couple of days."

Bubbe's soul departed before she had a chance to test us on the addresses of our relatives. She was buried next to her husband. On the way back from the burial Debra and I tested each other. We had the addresses perfectly memorized. Bubbe would have liked that.

Chapter 30
LIFE IS FICKLE

Meanwhile, the conditions we live in are deteriorating from day to day. Lice and flees are eating us alive. Fall has come. We worry about heat for the winter. The backlog of unburied bodies has reached staggering proportions. The grave diggers work overtime and get special food rations as incentives to catch up. The most vulnerable ones are the aged. My family has already lost them all. It seems to me that with the aged it is probably more psychological than physical. They feel hurt, confused, and useless. Like a fifth wheel in a wagon. They seem to suffer from the fact that they have to consume food which otherwise may be given to little children, and help their chance for survival. It is sad, but a fact of our ghetto life.

The next vulnerable group is the strong, big men. I have watched Motl, the smith who used to live before the war across the street from us, lose weight, weaken and shrink into a shadow of himself. He shortly died. So did others that we knew...Simcha, the horse cab driver, Shmil, the load carrier, Mojshe, the fish store owner, and many others that I personally knew before this monstrous war began. They are falling like flies. It is a fact of nature; the bigger ones body the more nourishment it needs for proper maintenance. Take away the food, and the man dies.

Yet, there are exceptions to this rule; the muscular ones, who by virtue of their strength and contacts manage to get jobs associated with food distribution, survive. So do their families. They benefit from the stolen staples they bring home after work.

The third most vulnerable group are the children. They need lots of basic staples and minerals to grow: vitamins, milk, butter, calcium, iron, says my Mother. Deprive them of these foods, and the child will eventually die.

In a way, I guess, we are fortunate after all. None of my closest family falls into that category. But a week following Grandmother's departure, Uncle Haim, who had a very bad cough, passed away. His wife Hannah, son Julek D. and daughter Itka mourned him at his open grave, surrounded by the rest of the family. Add another category; that of the chronically ill. So far, we have lost four family members in less than a year.

Winter is around the corner. Although our main concern hinges on the depletion of our food reserves, we also worry about heating materials - coal, wood, rags, anything that burns and provides heat. To make matters worse, the Germans have begun to ask for people who are a burden to the ghetto. They want criminals, loners, people unwilling or unable to work. Our authorities figure that about 20,000 people will fall into that category. The deportations have begun as the year was drawing to an end.

As our food supplies begin to dwindle one way of maintaining a somewhat increased intake of calories is by work. A job in one of the factories provides an additional serving of hot soup during the day. This kind of alleviates the constant feeling of hunger. Although the soups are watered down and thin in actual feeding staples, the atmosphere on the job does provide a kind of mental relief from hunger. One can talk about the arts, books and politics. This is as important to survival as food. Sitting home and constantly brooding over our fate can be self-consuming. So, by the end of this year I got a job as a finisher in our largest coat factory. Work starts at eight in the morning and goes on till six at night. There is only a slight break for the lunch soup. We are organized in groups. Each group has a leader who carries the responsibility for the group's performance. Our group produces military uniforms, starting with the supplied raw material and finishing with the final product. Groups are relatively small. Ours has twenty members. There are cutters, sewers, pressers and two finishers. I am one of the latter. My duty is to finish-stitch the linings and sew on the military buttons. The other finisher is a girl.

Her name is Genia. What a fascinating character this girl is. Tough, argumentative, and extremely confident in herself. Genia makes no secret of the fact that she is a member of a communist party cell. She constantly talks of the social injustices that have pervaded our society, about the

Soviet Union and its glorious leader Comrade Stalin, about the day of reckoning that is coming as surely as tomorrow's sunrise. All of this talk seems to me rather inconsequential at this time, but Genia persists that a glorious "Red" tomorrow is just about to dawn. A new world where all the social injustices will be eliminated together with the people who cause them. Meanwhile, today, she sits next to me frequently retreading her needle and singing old revolutionary songs. She seems to have acquired an inexhaustible number of them. Many deal with the Spanish Civil War, others with enslaved people of China. Our group leader, a young man in his thirties, also loves to sing. His repertoire is more subtle, his tunes are sad, almost haunting. His strong baritone belts out songs about the green fields full of fresh grass ready to be plucked by hungry sheep. About shepherds. About small villages once called home, about brooks and woods, waterfalls and butterflies. Many of us like to sing. Songs take one's mind off the ugly realities of the ghetto life. How nice it is to forget about the present and reach back into freer and happier times. So we join in whether we know the tune or not. In time I have learned many songs, most in Yiddish.

1941

Woe unto me for my hurt, my wound is severe.
I thought this is but a sickness, and I must bear it.

Jeremiah 10.

Chapter 31
THE ART OF SURVIVING

The cold weather sneaked in almost unnoticed, as did 1941. The calendar means little to us. To survive the day is our most significant goal. Mother, who has been sharing her rations with us insisting that we need the food more than she does, has taken ill. She cannot eat. Complains of pain in her stomach. Has lost quite some weight, and migraine headaches are fiercely pounding away at her brain. She lies in bed and refuses to take food. Debra quit school, against our advice, and in doing so lost her special food privileges. She is now taking care of Mother, watching her all day, like a hawk.

Today, Father asked us to meet him in the backyard, and informed us of the obvious; that Mother has been starving herself for some time now, and unless we do something drastic about it, she will die.

"What do you suggest?" I asked father, as tears come streaming from Debra's eyes.

"We must give her part of our rations to bring her back on her feet," Father suggests. "She also has a psychological problem. Her mind is made up that she will not survive. With this kind of attitude, she is accelerating her own demise."

"Saving part of our rations is doable, but we will not last long. You know it, Dad," Debra responds, sniffing and wiping her tears. "Why can't you find a job which will help us with food, like some other people do?"

Debra has just voiced one of my deepest concerns, which I did not dare to utter for fear of insulting Father. Our Father knew a lot of influential people, highly placed in the ghetto government. Yet he refused to contact them, either for a job for himself, for Mother, or for us. He is still as free from hypocrisy as before the war. Is it idealism, naiveté, or simply shyness on his part? I have trouble figuring it out.

"My children," Father looks down at the ground. "I am a man of principles.

Before the war, I belonged to a political party, believing in its program. I became disappointed when I realized that the party leaders were after personal power and did not care much how they got it, or over how many bodies they had to step to reach it. I still believe in my principles. I know that it is tragic, maybe even disastrous, to hold such beliefs under our present circumstances. That may cost us dearly. But this is the way I am." Tears are filling his eyes and begin to erratically roll down over his unshaven face.

"But Father," I cannot hold myself back. "This is a matter of life and death. This is a question of survival. What will you do with your principles when you are gone? Do you think anyone will care whether Abram W. was a principled man or not?"

"And even if anyone does care," Debra mixes in, "What about us? You live only once, and I would like to carry on and see the Germans defeated."

"My dear daughter, most of us, if not all, will die before this happens. So, will it really matter whether I have used my influences or not? This way I can at least part with a clear conscience."

Father's logic escapes me. With regard to Mother's condition he is a realist, but when it concerns his own outlook, he suddenly sees nothing but extinction ahead.

"Conscience, common sense. Why don't you put your priorities in proper order? First comes life, then conscience or whatever moral platitudes one may live by." I am now practically shouting. "When you die you are dead. Period. So is the moral code you have lived by."

"What makes you so sure that there is no life after death?"

We cannot believe our own ears. Here is our Father the agnostic, talking about life after death.

"Debra," I decide to switch the topic seeing that we are getting nowhere with this discussion. "Let's go to fetch some wood. I heard from Itka D. that people are in the process of tearing down a huge wood shack a couple of blocks away. There still may be time to get a couple of boards, or may be just enough splinters to get a fire going."

We depart leaving Father standing, drowned in his thoughts.

At the demolition site people are climbing over one another and fiercely fighting for every splinter of wood. I manage to get hold of an old door, and together with Debra we fight off any attempts to take it away from us. Finally, we carry our booty home, proud of our accomplishment. We quickly deposit the door at the entrance to our flat and return just in time to pick up some old, rotten window frames. There still appears to be enough wood in them to sustain a fire.

Back in the flat I start the fire in our stove. Within minutes the place begins to warm up. Zajvel and Rajzl are very appreciative and cannot stop thanking us. Mother lies in bed and hardly moves. Debra peels the last of our potato rations for this week. We will make a potato soup. The peels are ground and mixed with a little flour. These will be our dumplings. We still have some oil which we just got last week. Although the oil reminds one of dark and heavy machine oil, it apparently is edible and we make the best of it. Soon, the smell of freshly cooked soup fills the room and appears to cleanse it from the stench emanating from our "portable" toilet - the tin bucket.

Debra sets the table. We help mother get out of bed and take her usual place. Our preparations to consume the meal are more ceremonious than they were before the war. Ceremony plays an important part in the food, or what we have that substitutes for it, consumption process. It seems that the pleasure of filling one's empty stomach is at least greatly extended by the ceremonious approach. Alas! The actual consumption does not take very long. The measly bowl of soup is quickly gulped up including every trace of food, even one of microscopic proportions. The bowls are meticulously licked. By the end of the meal the plates are as clean as they were at the start. Unfortunately, we are not much better off than before the meal. Still hungry.

"Hey there! Open up the door. Quickly." We freeze in place. The voice, though, sounds familiar. I run up to the door and swing it open.

"Julek! What the hell are you doing?"

In front of me stands Julek D. A large sack hangs about his shoulders. It is full and heavy. He dumps the sack to the floor.

"Close the door! Someone may notice me!" He shouts.

Julek D. has developed connections with the produce department, and recently got a job unloading vegetables at the Old Square.

"I've managed to throw this over a wall where we were unloading potatoes. Moniek D. helped me. He also got one." Julek is obviously out of breath.

"Why did you bring this here?" Father is uncomfortable with the thought of having to hide stolen property.

"This is not the only one. I have some in our flat. It is not safe to harbor too much where you live. Let me store them here and I will give you some."

"I don't want to have anything to do with this. If you want to steal it is your business. Pick up the sack and get the hell out of here."

Father's objections are met with silence. His pride does not permit him to be a party to an illegal deal. I cannot hold myself back and object:

"Father, you know as well as we do that the guys close to the bowl eat best. Everybody does it. If Julek won't do it others will. Besides, Mother can use some of those potatoes. So can you. We'll keep them." I turn to Julek "There is some room under one of our beds. Let's shove it there."

"Have I ever taught you to steal, or accept stolen property?" Father's objections do become weaker.

"No you haven't. The Germans have. Can you call this stealing when the police and the so called officers of the ghetto administration give themselves big food bonuses. And for what? For letting the vegetables rot and freeze because of their own incompetence?"

"What this world has come to!" Father is beginning to give in. His objections grow weaker.

"Don't worry Uncle Abram," Julek attempts to allay Father's fears. "Mother will use up this sack in a week. Thanks for letting me hide it here. You can take a couple of potatoes each day for soup."

Don't thank us. I would have taken some anyhow even without your permission." I assure Julek "We are risking our own lives helping you hide this. It wouldn't be fair."

During the entire episode Zajvel and his wife were sleeping. Sala W. was out trying to develop some connections on her own. As the door noisily closes behind Julek, Zajvel wakes up:

"What's happened?"

"Nothing Zajvel. Go back to sleep."

"You guys woke me up. Now I am getting hungry and I finished my bread this morning. When I sleep I don't have to eat. So let it be quiet."

"Fine, Zajvel. Sleep! We will try not to disturb you".

"You already have. Now how can I sleep with a growling stomach."

"Plug your ears, Zajvel. Make believe you are so full after an excellent dinner at a restaurant that you cannot possibly eat any more. Sleep!" I raise my voice.

"I have eaten in some excellent restaurants in my life. O! What I would give to at least once more experience this pleasure."

"What do you mean 'restaurant'?" Rajzl suddenly wakes up and enters the conversation. She turns to her husband:

"Haven't I cooked some excellent meals for you? If I weren't so weak I would get up and smash your head in. What a nerve this man has. Esther," she turns to Mother, "Have you ever heard of something like this? I spent my entire life cooking for this man and now it all comes out - he never appreciated it!"

Mother, who has been listening in quietly to the conversation from her propped up position in bed, smiles.

"Rajzl. He didn't mean it. Right Zajvel?" She turns to Zajvel. "Tell her you liked her cooking best. She was an excellent cook. I can vouch for it."

"All right. I didn't mean it. Go to sleep Rajzl, and let me sleep."

It is getting dark and cool in the room. The fire we started to cook our "dinner" on is slowly expiring. I fetch a few pieces of wood from the outside storage hut and rekindle it. The bright, reborn flames play on the ceiling projecting all kinds of images. I gaze at this marvelous display. I see rainbows, castles, fields, exotic flowers, flames, all forming one huge, dynamic kaleidoscope. It is dark now. Although the hour is still early, we to go to bed. Bed is the only place where we can at least forget about the circumstances we are in. We can also dream of the past, of satiated bellies and of better worlds.

Zajvel and Rajzl died four weeks later. Zajvel died first. His death was greeted by Mother's screams. This woke up Rajzl. When informed of what happened, Rajzl, without saying one word, turned around and fell asleep. She never woke up

These are the fifth and sixth deaths in our family since the war began.

We have now much more room. Sara W. hardly sleeps here anymore. She found herself an older, but well padded, man. He is married, but his high position within the ghetto government allows him to keep a courtesan on the side. His food supply is not as limited as ours. As a matter of fact his rations could feed at least five people.

Speaking about rations, we have been given new allotments this week. A loaf of bread weighing two kilograms per week. Some margarine, potatoes, and special rations. The specials occasionally include vegetables, cheese, and even small rations of horse meat. Meat loaf made of horse meat tasted simply heavenly. Before the war I, probably wouldn't have touched it, but now it is a sheer delicacy. It tastes somewhat sweeter than beef, and is a little tougher. But it is meat! If only we could get more of it more often.

For some unknown reasons, Mother's health has substantially improved. She runs around and even thinks of getting a job. Debra started working as a seamstress in a factory employing only children from the ages of seven to sixteen. Father is still not fully convinced of the wisdom of using his connections.

Chapter 32
Typhus And Rumors

May flowers are in full bloom. The aroma of lilac blossoms permeate the entire house, alleviating the everlasting stench that seems to be present everywhere. At last, we can breathe some fresh, invigorating air. This is the only thing that is still free, and available in unlimited quantities. Or so it seems. Even the rats are having a field day. They seem to be frolicking happily in the sun on top of the garbage heaps that are yet to be collected. Collection is late because the transportation system seems to be overloaded with the removal of carcasses. The grave-digging details are working overtime digging graves in the now softened ground as fast as they can.

I have felt kind of ill lately and decided to stay home today. The advent of the long awaited warm weather has also brought an onset of a typhus epidemic. I have been having headaches and diarrhea. Mother is suspicious that I may have contracted the disease.

"Take your temperature," she asks, handing me a thermometer.

"OK. I will take it for you sake, Mother. There is nothing wrong with me." A couple of minutes pass by. Mother removes my thermometer.

"My God, you have 44. To bed with you. Right away."

I check the thermometer. Indeed, the mercury has drawn up to 44 degrees C. Quietly, I follow Mother's orders, undress, and hit the pillows, covering myself with the warm quilt. Soon I begin to shiver. Mother attempts to give me some herb tea. The room begins to spin, and I fall unconscious. I begin to hallucinate, and seem to have entered a new and different world of my own.

Presently, things are very peaceful. The quiet around me is so soothing. I am sitting on top of a beautiful mountain. Everything around me is covered with vivid and exciting colors, the looks of which I have never experienced before. There is an indescribable harmony and unison between sky and earth. No people. No animals. Not even insects. Only peace and beauty. Slowly, I move higher and higher, toward the very peak. The higher I reach the more joyous the experience. This progress is not paced by time. Time seems to be standing still. I really have no notion of time. On the peak I find a guitar. I very slowly, and with great deliberation, reach for it, and pick at its strings. The most entrancing, heavenly, melodies begin to fill the air. The more intensive my play the more beautiful the music. It is as if my mind had fully shut down, and only the senses prevail.

If there is such a thing as ecstasy than this must be its foremost expression. Is this Heaven?. Nirvana? I want to stay here forever, but all at once a figure appears at the bottom of my hill. Yes, this is my hill, and no one can be seen here! I look closer, and see it is my Father. He attempts to climb it, slips, resumes the climb, and slowly progresses toward the top. Is he going to end my paradise? Time starts to assume its normal dimension. I panic. Why does he disturb my peace? What does he want here? "Go away!" I can hear myself screaming. Father steadily moves upwards. I pluck at the strings of my guitar, harder and harder, but the music gets fainter and fainter until it dies out. He reaches me. I fight him off with all the strength that is left in me. He insists on grabbing me, and succeeds, slowly pulling me down my hill. The hill vanishes. The guitar is gone. My beautiful dream dissolves. I hear noises.

"Thank God! He is awake." Mother's screams bring me back to reality.

"What happened to me?" I am totally bewildered and surprised. I sit up on my bed and look around. It is as if I just woke up after a good night's sleep.

"You were sick. Very sick. We were extremely worried." Mother's voice sounds weak, but reassuring.

"How long was I out?" "Four days."

"What?"

"Yes. For four days you were lying here totally unconscious, just swinging the palm of your hand on the sheet, in an arc. Back and forth. Back and forth." Father hastens to fill in,

"Why, just yesterday, you jumped out of bed and began to hit your father. We could not hold you back." Mother complains.

"You know, a strange thing happened to me. I was in an entirely different world. On top of a fantastic mountain. It was so beautiful there. I dreamed that Father wanted to get me down, and I fought him off. What a beautiful place that was."

"It was the fever. When you began to dream that I tried to get you down, this is where the fever broke, and the crisis has passed." explains Father.

"Welcome back!" Debra moves closer and plants a kiss on my forehead. "Thank you. Back to our dreadful reality."

My illness did not stop time. The world seems to have been turning upside down as far as I was concerned. What keeps us in touch with the outside are rumors.

Rumors, always in ample supply, now flood the ghetto. It is hard for us to differentiate between rumor and fact, since we have no direct access to any official means of communication. There may be people in the ghetto who have receivers, but they remain hidden. Others have occasional access to old German newspapers. But are they reliable? We have no idea. Not long ago we heard that Italy, a major Axis partner, is having a tough time, with their invasion of Albania and particularly Greece. Then it looked like the Italian campaign against Greece may have fallen apart. Our hopes, and with them our speculations, were gone. When the Germans apparently attacked Yugoslavia and set up a government led by Croats. Greece, they say, was disposed of in a similar fashion. These latest rumors have been confirmed by Julek D. who found a late edition of the local German newspaper while unloading a truckload of potatoes.

It is a fact though that the German armies keep on rolling ahead. Their successes cannot be denied. Our concerns mount day by day. Just recently we heard of Hitler's attempts to invade Britain as early as last August. Apparently, London was subjected to heavy bombing raids. The fact that these raids did not bring Britain to its knees is a good omen. This gives us something to cling to. Also, hope remains that the Soviets may yet come through. Perhaps they can reach some kind of understanding with the Germans, leading to a German pullback which will place our city in Russian hands, as it was before World War One.. The Soviets cannot be worse than the Germans. No one can.

Chapter 33

A New Front

A few weeks have passed since my typhus episode. I am feeling well enough to work.

Today is Sunday. It is nice and sunny, so I decided to stretch out in a chair in the sun.

"Hey, you'll get burned," Julek D's voice booms suddenly right above me. "You are lying here while the world is burning."

"What else do you expect me to do? Today is my day off and I am still not in the greatest form. I sweat easily. You see I am all wet just lying here" I wipe my forehead and show the moist hand to Julek.

"Well, it looks like you haven't heard yet what happened overnight," Julek remarks casually.

"Is it true?" our next door neighbor bursts into our conversation.

"Yes! Yes! The Germans attacked the Soviets," Julek responds. "We have war on the eastern front now."

We really did not have the slightest idea of how these world-shattering events would affect us, but we desperately hoped that they would bring a quick end to our problems.

Soon, most of my cousins are here, everyone carrying the message of the German attack on his lips. No one knows how, but in this strange enclosed place fortified with electric fences and watched by guards, new developments have an arcane capability of penetrating and spreading over the entire ghetto with the speed of light.

"Now what?" asks Sara B.

"Let's wait and see," says David B. "Should the German Army prove as invincible as before, then Soviet Russia will be turned into mincemeat in no time"

"No need to become too pessimistic at this stage," says Julek R., who has just joined the conversation, but is apparently well aware of the latest happenings. "I think the Germans made a fatal error. They should have read their world history. Napoleon, the great conqueror, found his demise in the Russian frozen fields"

"I hope his defeat will come sooner than Napoleon's. This is his seventh year in power. Napoleon ruled for over fourteen years," I say, rushing to add, "Let him make his mistakes. May be he, too, will find his Waterloo. Hopefully in our lifetime."

Our discussion becomes heated. This, after all, may be our last chance. Should the Russian army prove to be strong enough to turn the Germans back, then by tomorrow we may be in Russian hands? Who knows? Stranger things have happened in war before. We are so deeply engrossed in our speculations that we haven't noticed one of our neighbors approaching.

"I have just come from the Old Market Square," he says. "Passing by Mr. B's office I heard the radio blare out news. I stopped and listened for a while pretending to be dusting off my clothing." He wears the uniform of flour workers which is eternally white with flour dust "The news is not good. At least according to their radio, the Germans managed to deeply penetrate into Russian territory. They expect the old Polish territory to be occupied by tonight. They say that the Russians are running away. There is mass surrender of entire armies. Yeah! That's what they said -- armies."

"They are saying that for the benefit of their people. What nation would admit, so soon after the start, that they lost a fight? I bet you the Soviets are knocking the shit out of them," says David, trying to put the best face on this grim story.

"Well, I hope you are right, but remember their invasion of Poland, Norway, Denmark, France." I respond. "They have done it before and can do it again."

The size of our group has by now grown to the point where it could be questioned by the Ghetto police.

"Look, what's the use of speculating? Let's wait," Father interjects, trying to break up the gathering. "Come into the house, I am making some herb tea."

Julek joins us as we enter our room where the pot is already puffing away. Father pours water into a small porcelain tea kettle, which we have had in the family for years, and permits it to brew for a few minutes. The tea is artificial… *ersatz*.

"This should fill your stomachs for an hour. Drink, it's good for you" Mother pours five glasses of tea for me, Julek, father, Debra, and herself.

"Thank you Aunt Esther," Julek D. sounds somewhat cheerful. "I brought you some good news." He turns to me. "You have been pale and skinny since you took sick. I talked to my foreman on the vegetable unloading station at the Old City Square. He can use some temporary help in unloading the vegetable leftovers which the Germans do not need now that a new season is upon us. It is really spoiled trash, some old potatoes, carrots, and beets."

"Would I? What a question. I cannot leave the job at the Taylor Shop without some kind of excuse. I may have to tell them that I am sick. They have lots of work now. New orders for reversible uniforms arrived. They are khaki green on the outside and white on the inside. It looks like the uniforms are for the Army. As they move, that is if they move, into Russia they will need them. With time, though, they will probably hire someone else to fill my spot. I am not that important to the output of the Jakuba Street Taylor Shop."

"A job at the vegetable station! This is terrific." Debra is all excited. "I am happy for you. Imagine; you can eat all the raw veggies you want while you work!"

I am equally excited by the thought of getting a job close to food. "What's more, I may even be able to "organize" some vegetables for all of you." We do not like the word "steal" and use "organize" in its place. "When can I start?" I ask Julek eagerly.

"Well, maybe the day after tomorrow. I will let you know tomorrow evening, after work. I know the guy who is in charge of hiring pretty well. It is almost certain that you will be hired," Julek responds, sipping the hot tea.

"Julek, we are all very thankful," says mother "He can use such a job."

In the evening we learned that, according to unnamed ghetto officials, Mr. R. was ordered by the German authorities to deliver 20,000 people for evacuation.

In December emerged other rumors about happenings in the far-away Pacific. We heard that the Japanese Navy and planes had attacked and destroyed the entire fleet of the United States, somewhere in Hawaii. The US declared war on Japan, and Hitler declared war on the United States

1942

My poor people put on sackcloth,
and strew dust on yourselves morn as if for an only child wail bitterly,
for suddenly the destroyer is coming upon us.

Jeremiah 6.26

Chapter 34

DEPORTATIONS

The onset of 1942 did not augur well for the ghetto population. Mr. R., our leader, announced that the Germans had requested the deportation of 20,000 "undesirables" from our midst. The ones to go first would be hospital patients, prisoners of the ghetto jails, thieves, black-marketers, etc. Although Mr. R. felt certain that he could bargain the number down to 10,000, as spring arrived nearly 40,000 people had been deported. By May, a new decree was issued, compelling all non-working people to be stamped. Fear and despair reached new heights.

So this is what it has come down to: We bargain for our lives with our lives, and Mr. R. is our advocate. He feels his duty is to keep the Germans happy at any price. I wonder if there ever was an historical precedent for this. Was there ever an instant in history where a victor in battle came to the head of a religious group in the camp of the losers, and asked them to deliver 20,000 people to be repatriated? Or probably, slaughtered?

What is the proper thing to do in a case like this? Should we lie down and give in, like meek sheep? Should we ask for time, if so-how? Or should we fight? If so with what?

The last option is to me the most attractive one, but there are realities to be faced. One needs weapons to fight a mighty power that has you tied up and on your knees. We have none. What are our chances for getting some? Probably zero. The Poles outside our fence do not really care what happens to us. They walk by every day, and cannot help but see the disaster that engulfed us. What are they doing? Nothing. Absolutely nothing. If they as much as hinted that we could count on them for arms, there would be no giving in to the German demands. Asking for time is out of the question; there is no negotiating with the Germans. Now, we are desperate, and Mr. R. says that the only option left is to meet the German demands. This way we may save the lives of the remaining population.

To say we are worried and scared would be to greatly understate our feelings. We are petrified, terrified, and intimidated. Rumors of horrors, similar deportations, and ghetto liquidations in the occupied, former Polish, territories have been penetrating the ghetto fences for some time now. We choose not to believe them. We are better off that way.

What good will it do to realize that we are really kept alive by the good will of the Germans and are completely at their mercy? No good at all; it may only accelerate the time of our demise. We may die of worries before we drop dead of overwork, beatings, and starvation. Take, for instance, the rumors of deportations to death camps. What good will it do to believe in such horrible prospects? Isn't it more comforting to believe that things aren't really that bad, that the sick and infirm are really going to hospitals and sanatoriums where they will get help? It may not be sensible to think that way, but it sure unburdens our minds, and keeps that tiny spark of hope still glowing.

In June, the ghetto was ordered to prepare itself for aircraft raids, the best news we have had in a couple of years. Raids meant bombings, and the fact that the defense was ordered suggested to us that the Germans expected to be bombed either by English or Russian aircraft. The news from the eastern front, however, grew dimmer by the day. There appeared to be little resistance to the advancing German troops. At least, that's what our rumor mills were telling us.

As the summer progressed, the invigorating effects of the warm, sunny days were being clouded over by the horrifying reality of daily tribulations and more terrible news. Rumors of new transports into our ghetto from Czechoslovakia, Germany, and Austria were growing in intensity.

One beautiful summer morning we were asked to assemble on one of the ghetto squares to witness another hanging. An old, or prematurely aged, man was led to a gallows by ghetto police. The German commander of this act, an SS officer, stood there with his handgun drawn, and in a quiet, controlled, voice issued orders for the execution. When the hangman's noose fell over the poor man's neck, he screamed out "Please, let me live! I have done nothing wrong." But the platform swung away and he remained shaking helplessly for a few minute, as his body twitched and twirled, and seemed to resist the final outcome. The crowd became restless. Voices to let him go rang out from all directions. The officer walked over to the gallows and very nonchalantly stretched out his arm and aimed the gun at the man's head. Three shots were heard. The body slumped, and sunk down, straining the rope. It was all over. The crowd quietly dispersed.

On the first of September the Germans asked for all children. We thought that the previous deportations were bad! This is totally devastating! Mr. R, our leader, has only one thing to say: "Jews, save yourselves and hand over your children". Save ourselves? Is it worth it? What mother could live with herself?

To soften the blow, we are told that the children are going to "*Kindersheimen,*" places where they will be well taken care of.

There are no words left to describe the state we are in. Though our family has no small children, my mother's cousins have young kids who are vulnerable. But does it really matter when all children must leave? Sooner or later all of us will be asked to report for exit. A certain date is set for the children's departure. That date passes without a single child being delivered.

On September eleventh, the German SS enters the ghetto accompanied by ghetto police. A house-to-house search for children begins. Frantically, parents try to hide their youngsters as well as they can. Alas, most are found. The mothers that won't let go of their kids are packed onto wagons with them.

At home there is more bad news from the eastern front:

Leningrad and Stalingrad seem to be encircled. Our only hope is that encirclement may also mean that the armies have been stalled.

Chapter 35
Vegetables And Sewing Machines

I spent most of the summer unloading vegetables off huge German trucks. It was a back-breaking job, but it paid off very handsomely. Not only could I eat all the carrots, beets, cabbages, and other assorted vegetables, but evenings, when going home, I would fill my pants pockets with some, and for good measure squeeze a potato or two under my armpits. That was enough for mother to cook a thick, healthy, vegetable soup for all four of us every day.

Alas, this life-saving arrangement didn't last long. One evening, a new ghetto policeman belonging to a special unit called "*Sonderkommando*" noticed my somewhat bulging pockets. He frisked me, found potatoes, and took me down to the police station. Following a good beating by some of the greatest abusers of the same "privilege", I was promptly fired. A couple of days later I was given a job as a yard worker in a sewing machine repair center. This, to me was the equivalent of being banished from Paradise forever. Now I know how poor Adam and Eve must have felt, but that brief experience reminded me what it means to be satiated. What a heavenly feeling it was to have a full stomach.

My job at the sewing machine repair shop wasn't as bad as I thought it would be. Six of us were given the title of yard workers. This meant that we were responsible for the loading, unloading, pick-up, and delivery of sewing machines.

The machines, confiscated from Jewish and Gentile homes, arrived twice weekly in trucks at the main ghetto square. There they were loaded by square workers onto small hand-drawn wagons with large steel-rimmed wheels. We pushed the wagons over the cobblestone streets, to the shop where we unloaded them and placed them in neat piles. Machines that had been serviced and were ready for production were also loaded onto our wagons, and delivered to the ghetto factories where they were employed in the production of German military uniforms.

The tailors tell me that their work on the new orders for convertible uniforms that can be changed from army blue to white by turning them inside out has been stepped up. The orders are connected with the winter campaign against Russia. They may be late for that. It will take a long time to manufacture, deliver, and distribute the new uniforms to soldiers on the front. They may not get the uniforms this winter. Maybe next. But this is the least of our worries. The main thing is that our jobs will be relatively secure, and so should we, for the next year or so. We hope.

Of the six of us, three carry most of the load. I, a dark haired, deeply religious young fellow named Motl, and a newcomer to the ghetto from a small nearby town, Simcha. The other three are too weak or too tired to do any heavy work. In some instances the machine probably weighs more than the individual. The weak among us are asked to hang on to the steering shaft, when working our wagons, and we, the stronger ones, push it through posts located above each of the wheels. In the shop, the weak are sweeping floors, and tidying up things in our yard worker's quarters, which are located in a windowless room kept light by a five watt bulb. At the center of the room is a long wooden table with benches on each side.

Our foreman, whom we call Mr. K, is a stocky and very crafty individual. I have seen him, at times when the unloading had to be done fast, carrying six Singer machines at the same time, three on each arm, while having a sewing machine table hung around his neck. Singer, Adler, and Pfaff machines were the most commonly encountered trade names. They were also the heaviest.

Mr. K is an orthodox Jew. Before the war he owned a small food store. His red, rough face seems to always carry a faint smile. At a time when our daily language is interlaced with profanities, this man never curses. He earned our respect by his actions, and now is unmistakably our boss. We never question his orders. We try to do the best we can to keep him satisfied.

Mr. K reports to Mr. P, who is our police commissar. Mr. P is always impeccably dressed in a dark suit, breeches, highly polished riding boots, and a blue police cap, fashioned after the French army officers' head attire. The cap is trimmed with yellow stripes, and a yellow star of David rests at the center above the visor. Mr. P, somehow, doesn't seem to be comfortable in his uniform. Behind his strong outer appearance there is a shy individual, who prefers to keep to himself. This seems to be strangely at odds with the duties of his position. His job is to see to it that things are properly run and work is carried out on time. He is directly responsible to the Ghetto government for the shop's operation.

The actual work of plant administration is carried out by a Mr. L, a bachelor obviously well raised. He walks with an aristocratic air about him, his steps brisk and light, as if he was always in a hurry. He lives on the plant premises in a three-room apartment with his elderly mother and a cat that he obviously adores. The animal causes him frequent problems and worries. Cats have not been seen in the ghetto in a long time, and when observed are usually good for a couple of delicious meals. It is the job of one of our weaker workers to walk the cat in the yard for an hour every day.

The technical work is supervised by a man named Mr. S. He claims to be a relative of the American Singers of sewing machine fame. A nice, distinguished looking gentleman, with a now somewhat stooped posture, he rarely loses his temper. Everyone in the shop is treated by him with infinite patience. When something in the shop does go awry, he assumes full responsibility for it. Never have I seen him blaming or bawling out others. He is always patient, and in a stable, good mood. I admire the man for his capacity to concentrate on what he is doing, while apparently being completely oblivious to the realities of our existence. Or, is this a face he is putting on to make life easier for the workers under his supervision? I think it is the latter.

At the gate before entering the plant, one has to pass through a small office where a clerk checks the credentials and makes sure that the time of arrival at work is properly entered.

Two people alternate on this job. One has the day shift, the other the night. Both of these men are always immaculately dressed. The younger one, whom we call Red, because of his red hair, works the day shift. He frequently wears golf pants tied up at the knees, with long socks covering his legs. His shoes are polished and neat-looking. Before the war, he belonged to a sports club, Maccabi, and was managing its soccer team. This is where he met Mr. P, our commissar, who gave him his current job. I never could figure out how, but Red always has the latest news first. We presume that either he or our commissar has a hidden receiver. His working hours are far longer than ours, and people who had to stay longer on the job saw him disappearing into Mr. P's quarters after the gate was closed. The other clerk, who shares the desk with Red at different hours, is a mild, elderly gentleman. With his neat, clean appearance and polite and ceremonious manners, he reminds me of an old Polish nobleman. Before the war, he was a professor at the Technical School. Now he is a gate keeper. He always carries a small bottle with nitroglycerin pills for his heart condition. The pills he acquired through the intervention of our commissar. It was from him that I first learned the term angina pectoris. To us he is Albert.

And so it is that at work I have found a heaven that I could not find at home or any other place. While at home I am constantly faced with sickness and hunger, here I forget about my hungry stomach, and find enough time to engage myself in thoughtful conversations with my co-workers, or hard work, either one of which makes life easier to bear. At times, when the loading and dragging gets really rough, Mr. K speaks up for us to Mr. P, and we usually get a coupon for an extra bowl of soup valid for the next day. When work loosens up I like to sneak under the wooden table in our quarters and write poetry.

It is a sunny day today, but cold. Unfortunately, the summer is gone and with it the warm climate. Because we ran out of fire wood yesterday, today my sister and I decide to stay home from work and try to organize some wood for the oncoming fall weather.

"Get warmly dressed, it is cold outside," mother reminds us before we leave.

"Fine, mother. Don't worry about us now. Go to bed and relax a bit. It is warmer under the goose feathered cover."

We leave the house, worrying about mother's health. She has had a bad relapse lately, and we took her to the doctor. He examined her, and thought that she might have tuberculosis. They took a saliva sample for examination, and the results should be in by today, so we are planning to stop by at the hospital on our way.

The streets are full of newcomers; well-dressed and well-fed people who stand out from our dreary crowd. The first transports arrived a week ago, and more keep on coming. We hear German and Czech being spoken. Those people came from Prague, Berlin, Frankfurt, Vienna and other places.

"They look good, no? Give them another month or so and they will quickly disintegrate," says Debra, who seems to be a little jealous of the state these new people are in.

"I am afraid you are right. As soon as they have traded their clothing and goods for food they will begin to starve at a faster rate than we. Remember at the start of the ghetto? The strong ones didn't last very long without food."

We are approaching the hospital. Things here are in great disarray. Apparently, the nurses are expecting a new evacuation of all sick people. Rumors to this effect have been making their rounds for some time now. The presence of new transports into the ghetto will probably give the Germans an excuse to clear the dead wood and make room for the newcomers.

After a lot of running and begging we finally find a nurse who takes pity on us and looks up mother's test results. They are positive. Koch bacteria was present in substantially large amounts. The nurse suggests that we too, get tested, and soon.

"I really don't care," Debra responds to the nurse's urging.

"Look," I turn to the nurse "She is right. What if we were to be found infected. What can we do?"

"I am afraid nothing at this time," answers the nurse matter-of-factly.

Having digested the bad news, we proceed to look around for places where some wood-prying of old, abandoned, houses may be in progress. Soon we find a place following the track of people running with old planks, doors, and windows. There is still some wood left on the site, but just enough to light our stove a couple of times. It will have to do for now.

About a block from our house we meet father. He looks strange wearing his "new" winter coat which he had made to order just before the outbreak of the war. It seems that the coat can now accommodate at least two fathers, he is so thin. Each one of his steps seems to be premeditated. His swollen ankles are dragging his nearly limp feet along the sidewalk. He still wears leather shoes. I have given him mine since his own wore out about two weeks ago. I am now wearing the latest in ghetto foot wear -- cloth uppers and wooden soles. They make me look taller than I really am, but comfort is not one of their virtues. At least they can be stuffed with layers of old socks to keep one warm.

"How are you, father?" Debra is first to catch up with him

"I am weak. Very weak."

"We got some wood. It is better than none at all. At least we will be able to keep the place warm for a couple of days," says Debra, proudly showing off our treasure.

"Father," I rush to add, "We also got the results of mother's test. They are positive."

"Well, I am not surprised. I too have been coughing lately, and may even have some fever. But at this time...who cares?" Father is trying to be realistic. "But I pulled myself together this morning and went over to see Mr. G, you know, the one I worked for before the war. He is now in charge of ghetto security, and guess what? He gave me a job."

"Really?" We are having trouble holding back our enthusiasm. "Finally. You should have done this a long time ago. Where will you work? When do you start? What job is it?" Our questions are pouring out faster than bullets from a machine gun.

"Well, let's get into the house. I will tell you all"

Once inside, father slowly removes his coat, and sits down to unlace his shoes which have by now deeply cut into his swollen ankles.

"Now I feel better," he says with a sigh of relief. "So, I finally got up all my guts, and decided to see Mr. G. He gave me a broad welcome and asked why I had not contacted him sooner. Obviously, he was much concerned by my looks and appearance. We talked for a while about the "good old times" and finally I stated my reason for being there. He thought for a while, called in his secretary, made some checks, and offered me a job as night watchman for a salad distribution center, around the corner from our home. That means that I will be working from eight at night to eight in the morning. He says that I can put up a comfortable chair and sleep most of the time. The most important thing is that once in the store I will get a special portion of *salad de jour* to eat instead of the traditional soup."

"This is terrific. Dad, imagine those salads can be more nourishing than the soup." Although the vegetables they are made of are old and frequently rotten or frozen, they nevertheless contain iron, vitamins and sugars. I find it difficult to restrain my enthusiasm. "Dad, this may get you back on your feet.

"And once inside, who is there to hold you back from eating a little more?" Debra is sharing in my excitement.

"Well, let's wait and see. I am supposed to start tomorrow night."

Mother does not hear a thing. She is in bed peacefully asleep, resting her aching head on a fluffy pillow. Food is scarce. Our bread rations were consumed yesterday, and there are two more days to go. I managed to get some potato peels from the kitchen, which should help. Tomorrow we will be back at work and are certain to get at least a bowl of soup. Father's job may also bring in some extra food. We hope.

Chapter 36

RATIONS AND NEWS

Time is of little consequence in our environment. It is measured not by minutes, hours, days or months, but by rations. The time to pick our rations is like sunrise, or the beginning of a new day. When the rations run out it is like sunset: Frequently, much too frequently, the sunset is very ominous, leading into long nights of starvation. Then the time for new rations arrives. The time gap between meals is filled with backbreaking work and worries.

December has come, and with it the long cold winter nights. Red was busy at work disseminating a huge collection of the latest news. Normally we would have greeted these tidings with happy outcries, but this time we are slowly growing numb, and our reaction is limited to a few words of consolation.

According to Red, the Russians launched a massive offensive that repulsed German attacks, and began a long-awaited counter-offensive. It is led by a General Zsukov. Red says the winter there is terrible, and the Germans are not used to it. Like Napoleon's soldiers, they are freezing to death.

The other news was even better; a new front was opened by the Allies in Africa, and the German troops there, after considerable initial successes, are in retreat.

So now, after two years, the chips seem to be all in place. Soon we may have another front opened in Europe, and before we know it, the war will be over. How we wish we could believe in all that. Alas! Our skepticism is by now too deeply entrenched in our thinking, and the realities of our life totally disconnect us from the outside world. To live, means to have something to eat, work, and sleep. Every once in a while there is a concert of the Ghetto symphony orchestra, to raise the inhabitants' spirits, but this is mainly for the "upper class," those in or associated with the ghetto administration: *The Judenrat.*. They still find time for entertainment even now after we lost almost all of our elders and small children.

1943

You will win, O! Lord If I make claim against you
yet, I shall present charges against you
Why does the way of the wicked prosper? Why
are the workers of treachery at ease?

You have planted them. And they have taken
root, they spread, they even bear fruit....

Jeremiah 12.

Chapter 37
A Painful Departure

About sixty thousand, or more, people have already been "repatriated". No one knows where they were sent to. The reparations, which we have learned to call "akcja" or "Aussiedlung" continue. Almost every day new people are marched off to the railroad station where they are loaded onto trains and driven to an unknown destination. The Germans tell the ghetto leader, Mr. R, that they are needed to work in other places in the Polish Protectorate. If so then why don't they write, or try to communicate in one way or another? Why don't they tell us that they are well? Could it be that the rumors of gas chambers being used to exterminate them are true?

One institution is cluttered in this chaos -- the funeral establishment. They are busy working overtime for which they get special rations. What would the ghetto look like without them?

I used to love the winter season. For one reason or another the air was much clearer, cleaner, and obviously crisper. I loved the feel of the frost pinching my nose and cheeks. The sledding. The snow ball fights. What joy! When the snow was heavy, the wheels of the horse-drawn wagons were replaced by sleigh guides. The packed snow provided a smooth riding surface filling in all the bumps between the stones, and the street noise level drastically dropped. The warmth of our apartment was so euphoric and welcome following a few hours of play in the biting frost. Today winter is a killer -- an ally of the Nazis -and seems to be collaborating with them to an indescribably cruel extent.

The year 1943 has brought with it very cold weather. Like in other, tough winters the walls in our room are glittering with stars. It is as if they were specially decorated for Christmas and New Year. These "ornaments" are formed by the frozen moisture, part of which is exhaled from our sick lungs. Father Frost freezes it on the walls and creates the loveliest of patterns. Eventually, layers grow on top of each other until they resemble frozen mosaics landscapes of snow and ice.

Mother's condition is deteriorating rapidly. We talked to the doctor about her. He has doubts whether she will survive to see warm weather again. Father works now, dragging himself home each morning before we leave, holding his tin soup can. It usually contains a little salad which all of us share, each getting a spoonful.

January is one of the toughest months to endure. Vegetables, which are important staples in our diet, are ether rotten or absent in our rations. The bone- chilling cold taxes our wood-gathering opportunities, the ground is frozen, and the wagon-pulling is a horrible chore.

Yesterday was a tough working day. I am still exhausted and hungry. Our food rations are almost all consumed, so I decide to stay home today. My sister, too, skipped work. As usual, the weather was harsh.

"I am not going to let mother freeze in bed," says Debra. "We have the solid black mahogany breakfront -- let's burn it"

"Do you realize that this is our most precious possession? That's the only thing we own that has some worth," says Father, obviously not yet ready to part with the antique that means so much to him and that he associates with another lifetime, filled with pleasant memories.

"Dad, don't you think that to stay alive is more important?" I ask. "If, and when, we survive we can always get a new one. Should we die, than who gives a damn? Now we all freeze, especially mother who even under the goose feather comforter seems to be stiff from cold." I cannot see the value of keeping something around that may relieve our pain, even if only temporarily.

Debra empties the cabinet of all the junk we have kept there. There are old pictures, Father's notebooks from technical school, a small collection of coins, an American eagle quarter, an Indian head nickel, some old Roman coins. More pictures of our American uncle Hyman alone in a US Army uniform, another with his family, my Belgian uncle Leon, mother's cousins in the US and England. Mother's parents, and uncle Izaak dressed in a Russian officer's uniform. Also lots of old clothes which can be rightfully called "shmates", or old rags.

A few moments, and the beautiful old breakfront yields its beauty to an ugly sharp ax. The pieces of cinder are quickly ignited and warmth begins to spread across the room. I watch the antique wood slowly ignite, turn red, and burst into flames that gradually consume it. Soon it will be gone. Converted into grey ashes...

Mother raises her head as she feels the heat emanating from the stove. "Please, raise me up. I want to look around a bit."

Debra and I quickly raise the pillows, and pull her up. Both of us sit down on the edge of the bed. "How do you feel today, mom?"

Mother does not answer. Her eyelids drop. She sighs. Her facial muscles begin to tremble and dither. A faint smile appears on her face as she utters, "My children, I am kaput, finished." A loud puff exits her mouth. Her body slumps] and relaxes.

I grab her pulse. Father takes a mirror and puts it in front of her mouth, then nose. There is no more sign of life. She has departed -- forever.

"God. If there is a heaven, please let her in," Debra sobs quietly. "She was a saint. She sacrificed her entire life for her kids. God! Why did you take her away? This is so unfair."

I embrace Debra and we stand there looking at the lifeless body of our mother. Here lies the bundle of flesh and bone that once was a living creature that gave us life, and sacrificed her own so that we can live. Debra's laments continue. Tears are streaming from her eyes. I cannot cry. I just stand there and look at my mother's body, contemplating the meaning of it all. Yes, death is cruel, but it also can be merciful. She suffered so much in her lifetime, maybe this is her liberation. I guess, many of us do envy her. At least she has now reached the stage where Hitler and his likes cannot touch her anymore. No more worries, fears, starvation, disease, or deportations, no more headaches for her. She is now at peace.

The life that was is no more. It was just a matter of time, and time is only an active dimension as long as life is there. Once life stops, so does time.

Father sits stooped in his chair. His arms cover his face. I cannot tell whether he cries or not. He looks so shrunken, and old, and sick. A sudden burst of a spasmodic cough breaks his silence. The phlegm he coughs up and spits out on the floor is red with blood. God, how long will it be before he too departs?

Mother was buried the evening of the day she died. She had a decent burial considering the circumstances. An old acquaintance, a cantor before the war, worked at the cemetery. He saw to it that the burial was performed according to the Jewish ritual. The grave was not yet fully dug. The earth was frozen. I helped cousins Dave and Julek finish the digging to the proper depth. The body was cleaned by a woman of the burial squad according to our Jewish ritual, and dressed in white linen. We gently lowered her onto a few planks of wood. The cantor sang the prayer for the dead, and father and I recited Kaddish. At the end of the ceremony the grave was gently filled by me and my cousins as if there was a danger of hurting her. On top we placed a small sign with my mother's name and dates of birth and death.

Finally she managed to escape the insanity and cruelty besieging us all. No harm can be done to her anymore. She is safe in the arms of death.

Chapter 38
WHERE IS GOD?

I woke up this morning feeling very stiff. It was a cold night and it took me quite a few hours to warm up cuddled up to father's cold, almost lifeless body. I rinsed my face in the washbowl's frozen water, got quickly dressed and walked off to work.

"Good morning. A nice quiet day so far," Red extends his friendly greeting as I punch in my time card.

"I hope it stays that way. This is no time for wagon pushing. There is too much snow on the ground. Let's hope that there will be no incoming machines to be picked up. Anything new on the fronts?"

"Hmm...Do you really want to know?" Red teases me. I know what that means. There is some good news, somewhere.

"The Russians took back Stalingrad. This is final. All German Armies under Field Marshal Paulus have surrendered."

The news explodes into my face like a petard. Its impact practically knocks me off my feet. I lean against the wall to retain my footing. Seeing my reaction,

Red adds, "No reason to get overly excited. The Germans are also taking a beating in Africa. Finally, bombing of German cities continues. How do you like that for an early morning report? As good as a couple of scrambled eggs, fresh rolls, butter, and a glass of cocoa."

"Oh, stop it! I was dreaming all night about food. Ate myself silly, yet got up hungry. But you are right. In many ways this is better than food." Actually, it is food. Food for the soul. I am beginning to believe that with more news like this we may manage to survive.

"Yes. The best meal I've had in a long time," says Red enthusiastically. I'd never seen him so upbeat.

"It is time to go to work. See you later."

In the worker's quarters, things are quiet. A couple of our co-workers are already there. They lie on the floor and try to catch some sleep all cuddled up in rags and some old torn blankets. Mr. K sits at the table, a hot cup of ersatz coffee in front of him and next to it a small meticulously wrapped package, which he now unwraps, gently, and with loving care. The bottom of the package contains two thinly sliced, dry pieces of bread with a sliced carrot sandwiched in between.

Mr. K takes a small bite and gently chews on it as if it were the dearest treat. His tongue slaps loudly against the pallet as he softens the delicacy with a sip of coffee.

"Good morning, Mr. K"

"Good morning. Looks like we will have a slow day today. You guys take it easy. I have an errand to run for Mr. P this morning, so should anything happen you are in charge"

"OK." At this moment Motl and Simcha enter the room. "Good morning, guys." "Good morning everybody."

Motl, as usual, displays a cheerful smile. Simcha seems somewhat depressed.

"What happened, Simcha? You do not seem to be your usual self this morning," asks Mr. K, who knows his people well.

"You are right. My father is now critically ill. I don't know how long he'll last." "Simcha, with God's help, he will survive," Motl says consolingly. "Don't worry. There is nothing you can do about it anyhow. It is all in His hands. He will take care of us all, like he always has." Motl's reaction is not fully appreciated by Simcha, whose face has taken on a sad grin.

I, too, get aggravated by the constant reminder of God. If he is that powerful, where is he now, when we need him so badly?

"C'mon, you keep talking about our merciful God. Why did he select us for this cruel punishment? Aren't we supposed to be his chosen people?" I ask.

"This is a question most non-believers like to ask," Mr. K replies. "Sure, we are his chosen people. We have been chosen to carry out good deeds on this earth. But with this choice comes also a great responsibility.

When we do not comply with the Almighty's expectations we get punished. This is not the first time we have been subjected to the wrath of the Almighty. There were Hamman's, Torquemada's, Chmielnicki's throughout the centuries that were sent by the Almighty to punish us for our excesses. They did their job and quickly disappeared to allow the Jewish people to regain their faith and strength, and become a light onto other nations."

"I hear you. If God keeps on treating us like this, alternately loving and punishing, I think it is time to recall Sholem Alejchem who asked God through his Tevye character to find some other nation to bestow this honor on. Seriously though, I am a believer, Mr. K. God is alive and well. In this world of ours it is impossible to deny his existence. All one has to do to become convinced is look at a flower, tree, animal, or, for that matter, any living thing that inhabits our globe. The marvels of life are unexplainable by the limited capacity of our minds to observe, comprehend, absorb, and interpret. The complexities of life are so enormous that only God can explain them."

"But, the concept of being a chosen people does not reflect the realities of our life," says Simcha. "It has been engraved in our minds to keep hope alive even under the most adverse of circumstances."

"I agree, Simcha, but this concept is part of the general dogma which has been programmed into us by the interpreters of God's will," I continue. "In almost all of the modern religions, particularly those that evolved from the old Hebrew Bible, God has been defined as the Almighty being that can feel, see, follow and control all our actions anywhere and at any time. This was done to keep believers in line, and compel them to behave in an acceptable way. Moreover, He, or the carefully selected and anointed executors of His will, possess the awesome power of punishment which includes the ultimate excommunication from society to death. Act against His will and the ultimate punishment will engulf you. Not only will you die, but even after death you will wind up in a horrible place called Hell, where your punishment will continue ad infinitum. On the other hand, conform to His dictum and you will forever live a beautiful life in a much more agreeable place called Heaven. In other words, when things are good, God is to be thanked for it because He willed it so, and when they are bad, it is your fault, buddy, and God can be merciless."

"You say you believe in God and yet you talk like an atheist," says Motl. "God is mighty. God is strong. God follows every individual's behavior, and determines his fortune. You will see God will eventually punish those who do us harm. His ire will be severe. He'll kill them and destroy their cities. Moreover, the concept of Heaven and Hell is not really well developed in the Bible." Motl's Orthodox upbringing comes to the fore.

"Perhaps, eventually, those who do us harm will be severely punished. Our history is full of fallen Jew-haters. But, shall we live long enough to witness the demise of our enemies?" I wonder.

"Whether we will survive this disaster or perish I don't know, says Simcha. But I agree with you that God is indeed present everywhere. One cannot escape his watchful eye. God's creative and corrective ability knows no limits. He represents the ultimate force that keeps our globe, if not the entire universe, under control. He employs a grand master plan for the maintenance of balance in our world, which includes even the tiniest creation, or living matter, from single cells to ants to people. God cares for humans in the same way he cares for plants, animals or any other being he created. He also makes mistakes. Sometimes his creations run amok, but in his infinite wisdom he managed to build in special provisions for correcting the un-manageable... Sometimes he can be merciless. Entire species have been known to vanish in his wrath."

I am glad to hear Simcha come to my rescue with this lengthy explanation, although frankly, I did not expect him to share my philosophies of life. He is usually very quiet, and hardly ever takes part in any discussions.

"That's right, Simcha, but let me add that God has no mercy in the sense that we understand it," I add. "Had he been merciful, in our meaning of the word, his plan for creation and re-creation would not have included death as the terminator of life. The very merciless idea of a predator is God-created. It is a necessary link in his vast chain of control and sustenance." Now I'm getting really worked up as I keep rambling on, "God is not concerned with the fate of a specific individual. The fate of one or for that matter even a group of individuals is of no concern to God. The behavior of a species can, however, bring down his wrath if it gets out of control. Remember Noah and the Flood?"

"I strongly differ with you," chimes in Mr. K, who has now finished his sandwich, leaving him freer to engage in the argument. "Your notion of God leaves us without hope. Motl had it right. God cares. God is a loving God. He watches over every individual. All you have to do is read the Bible and you will find there that the Almighty, blessed be his name, has been lovingly caring for us since our forefather Abraham's times. True, every once in a while he will test us, and rightly so. It is easy to forget that we disavowed him the moment Moses disappeared onto Mount Sinai. Wasn't he right to punish us? The instant we felt a bit secure we turned from him and began to believe in other gods. Apparently, we must have sinned again. Our current punishment is not imposed on us by Hitler, although he has a hand in meting it out. It is being conceived and directed by God himself. Therefore, there is little we can do to avert it. We must let things run their course. Eventually, His mercy will reappear. We will and shall be saved."

"Believe what you wish. This is your business, Mr. K. Let me only correct myself. In saying that God knows no mercy, I may be misstating my case. The fact is, that in a certain way, God is merciful. One has only to note the self-healing aspects of any creation to comprehend this form of mercy. Or, take the fact that plants, animals, and insects, when faced with a sudden, detrimental change in their environment or in the presence of a predator, will change their texture, color, general appearance, and even biological make-up so that they may survive. This is a God-given blessing. You can call that mercy."

As I finish my sentence, the voice of Mr. P can be heard calling for Mr. K. Mr. K jumps up and runs out. For a while silence envelopes the room, but not for long. Soon Mr. K reappears.

"Well, you guys," he says apologetically. "I thought we may have a quiet day today. Unfortunately, a small shipment of machines arrived at the Central Square. Let's go!"

Later, as we pushed the sewing machine-laden wagon over the rough cobblestone streets, I asked Simcha whether he lived before the war in the ghetto area or in the city. His answer surprised me. Three years ago his family moved to Argentina, and returned to Poland only three weeks before the start of the war. What unfortunate timing. He fell right into the fox's den. No wonder he is so serious and quiet most of the time. I could have never forgiven myself had this happened to me.

Chapter 39

CHAOS

Winter has departed, leaving in its wake thousands of new graves and empty homes. Our house is surrounded by SS and local police. They demand all children. Julek R and his wife respond, hoping that their children, who are aged 10 to 18, will not be taken. The older kids are not. The SS wants only the two youngest. The family refuses to let them go. After a brief struggle the entire family volunteers to leave with their children.. We wave good-bye as the wagons leave the place. We have now lost eleven family members.

Although the factories still function, their output has drastically declined. It is April and the trees are beginning to yield signs of life after the long and dreary winter. The tiny buds which were a dirty brown during the winter slumber are beginning to turn green. Mounds of snow still to be found in deep shady spots, are rapidly melting away, disclosing the filth and dirt hidden under them. The air carries with it the fresh breath of spring mixed with an awful stench of rot and human feces. It is hard to understand how any living creature can thrive in this environment. Yet, the twittering birds and frolicking rats seem to be having a ball in the midst of this mess. This is their nirvana.

Now that the subject of rats has entered my mind, I wonder why we don't eat them to stay alive. After all throughout history, when faced with starvation, people have eaten rats. I remember reading about the Franco-Prussian wars and the blockade of Paris. People ate rats then; they even became cannibals. I have heard that in some Asian countries rats are delicacies. So why do we look at these animals with disgust? The only reason I can think of is our tradition. Our upbringing, whether religious or agnostic, is steeped in tradition. Regardless of our convictions, I think that deep in our souls, most of us believe that there is a God who decides how we are to live as individuals, and how we are to die. Faith is the only positive thing we have left to latch on to. I, too, begin to think that maybe, just maybe, our God is watching over me.

I drag myself out of bed. It is still cold in the mornings, and the fire in our stove has long since died out. Yesterday we decided to burn some of our chairs. I ignite the remnants of wood left under the table, and place them into the stove. Soon they come alive with red jumping flames, bringing warmth into the room.

Debra has raised her head from under the bedding, asking, "Is it time to get up?"

"Yes, it is getting late. You'd better hurry," I admonish her.

"Don't scream so loud. Father is still asleep. He was up all night," she whispers. Debra gets up, reaches for the bucket of water and pours some into the washbowl.

"The water is freezing cold."

"What do you expect? There is fire in the oven; you can put some of it into the tea kettle and warm it up."

"It will take too long," Debra complains, looking at the clock on our wall. "I'm late as it is."

As she washes herself, I prepare the razor, sharpening it on father's old leather belt. I have taken to shaving, since my beard has grown too thick and bushy, and is hard to keep clean. The lice, which seem to be collaborating with the Germans to suck our blood, are so pervasive, they are everywhere. Why give them more room to lay eggs and multiply? So now I am shaving at least once a week.

As soon as Debra finishes washing I empty the washbowl into our waste bucket which is filled to the rim after the long, cold night. I carry the bucket outside into the freezing morning air, and dump its contents into the ditch of the outhouse. I rush back into the room, shave, and, after making sure that father is comfortable in bed, leave the house in a hurry. Debra is already gone. At work, Red greets me with a sad "Good morning."

"What happened?" I ask "Has the world fallen apart?"

"Believe me. I wouldn't mind that. At least everyone would have been in the same boat."

"So what is happening? Tell me; I can't stand the suspense."

"Well, brace yourself. This is not from the press or radio. My sources tell me that a disaster has struck the Warsaw ghetto. At first there was a large deportation, they say to death camps, then some of the youth revolted, and now there is house-to-house fighting going on."

"Interesting. How will this affect us? You know who will win." I am by now also deeply upset. "No one will help the Jews. The Poles probably welcome the Jewish uprising. This will help to eliminate more Jews, and most of them would like to see that happen."

"I agree with you," says Red. "There's one thing I am sure of, and that is that our time in this ghetto may be up soon." Red abruptly cuts our conversation as more people arrive to check in for work.

This news makes my misery even worse, if that is possible. This is the first time I have heard of any Jewish resistance. Perhaps we should take it as an example and rise up on our own, I ponder as I carry out my daily chores. But then, who will support us? Since our city has been annexed to the Reich, we live in Germany, The few Poles who might be inclined to help us would find it very difficult to get through the ghetto fences and guards. For all practical purposes there is no interaction with people on the outside. The only contacts some of us have with "the other side" is on the market square where our daily food subsidies arrive, and where the wares produced in the ghetto are delivered for further distribution. The only people present there are truck drivers, German soldiers or police.

"Hey, wake up," I hear a familiar voice behind me call.

I quickly turn around. "What the hell are you doing here?" I ask.

"Believe it or not, I was sent here by the Labor Office to be interviewed for a job as a yard worker," answers my cousin Julek D.

"What happened to your job at the vegetable market?"

"Oh! I will give it to you in shorthand: I was fired. They caught me stealing." "Well, I knew that sooner or later that would happen."

"How's your girlfriend Sala?"

"She is fine," replies my cousin. "Still working. We got married, you know." No, I didn't know they got married, although we lived only a few yards away from each other. The close contacts we had with our aunts, uncles, and cousins had begun to disintegrate as times grew worse. All of us are now concerned only with our own survival. We are so obsessed by the tenacious feelings of hunger that there is no place in our daily lives for maintaining relationships, aside from those we have to nourish to carry out our work so that we may earn our daily bowl of soup.

"Who is in charge here?" asks Julek.

"I think you should first go to the front office. The receptionist will tell you what to do," I reply.

As Julek disappears into the office building, I run toward our shed to share the news with my co-workers. At least we finally got a strong guy who will share the hard work with us. We have lately lost two of our weak compatriots. They worked until they could not move anymore. Then one day they did not show up, and that was that. Now, I am elated. Julek is a reasonably well fed and strong individual. He should be able to relieve us of some of the heavy work.

"Hey, Motl, Simcha, we got a new guy in," I shout as I enter the shed. "What guy? What are you talking about?" asks Mr.K, appearing puzzled.

"My cousin. He has been referred to us by the Labor Office. Boy is he strong."

"Well, it seems the Labor Office finally came through. I asked Mr. P months ago to put in a request for two more men. Maybe we got one."

"And a good one at that," I say. "I can vouch for that."

No sooner have I finished my sentence than Julek D. appears in the door. "Julek, come meet your new supervisor. This is Mr. K," I say by way of introduction.

"Nice to meet you. I hope I can be of help here."

"I am sure you can," says Mr. K, who apparently likes what he sees when he looks over the addition to his new staff. "Where did you work before?"

"At the vegetable market."

"What brings you here? You know you'll be lucky if you get an extra soup here." Mr. K is more than curious.

"Well, to be truthful, I was fired because they caught me taking home some vegetables."

"So, to put it plainly, you are a thief. Is it nice to steal from your brethren?"

"It depends how you look at it. First of all, everyone in the ghetto who is in a similar position steals. And second, imagine that there are about 150,000 people here. What does a pound of potatoes, or even ten thousand pounds of potatoes, mean to the average Joe in the street? He cannot tell the difference in the size of his rations. At least this way some people have a chance to eat slightly better and perhaps survive this mess so as to be able to tell the world what really happened here."

Julek's excuses are not very well received by Mr.K, "Your argument is as old as our civilization. I have heard and read it before. That doesn't make it right. God has given us Ten Commandments and not to steal is one of them."

"Look Mr. K, I have come here to work, that is if you want to have me, and not to debate."

"All right, then, work you will get. There are fifteen machines to be moved to the factory from the storage shed. Your cousin will show you where they are and where to carry them to."

Outside I whisper to Julek, "This wasn't the best of starts. Be nice to the guy. It is good to be on his side when he has the power to give you a very tough assignment, and perhaps an extra bowl of soup."

"Yes, I know, but I didn't start this discussion. He did. In the future I'll try to stay out of his way."

Julek didn't stay with us very long. In July he received an order from the Ghetto Administration to report to the jail. He was subsequently put on a train together with a number of other perpetrators, and sent to an unknown destination. His wife Sala, now pregnant, was left behind.

The news from the outside, as relayed on an almost daily basis by Red, was mixed. On one hand, the ghetto of Warsaw was apparently liquidated after a fight that lasted a couple of weeks. Red has it from a "reliable source" that the ghetto is completely burned out. How this will affect our miserable existence is not clear.

On the other hand, it is clear that the tide has turned on all fronts. Red's sources speak of a broad Soviet offensive following the fall of Stalingrad. The war in North Africa is over. It ended with the defeat of the German invaders. A new front has been opened in Italy. The Allied troops have landed, and by September Italy had surrendered. Unfortunately, German troops have entered Italy, and reoccupied a good part of it.

In the ghetto things are going from bad to worse. At a time when we are convinced that things cannot be any more miserable, they become intolerable to the point where we begin to question the need to remain alive. Every day, on my way to work I stumble upon new corpses. They are now left in the street, disintegrating, because there are fewer workers available to remove and bury them. Deportations also take their toll, with lots of people taken away, sent to unknown destinations. The entire ghetto is in an uproar. Why do they pick on children, the old, and the sick? Where are they sending them?

Fall has arrived once again, and the nights are getting cold. We have little wood in store to keep the house warm. All the furniture is gone; even the chairs have been burned, leaving us with nowhere to sit but on our beds. Luckily for us, as more people die or get deported, more houses become available for tear-down. Actually tear-down is now one of our busiest industries. The empty houses are being dismantled by squads of people who were given this job as punishment for stealing or talking against the ghetto government. Wood gets saved for distribution as fire wood to the ghetto inhabitants. Bricks are cleaned and stacked for shipment outside the ghetto. The meager wood rations from the tear-downs are just about enough to keep the stove burning for an hour or so. We stay alive because Debra still works, and gets her extra ration of soup; father, although greatly weakened, still manages to drag himself every evening to the salad store, while my sister and I make the best of our meager weekly rations ensuring that they are not instantly consumed.

This morning I was terribly depressed. On the way to work I had to push aside a number of corpses at different times to clear the sidewalk. Their stiff, lifeless bodies lie there, each in a different grotesque position.

"Good morning, Red," I say morosely as I enter the office. "Good morning." "Anything new today?"

"No. It is quiet. Very quiet."

"Do you think it might be the lull before the storm?"

"May well be. The talk of ghetto liquidation has resumed."

"There are hardly any people left here."

"You'd be surprised. I heard from a friend of mine who works in the administration that there are still over 80,000 people left in this cesspool."

"Now, Red, we may be disintegrating, but haven't turned into shit yet, as long as we are still alive. See you later." I check in my time card and leave the office.

In the workers' shack there are only three active workers left; Motl, Simcha and I. Julek has been deported and the others simply departed into God's domain. The Labor Department has yet to send someone to replace the ones that are gone. Mr. K is already there ceremoniously unpacking his "breakfast." It consists of a dry piece of bread, meticulously cut into tiny bits. A drop of salad covers every piece of bread. The pot of water on the stove is boiling.

"Good Morning, Mr. K."

"I have had better mornings in my life," says Mr. K, pouring hot water into his coffee cup, where a bit of ersatz coffee, mostly chicory, has been placed.

"You know, walking to work I noticed more corpses on the streets than usual. I wonder, with all the starvation and disease all around us, how can the inhabitants of the city escape a major epidemic? One can surround the ghetto with wire fences and guards, but flies, mosquitoes, and pests do not recognize the Fuehrer's authority, and freely pass over onto the "other side."

"You've got a good point there. God endowed them with freedoms which are denied to us. But, in due time God will see to it that the perpetrators of this monstrous crime will get their punishment. We are but God's creatures, and have to do what he commanded us to do through our father Abraham, Moses and the prophets."

"You are a lucky man, Mr. K. I wish I had the strength of your convictions. It surely makes it much easier to get through a day."

"Well, all you have to do is say your prayers three times a day and you'll see, you'll feel much better."

Mr. K has finished his breakfast. He now pulls out a set of prophylactics, and his prayer shawl. Slowly he tapes the leather straps on his left arm murmuring quietly the Morning Prayer as he turns south, facing Jerusalem.

As Mr. K prays, Motl enters the room wrapped up in a woolen shawl. It seems to me that his beard has grown much longer, and his alert, friendly, black eyes have recessed in their sockets and taken on a melancholy look.

"Well, another day." Motl's greeting sounds more depressing than usual.

"Are you out of your rations already? What makes you so sour today? You are the one who is usually the most cheerful of all of us," I wonder out loud.

"A couple of things, I guess. My parents do not feel too well lately. And this morning going to work I met a neighbor who works in the administration. He told me that rumors of ghetto liquidation are very persistent."

"Let's go" interrupts Mr. K, who has quickly disposed of his prayers, "Whatever happens, happens. It has been all predetermined in Heaven above. Meantime we have a job to do. Where is Simcha?"

"He was not very far behind me when I clocked in. I bet you Red got a hold of him. Speak of the devil, here he comes."

"Good morning," says Simcha, entering the room. "I am sorry I'm a bit late.

Red has the latest news and was eager to unload it. It seems things are not as good as we thought. The Germans are putting up a hell of a fight in Italy. There is savage fighting there. Boss, what do we do today?"

"Follow me," says Mr. K. "We have some cleaning and sweeping up to do. We also have to ship out the machines that cannot be repaired."

Thus, a new working day has begun at the Sewing Machine Repair Center.

1944

Disaster overtakes disaster
for all my tents have been ravaged. In a moment...my tent cloths..
How long must I see standards and hear the blare of horns?

Jeremiah 4.2

Chapter 40
ONE SOLUTION

The night of the New Year 1944 we spent rolled up in bed, trying to keep each other warm. Most of the non-working hours, be it day or night, we spend in bed. First of all it is warmer. Secondly, we save energy and do not feel as hungry as we do running around.

The New Year arrived on the wings of excellent news. There is talk of an Allied invasion of France, the Soviets are moving ahead registering one victory after another. Our rumor mill has it that the situation in the east is so critical that the Fuehrer has taken personal charge, and moved his headquarters close to the front. That, indeed, is good news but our personal situation does not seem to change. We are as miserable as ever. Perhaps even more so. Our anxiety rises; shall we survive, or will we die just as we are about to be freed?

Rumors concerning the fate of our ghetto and its inhabitants have taken off, and whirl around increasing our desperation and feeling of helplessness. The ghetto is about to be liquidated. No, it will stay; more work orders have been received for our factories. We are about to be shot. No, we won't; they need us. Their men are all on the fronts now. The Germans will take away all our food; they need it for the Germans. No. They will increase our rations, they need our work. The Soviets are expected soon. No, the offensive was stopped by the Germans, how can it be when Red is telling stories to the contrary?

So it goes from morning till night. We do not know any more who or what to believe.

Father died as this spring was coming to an end. In the last few weeks of his life his health completely deteriorated and he remained bedridden. One day while pushing a wagon with a load of machines through our neighborhood I suddenly got a premonition that something bad had happened. I asked my comrades to take over and ran to our house. As I entered the room I saw father's body slumped at the edge of the bed. He apparently tried to get out of bed, when death finally freed him from his misery. I called in a neighbor of ours, an Orthodox Jew, who was familiar with the religious rules guiding the cleaning ritual, and together we washed and cleansed his body, wrapped it in a sheet, and put it down on the floor. My cousin David B. helped me bring one of our wagons from work, while his sisters Ita and Sara informed my sister of his death. His sisters Bajla W. and Rose R. showed up just in time to follow the wagon out to the cemetery. Once there, we gave part of father's rations to a grave digger with whose help we dug a grave, lowered the body, said *Kaddish,* and covered it with dirt.

Not a tear was shed during the entire ceremony. Our eyes have dried out. We cannot cry anymore. Besides, we honestly envy the departed. From now on our father is definitely out of the hell we have been in for so long. He has been liberated in the most absolute sense of the word. Who knows, perhaps, up there, there is a heaven where our souls can live in peace forever. Perhaps, we shall all meet there one day. Perhaps...

Chapter 41
THE TRAINS

When I was very young, we would spend our summer vacations in a rented cottage in the countryside. The village in which our cottage was located could be easily reached by train. Train rides were fun. We would roam and play in the isles, or simply sit still and observe the countryside passing before our eyes. At times I wasn't sure whether I was standing still and the country was rapidly moving in front of me, or vice versa. I loved to stick out my head through the window, look towards the panting locomotive, and feel the wind striking my face. The fresh air was exhilarating. I would breathe deeply, and enjoy its purity and the fragrance of spring flowers it carried. After a while the constant grinding of the wheels would put me to sleep only to be awakened by the train's whistle, followed by a sudden jolt and squeaks of the brakes as the train came to a halt at the station.

Now, the sight of trains disturbs me. There is something ominous about them. All deportees are forced to take trains to bring them to their new destination. Where they are going remains a mystery, perhaps because we will it so. In spite of many rumors that the trains move their burden towards a deadly destination, we have convinced ourselves that the ghetto people will reach a new haven, where they will be fed and cured of their diseases. If this is an illusion, a Fatah Morgana, so be it! We will never know for sure until our time has come to board, and we exit the ugly box cars at our destination.

The trains have been very busy this spring. New orders have arrived to evacuate the ghetto. This morning on my way to work I see many people moving with their measly goods in the direction of the prison from where they are loaded onto the trains, destination unknown.

In the front office Red is busy scanning a list about four pages long. "What's going on?" I ask, surprised to see him doing office work.

"Do you really want to know?"

"Come on, I can see you have some news."

"Well, as usual, there's good news and bad news. They come wrapped in the same package, you know."

"Stop stretching it out. Let's hear it," I urge impatiently.

"The good news is that an invasion of France by Allied troops is expected any day now. The bad news is that our factory has been asked to prepare a list of dispensable people for transports to unknown destinations."

"Am I on it?"

"Not yet. But I don't believe it ends here. I think this is only the beginning of the final evacuation of the entire ghetto."

"Well, there isn't much we can do about it, is there?"

"That depends how much of a chance you are willing to take."

"This is not up to me. Are you talking of hiding someplace? Where can we hide? Where will we get our food from?"

"Well, it's up to you. If you feel you are ready to take a chance then prepare some place where you can safely hide. The Soviets are not far. They are approaching Warsaw. Take my word for it; I know it from a very reliable source."

"I'll think about it. See you later."

Mr. K, Motl, and Simcha are already in the workers' shack. They have already heard the news that Red had to dispose of. Today will be a very slow day. The taylor shops are cutting back on personnel because they got orders to prepare lists of "non-essential" people. Production is very slow, almost at standstill.

Chapter 42

A God-Send

The work slow-down we currently experience is welcomed by all of us. Time for a well-deserved rest. No one knows what may come next, and a bit of rest may help to strengthen our aching bones and muscles. Judging by what we have so far experienced, we must be ready for evil and cruel treatment. That is, if we are left alive by our persecutors.

At work, there is plenty of time to kill. I take off my jacket, sit down in a corner, which I have managed to claim my own, pull out a notebook and begin to write a poem.

This is not the first time I have written poetry. Before the war I wrote verses which were frequently read in class. The year before Pilsudski's death I remember writing a long poem for his birthday. It began with "O! Chief, our Chief, Your valiant struggle to render Poland free, raises great pride in kids like me." I scribbled down the poem on a sheet of paper and placed in an envelope which I addressed to: Marshal Pilsudski, The Belweder, Warsaw. Four weeks later the mailman knocked at our door with a special delivery letter addressed to me. Mother, who signed the receipt couldn't understand what it was all about and was outright frightened. She opened the envelope with trembling hands, and pulled out a neatly folded letter from the Marshal himself with a few words from his secretary, a Miss Illakowicz, who, I later learned, was a poet of renown in her own right. It contained thanks for the birthday wishes and the enclosed poem. .Needless to say, I became a celebrity in school, and the entire neighborhood was extremely proud of me.

When the ghetto closed, I started to write whenever I was inspired and had ample time on my hands. Many here keep diaries or write poetry or prose. In spite of the hunger, rumbling stomachs, and swollen hands, we write in the hope that someday, in a different, peaceful world, someone, somewhere, will find our writings, and hopefully learn from them of from our experiences.

In my opinion, ghetto politics are cruel, insane, and totally out of place. Perhaps I am wrong. Maybe this is the way people, who find themselves in a desperate situation, behave. Everyone tries to get closer to the bowl, and grab whatever he can to sustain himself and stay alive. I decide to describe our ghetto. If I perish, perhaps these poems will remain to tell our tragic story. I start writing. After about an hour the poem has taken shape:

The Ghetto

Dark, sunken, foul, narrow streets
old church's steeples. All around fences.
Shields with factory names one meets
Three bridges. Commissar's pretenses

Made up girls in loud colored dresses
Iron, Calcium, only drugs for healing
Work for children instead of caresses
Coal and potatoes stolen without stealing

Hunger, disease, plagues we can't afford
bodies and burials, there are no defections,
but over this mess sounds out one word:
Connections! Connections!

This is existence without any reason
Let truth be known for times to come
Connections ease life no matter what season
Cause here connection mean a better home.

That's enough for the day. I get up and stretch my legs. My stomach grumbles. Soup time is here; lunch break. I take my tin-plated soup canister and move towards the kitchen. A line has already formed and the sweet smell of potato soup permeates the air. The window opens up. A cloud of steam escapes. The kettle of soup is standing ready for distribution. The line moves very fast. As I near the window I notice a girl whom I have not seen here before. She dips the ladle and mixes the soup. She apparently is the new soup disburser.

"Hey, could you move that ladle a little deeper?" I ask hopefully.

"Who do you think you are?" she replies. "Everyone is entitled to his share. I make no exceptions."

"I'm not asking for special privileges. All I want is for you to stir up the kettle so that I may find a couple of potatoes in there."

"All right." She submerges the ladle and brings up a nice thick mixture of potatoes and carrots. "Here; don't complain."

This makes my day. I was really hungry and that soup should go a long way to still my appetite. I walk back to our shack holding the soup can as if it was a Wimbledon trophy.

"Guys, I hit the jackpot today. There is a new girl working in the kitchen. I figured there is nothing to lose so I asked her to give me somewhat thicker soup. And take a look at that." I proudly display my soup, mixing it with the spoon to bring up the thick stuff.

"You lucky stiff." Motl is jealous. "I got mostly water," he says, showing me his soup. Indeed, he has to fish around for quite a while to catch a potato.

"Well, tough luck. Smile at her. Maybe the next time she'll dig deeper."

I consume the soup sitting on the floor in my little corner. Each spoonful gets thoroughly dissolved and slowly swallowed. As with our home rations, the trick is to make it last as long as possible, because soon after the soup gets consumed one becomes hungry again. To make it last we have developed all kinds of strategies. At first the soup gets heated up on our stove. When it is hot it takes longer to consume. Then, while eating, I first skim the water off the top. This leaves the thick, hot ingredients on the bottom to be eaten last. Finally, when I eat I keep my lips closed leaving only a fine split though which I suck in the precious stuff. Regardless of all the tricks used, however, when the bottom of the can is reached, the feeling of having lost something precious engulfs me. And why not? There won't be any more soup until the following noon.

Lunch time is over. Mr. K is anxious to clean up the yard. Though it looks pretty clean to me, he thinks it should look still better.

"Who do you expect here today? The Fuhrer himself?" I cannot stand futile work.

"Since we have had a pretty slow day today, it won't hurt you to get some exercise." Mr K has a job to do and he will do it regardless of what we say.

"That's the last thing I need; exercise," I mumble as we leave the shack to pick up our shovels and brooms.

Outside, the weather is nice. The shining sun reassures me that the world goes on; the fresh air, full of spring fragrance invigorates me and lifts my spirits. My hunger is temporarily satisfied. I feel good. I see a bunch of old potato peels next to the kitchen and move over to examine whether they are still edible. Potato peels are at a premium and hard to get. Usually you must know someone from the kitchen staff to have access to them. Most of the time the staff keeps them for their own consumption, or trades them for bread.

As I bend down to pick one up I hear a girl's voice, "Are you still hungry? I thought I gave you a good dipping."

I turn around and see the kitchen worker who distributed the soup this noon. "Am I hungry? What a silly question. I have been hungry for the last four years. Where are you from? I have seen you here for the first time today."

"I worked in another kitchen but the factory was closed down. No more work. So they transferred me to this place."

"I hope our place stays open. The rumor mills have it that we will all have to leave soon."

"That is more than a rumor. The transports keep on leaving almost on a daily basis. But, why worry? It won't help you anyhow. Enjoy."

I wish I could enjoy life, especially now, but under the circumstances sex is the last thing I crave. Food, and only food, makes my world turn.

Looking at her I see her round face, big blue eyes, a gorgeous little mouth, and a figure that would stand up to Venus de Milo's and win the comparison.

"What's your name?"

"Mania. What are you doing here?"

"I am a yard-worker. I am supposed to sweep this place. My boss will soon remind me of my duties when he sees me standing and chatting with you."

"Don't worry about that; I can get even with him when he comes for his soup." "What are you doing after work?"

"Going home."

"Where do you live?"

"On Zawiszy Street."

"Funny. So do I."

"Let's go home together." "OK."

This evening, as I leave work, Mania is already waiting in the front office, and we start on our way home. Mania keeps on talking about her work in the kitchen, the kitchen chief, his sexual advances. She despises him. If he won't stop she will either ask for a transfer or leave this work altogether. I suggest she be more diplomatic about it. Brush him off, but with courtesy and firmness. Perhaps threaten to tell his wife and children. Mania thinks I am naive. His wife doesn't give a damn as long as he brings home food, and neither do his grown-up children. But I insist the last thing I would do is leave the job. She will have trouble finding another of equal value. Later, our talk turns to pre-war movies. She loves Janette McDonald, and would, one day, like to sing professionally. Could I be her Nelson Eddy? She laughs. She reminds me of Lola. That would be great, I add, but for the time being we have to first survive. We reach her house and part, hoping to see each other again tomorrow.

Chapter 43

A False Alarm

The last few days have been, politically speaking, most refreshing and invigorating. Red tells us that Rome was retaken by Allied forces; Allied armadas have finally landed on the north coast of France, and are proceeding toward Paris; the Red Armies have begun an offensive that in some spots got up to the Vistula River. Finally, this is the news we have been waiting for. It cannot get any better. We pray it is true. So far we have not been able to confirm any of Red's stories, and we have no sources of our own.

This week, though, things began to happen. In the quiet of the night, we can hear distinct rumblings. Either cannons or bombs are going off not too far from our city. All kind of stories are sweeping the ghetto like wildfire. They are pervasive, and in most cases true. Red is no longer my original source of news; we get it in the streets as if it was carried on waves of ether, and Red confirms it.

The good news has a bad side to it; the Germans have apparently sped up the enactment of their plans vis-à-vis the Jews. Deportations are in full swing. Sara B and her sister Ita have been placed on the deportation list. My aunt Hannah and her daughter Itka also received "invitations" by ghetto mail, to leave their home. All four of them decided to go together. David B will stay behind and perhaps join them at a later date. At least those are his plans.

It is July, and Aunt Hannah and my cousins left yesterday with one of the transports. Today Red tells me that the trains turn around reasonably fast. A friend of his who works at the station has told him that it takes a day for the same trains to return. They cannot be going too far.

"Is this good or bad?" I ask.

"It cannot be very good. A station attendant found a note in one of the trains that told the people to stay home, lest they wish to die."

"Another one of these scare rumors?"

"Who knows?" Red prefers not to speculate.

On the way to our shack, I pass the kitchen. Mania is waiting to greet me. She has been doing this since I first took her home.

"Good morning!" Her melodious voice is very soothing.

"Good morning," I respond. "Forgive me for not being more cheerful. My aunt and cousins left with yesterday's transport."

"I know how you feel; a couple of my uncles also left with their families. Where do you think are they going?"

"That depends on you--if you are a rosy optimist than you'll believe the Germans: They are going to work in a better place than the ghetto. But if you are a realist, then you believe my pal, Red: they are going to meet their Maker."

"I don't want to talk about that. No one knows what tomorrow will bring, why mess up today?"

In a way she is right. In a situation like the one we find ourselves in, it is better to live with today. Tomorrow? We shall face it if, or when, we get there.

"I have to report to work. See you later," she says as we approach the kitchen. "Don't forget to be last in line."

"I won't." How could I? For the last couple of weeks I have been rewarded with a can of good, thick soup every working day.

Motl is already there firing up a couple of branches in the stove, to warm up his coffee.

"Where is Mr. K?" I ask. He usually arrives much earlier than the other workers.

"He was here this morning, but then he was called in to the Commissar's office."

"What the hell does this mean?"

"Well, it could be an unusual working assignment, but then again, it could have something to do with our marching orders."

"I hope it is the former, not the latter." I say, although I have a feeling that the latter is more likely.

I try to make myself comfortable in my favorite corner when the door swings open. Mr. K appears holding a piece of paper in his hand. His face is somber. He looks down as he straightens out the sheet of paper.

"Guys, I never thought I would live to have to do this. Mr. P has received new orders. The remaining working force must be cut down to a skeleton crew. I am sure that soon all of us will be out of here, but for now, I was asked to notify you that all of the yard workers must report to the jail by the middle of this month. I am the only one that will remain to help liquidate the plant, whatever that means. Most shop workers are subject to the same orders."

"Does that mean that the entire ghetto is about to be liquidated?" Motl knows what the answer to his question is. He is just trying to get final confirmation.

"I cannot officially tell you, because I have not been given any further details. All I can say is follow your own reasoning."

"Can we, in the interim, come to work?" I am curious because of my noontime soup.

"Yes, you can. But, for all practical purposes, you will cease to exist after the date given on your slip. Whether you go or stay in the ghetto is none of my business."

Simcha shows up a little late. He says he has a problem. His wife has received marching orders. His problem is quickly resolved when he learns that he is free to join her. We talk until noon. Mostly repetitious, empty, hopeless talk, but not useless. We need to somehow reassure ourselves that all will be fine, though we know very well that it will not.

At the soup distribution window I learn that Mania, too, has been asked to report together with most of the kitchen staff. Only a skeleton crew will remain. Hard to tell what they mean by a "skeleton crew". I hope it doesn't mean a crew of skeletons, but then again…does it really make a difference?

At home, Debra is waiting with bad news. She has been asked to report. Well, so have I. What should we do? We decide there is no choice but to go. What would we live on if we remained here after the ghetto gets liquidated? Our food reserve consists of a bottle of oil that looks like heavy machine oil. We have managed to save it because there was little stuff to fry, and also because oil doesn't spoil.

Out of the twenty relatives that occupied our apartment house when the ghetto closed, only David and the two of us remain. David wants to stay. Let him stay. We will leave.

Two weeks have gone by, and the day to report has arrived. Although the summer is in full swing, we do not see or feel the blessings of this season. All we know is that soon our lives will drastically change. Where are we going? Who cares? If there is a tomorrow it must be a better one because things cannot get any worse. If there is no tomorrow, then so be it. We certainly have had enough of this miserable existence.

We decide that I shall report late today since the best time to go is after the day's transports have stopped. I will take our measly belongings with me, at least as much as I can carry. In the meantime, Debra will try to sell some of our feather bedding. Apparently, one can get German Marks at the collection station in the old church. Debra will join me tomorrow morning for the noontime departure. I pack my knapsack full, and report to the jail.

The ghetto policeman at the entrance notes my name, address, place of work, and hands me over to another policeman who leads me into a huge room. The place is half filled with people and their belongings. I tell him that I expect my sister to report tomorrow morning, and wonder if she could find me. No problem. He assures me that if she reports before ten in the morning she will be able to locate me. I find a spot near one corner where I put down my belongings and make myself as comfortable as I can. The people around me seem resigned, but they are certain that we are being shipped to work in Germany. I agree. What else can one do?

A man with a kettle full of soup arrives, and there are girls distributing food rations. We get a piece of bread, some margarine, and a bowl of fairly thick soup. Soon we feel better. Nothing like a decent meal. Our spirits rise. The guy next to me, a friendly and talkative chap, tells a joke.

"You see, when Hitler came to power in Germany the economic situation was such that the German people had to make a choice between guns and butter. Well, this did not go over very well with the populace and the Fuehrer knew it. One day he called in his science advisor and ordered him to start a program that will result in the production of enough ersatz butter to satisfy the needs of the people. The scientist didn't know what substance to start off with. "Start with human excrement" said the Fuehrer. "It is plentiful and won't burden our strained natural resources." The horrified science advisor knew that he could not object; an order is an order. Resisting it might land him in jail. So he sets out to find a scientist who would undertake this work. He asks around and soon gets a call from the Rector of the University in Berlin saying that he may have the right candidate. He used to be acquainted with a professor of chemistry, a Jew. Since Hitler came to power this Professor, a certain Dr. Schmeckl, wound up in a concentration camp."

Our storyteller laughs and continues. "Yes, Schmekl was his name. He is a brilliant man, and if anybody can do it he is the one. Orders went out to release Mr. Schmeckl from camp. A meeting was set up with the Fuehrer, and the professor was asked to present a program to turn human waste into butter within three months. But, Herr Fuehrer, this is a tremendously complicated task," said Dr. Schmeckl. "I'll need a few years to do that." "We do not have time to fool around" the Fuehrer told him firmly. "You do it, or we'll do you in. In one week I want to see a detailed program and schedule for this task" So Dr. Schmeckl went to work. The next week, when meeting the Fuehrer, Schmeckl presented a detailed program and schedule."

More people join me to listen to the storyteller, as he continues with his joke. "The program the scientist presented took four months, but the Fuehrer, though unhappy, agreed to the extension. After the first month the professor was to report on the detailed approaches. The making of a prototype sample was scheduled for the second month. Production plans were to be developed in the third month, and a sample of the final, mass-produced product presented to the Fuehrer for tasting at the end of four months. The first meeting went well, and the Fuehrer said, "Keep it up, Jew, and I may let you go free." In the second month a prototype sample was shown, but it fell short of the goal. The Fuehrer was furious. "One more failure and you'll be shot! I want to see a really good prototype the next time." Dr. Schmeckl got worried, and began to work day and night. When the time for the third meeting arrived, he had a prototype ready. The meeting began with Mr. Schmekl showing off a bar of what appeared to be butter. The Fuehrer looked at it. "Hmm, it looks good, Jew. When will you be ready with the production plans?" "Well, Mr. Fuehrer" replied

Professor Schmekl, "Before we get that far you should understand that this is an achievement unprecedented in the annals of science. Just look at it. It looks like genuine butter. It has the consistency of butter. It smears like butter. It melts like butter. It even smells like butter." The fuehrer by this time was indeed elated. "Then go ahead with the production plans," he urged.

"Schmeckl appeared a little concerned," our storyteller continued. "My Fuehrer," he uttered. "It has only one little problem." "What is it?" demanded the Fuehrer. Dr. Schmeckl cringed, saluted, and said in a soft, quiet voice, "My Fuehrer, it still tastes like shit."

At the end of his story my neighbor bursts out laughing. "Get it? It still tastes like shit. Hah, Hah, hah."

It's funny, but also true. Most of the ersatz stuff they make today tastes like shit. I find this joke amusing. It is representative of the times we live in.

This little interlude of comedy has taken my mind off my problems for a few minutes. The way he stretched the story helped. Now I am ready to fall asleep.

The floor is hard but I manage to get in a good night's sleep. For one reason or another, my problems seem behind me. My mind is at peace. The smell of brewed chickaree coffee wakes me up. I am now looking around to see if my sister has managed to check in.

"Line up for breakfast," comes the order from a ghetto policeman. "The trains may come earlier today. We have to get ready."

I get in line, and pick up a cup of hot ersatz coffee and a piece of bread. My new friend, last night's storyteller, is right behind me. We sit down on the floor next to our belongings and slowly start consuming our food. Suddenly, there is commotion at the main gate. We jump to our feet. I run over to the window. A horse-drawn carriage is approaching with the horse in full gallop. The driver keeps on whipping the horse, which is running as fast as it can. In the rear of the carriage, a man is standing. His white hair blows in the wind. It makes him look like a biblical prophet. Why, it's Mr.R, our leader! He shouts something at the top of his lungs.

As he nears our window, I can distinctly hear, "Jews, you can go home. The transports are stopped. Go home."

I don't believe my own ears. Can it be? Is it true? Mr. R's carriage turns around at the end of the prison road. I can hear him shout again and again,

"Go home. No more deportations." Soon, the police arrive. "Start packing" they yell. "Get out of here. He saved your lives."

Slowly the message begins to sink in. We are free to go back home. I don't know whether to laugh or cry. The policemen's words that Mr. R has saved our lives suddenly crystallize in my mind. So Mr. R knew all along where he was sending his people. The dreadful rumors must have been true. All those who preceded us are dead. I pick up my goods and run as fast as I can towards the gate. I want to get out of here. Where is Debra?

As I run, the ghetto suddenly appears to me a place where freedom reigns supreme. There are no Germans to be seen. No guns. No shootings. It seems I am a free man!

Debra is waiting in our flat. She heard a rumor this morning that the deportations had been stopped, and decided to sit it out and wait. We embrace, squeezing each other as if to make certain that we are still alive. "From what I heard at the jail, there is little doubt that the ones who went before us will never return," I tell her, recounting what the policemen had said. She heard the same thing here. Hopefully, this was the last attempt to empty the ghetto.

A couple of days have passed and I am back at work. Lucky for me so is Mania. As soon as the deportations came to a halt, Mr. R, the ghetto's German manager, decided to resume all working activities.

Simcha isn't there, he reported in time to be deported. Motl feels somehow invigorated, and full of pep. His father, who had been losing strength, is feeling better, and runs around the house. The distant rumblings of cannon and exploding bombs have a terrifically soothing, and one might say, healing effect on us all.

We work, trying to separate good sewing machines from trash. Each machine gets inspected on a table. We attempt to turn the wheel to see if it turns and if the entire system responds. The final test consists of holding the wheel still and pulling it in all directions to see if excessive clearance is present. The good machines are carefully lined up on a set of shelves. The bad ones are crushed with a heavy steel hammer. The cast iron housings crack like eggshells. Trash, thus generated, gets piled up on the floor. Lunch time is here. I am starved, since we consumed all our food before reporting to the jail. A hot cup of soup will do me an awful lot of good.

Mania doesn't disappoint. As soon as I hand her my soup can, she reaches in to the very bottom of the kettle and comes up with a nice, thick serving. I return to the shack and join Motl at the table.

"Boy, you're in luck again today. Where did you get your soup, at a restaurant? Motl peeks at my can and quickly compares it with his, which he stirs with the spoon. It seems to be very watery.

"You know it's good to have connections. I told you before, this girl, Mania, who dishes out the soup, must have a special liking for me. I have walked her home a couple of times."

"How lucky can you get? The next time I will line up after you. Maybe her generosity will carry over to the next guy."

"Good idea. Have you heard any news today? Any rumors?"

"Not much, but from what I hear the Germans have definitely lost the war."

"It's just a matter of time. Unfortunately we have no control over time. The Germans may lose the war but we may not be here to enjoy it."

"Don't be so pessimistic. We'll survive. You and I will live to enjoy freedom once again. You'll see."

"From your mouth to God's ears; that's what my grandmother used to say. I hope you're right."

The summer of 1944 is about to begin, and the news from all fronts were exhilarating. The greatest lift and, unfortunately, the greatest let down came when a rumor swept the ghetto of Lodz that Hitler had been killed by a German officer somewhere in Prussia. At first we were stunned, but soon the thought of being finally free exploded in crazy celebrations. Unfortunately, a couple of hours later the radio announced that the Fuehrer was alive and well. According to Red, my friend who was the source of all that information, it was announced that all conspirators would be tried by military courts, and properly punished. We knew what proper punishment meant

Soon, ghetto life returned to normal. It was quiet, but for the rumors of "liquidation" that refused to go away.

My sister Debra had not been recalled to work. The factory that employed young kids, was closed, she had no choice but to stay home all day, with no one to talk to. This took a terrible toll on her weekly food rations. Out of boredom she kept on nibbling away at her bread, and before even realizing it, the bread was gone and she faced a couple of days of starvation before the distribution of the next rations.. I had taken to bringing home most of my soup. Debra would add some water to it and make dinner for both of us.

My new friend, the soup handler, has been awfully good to me. She still dips deeper into the kettle and brings up thicker soup when I show up. Without her I don't know if I could survive. I see her every evening on our way home. She frequently visits our flat. We talk and sing. The thought of getting closer to each other is as distant as the North Pole. I am too starved and depressed for that.

A new day. The sunrise brings new orders from the German Administration. This time there are no rumors. It is official. It is final. The ghetto must be emptied of all inhabitants. All factories have been closed. Only skeleton crews will remain to clean up and lock the doors.

At noon, our Aunt Rose and Uncle David pay us a visit. We haven't seen them since my father's funeral. My cousin David also shows up.

"We have come to find out what you kids intend to do." Aunt Rose is childless, and feels somewhat responsible for us now that we are orphans.

"I discussed it with Debra," I tell her. "As you know, we did join in the last transport. Fortunately, or unfortunately, we were spared. The deportation was called off at the last minute. We think we ought to go, but we are still not positive."

"Let us assume we stay," our cousin David, whose sisters left with the last transports, cuts in. "What can we do to sustain ourselves?"

"We don't have any food reserves. Do you?" asks Debra

"Neither do we" affirms Aunt Rose.

"Even if we had food, we would need a good hiding place to stay out of reach of the Germans who I am sure will leave no stone unturned to make the ghetto *Judenrein,* free of Jews." David adds. Silently, I agree with him.

"Besides, who knows how long we'll have to wait before we are liberated?" I add

"Well, do I sense that we are going?" asks Uncle David.

"I guess we are. Anyone against it?" Debra is anxious to get to the point.

"It seems we are all in agreement. Let us then set a definite day, How about a week from today?" Asks Cousin David.

"That's OK, but let us not get caught by our overzealous police. Stick to your homes," cautions Uncle David.

"OK then. Next week at 10 am right here is our meeting place," I say, and all agree.

Now that the die has been cast, we all feel better. Somehow, after every life shaping decision we feel good. It looks as if we have abdicated our own responsibilities and left our fate up to God. My mind is at peace, as it was a few weeks ago in jail awaiting transport. That night I slept like a baby.

A week after the family (what is left of it) meeting. Debra and I start packing. Actually it is easy. Most of the junk we disposed of for the last evacuation. I fill my knapsack with a few sets of underwear, father's shoes, family photos, one sweater, some shirts, and two winter shawls. Debra packs her knapsack. We take the coins that father used to collect, a silver-covered notebook with a pencil. We put it all into Debra's coat pockets. Should we get searched it is easier for a woman than a man to hide small stuff.

Cousin David arrives with his luggage. He is ready to go. I hear a commotion outside. Aunt Rose's voice is loud. She curses her husband for having left her gloves behind. He assures her that when the war is over he will get her ten pairs of gloves. The door opens and both stumble in with their rucksacks on their backs, and drop down on one of our beds.

"I walked only from our place to yours and I am half dead already," gasps Uncle David, who obviously has trouble breathing.

"Sit down and relax for a few minutes. We can take our time. It is only ten in the morning." I advise Uncle David. "By the way, Debra, did you remember to pack our bottle of oil?"

"I am glad you reminded me of it. Open up your knapsack and I will put it in" I untie the knots of the pull-string and Debra inserts the bottle.

"Are you sure it is well closed?"

"Yes I pushed the cork down as hard as I could."

We talk for a while about the new place we are going to. Hopefully it is better than the one we leave. After all, what can be worse? An hour has passed and we are ready to go. I put on my father's "new" winter coat although it is terribly hot outside. Debra puts on mother's warm coat, and we march off towards the jail.

On the way we meet many people, strapped like us to their measly belongings, huffing and puffing as they make their way to the jail. I sweat like a pig. So do the others. For us, the easiest way to transport warm clothing is to wear it, but the heat is killing us. Now, we are not at all sure whether we will have the strength to make it to the jail. Somehow, we muster our last reserves and arrive at the train depot near the jail.

We form a chain holding hands as we get pushed towards the trains. There is tumult everywhere. Mothers looking for children, people screaming out names of relatives lost in the crowd; shouts of the SS men; yelling Jewish policemen. In all this chaos, order somehow prevails and we soon reach the top of the line. Here we are given a loaf of bread, our soup canisters are filled with some kind of fluid, and we are urged and pushed into the boxcars. Our car quickly fills up. An SS man yells out to shut the door. The door rolls into place and closes with a loud bang. Now, it is dark. We call out to each other. Thank God, we are all here. Ours is probably one of the last cars to be filled. Soon after we manage to find some free floor space and settle down, the wagons jerk; couplings collide, and bump. Loud bangs penetrate our wagon. The steam whistle blows. We are on our way.

Chapter 44
THE CAMP

Rah-ta-ta. Rah-ta-ta....the steam engine keeps repeating its refrain, forcing the wheels to pull forward on the barren rails which squeak ever so often in helpless disapproval. The train slides and shakes having encountered a sharp turn.

The rapid review of my life has suddenly stopped. A few jerks of the locomotive have brought me back to grim reality. I open up my eyes, and look around. The train wagon looks so familiar.

It is amazing how, sometimes, one can get quickly used to new surroundings and circumstances. Just less than ten years ago I got the shock of my life when, returning from camp as a young boy, I saw the covered body of one of our neighbors. Now, there are at least three corpses in our boxcar, one lying right next to me. It is the fellow who first made us aware of the presence of two refuse buckets. That is not shocking anymore. Soon my turn may come. I only hope that at the next stop the SS guards will remove the corpses and give them some kind of decent burial.

This train of ours has been on the road for at least three days. We stopped counting them, and are totally disoriented. We sleep a lot because of the poor nourishment and cramped quarters. There is simply nowhere to go, and the train keeps rumbling on.

Suddenly… a surprise. The train stops suddenly in the middle of a bridge span. I look out through my peep hole, and saw a huge river beneath us. This is the first time in my life I have seen that large a body of flowing water. On both sides of the river as far as the eye can see are apartment buildings, steeples of churches and formal structures. It must have been a very large city. David suggested it was Vienna, but I thought it might be Prague or maybe even Krakow Soon the train moves on.to our mysterious destination. I have a premonition we are better off not knowing where we are going to. The enclosure we have been packed into is something we have accepted and grown used to. After all, what else can we do? The tiny space I have claimed for myself is now my territory. I staked it out and have absolutely no tolerance for anyone encroaching on it. Only my sister enjoys the privilege of stretching into it. This trip has taxed her tremendously. She looks more like a ghost than a human being. I guess I probably look like that, too. Constantly, I keep on telling her: "Hang on. We'll make it." She grins, and shakes her head. Her beautiful brown eyes, so full of life before this war began, have lost their luster, and stare into space void of emotion.

Since I awoke from my dreams my mind still intermittently plays tricks on me. It wanders to beautiful places, where the smell is that of spring grasses and flowers, rather than human waste. I make believe I am in a place where food is plentiful, and freedom everlasting. If these are hallucinations, or nightmares, so be it. They help to kill time. Sometimes I talk and brood to myself, only to be rudely awakened by "Are you all right?" My sister cannot do that. She prefers to stay alert. How she does it, when the steady rumbling of the train's wheels is so conducive to slumber, I do not know. Nor do I care at this time. The wandering of my mind and my dreams help me to escape the brutal reality of my immediate environment.

The train has stopped for the normal routines of cleaning the buckets and refilling the water barrel. We are not given any food at this stop. Instead we are told that the next stop will be our final destination. The joy with which we greet this news is indescribable. Even the people we thought were in the process of dying suddenly jump up, begin to smile, and clean themselves. David embraces me and my sister. "We made it!" he cries. The train moves on and resumes its normal, monotonous run.

A few hours pass. All at once the locomotive's siren blasts off with a shrill sound, and the train begins to slow down. I can see through the cracks in my wall the outline of fences very similar to the ones that surrounded the ghetto. Could this be another ghetto? The mere thought of it wipes out all the hope I managed to gather when it was announced that we are about to reach our final destination.

"David, look through this crack and tell me what you see," I say, moving aside. David presses his face against the wall, and looks intently for a while.

"I see fences. Are we back in our ghetto? Or is this a camp?"

"Let me see," says Debra, pushing David away from the peep hole. "My God," she whispers. "I have the feeling that we are in for another ghetto tour!"

Soon, the train stops with a loud squeal. Before we get a chance to become oriented, the doors swing open. I grab my bag, while Debra and David grab their belongings. All of a sudden I feel some slimy fluid running down my pants. I touch it, smell it. It is oil. The bottle of oil that Debra packed into my knapsack opened up, and the oil is flowing, messing up all my stuff.

"How could you do this to me?" I scream at Debra. I am horrified. "What will I wear? How will I look in this new place?"

Debra doesn't answer, instead she grabs her bags and moves toward Aunt Rose.

"Where are you going?" I shout.

At this moment a man dressed in a striped gray prisoner's suit, familiar to me from so many movies I had seen, grabs me by my arm and pushes me towards the open doors.

"*Raus. Schnell,*" he orders in German. Then in Polish: "*Nie trzeba sie klucic*" Stop arguing, you must leave this stuff on the train anyway. You'll never see it again. *Raus*! Out!"

"But where are we? What does all this mean?" I ask in Polish.

"You'll soon find out. Schnell. When you get out you'll be taken to a uniformed SS man. This is Dr. Mengele. Remember this name. *Raus. Schnell. Lausige Schweine.*"

Why is he telling me that and cursing at me at the same time? I wonder. Soon my answer appears in the form of a uniformed SS man who now screams at the man in the prisoner's suit, "*Ruhe. Sprechen verboten.î* No talking here. *Raus mit den dreckigen Juden.*"

"*Jawohl, Herr Oberscharfuehrer. Macht das Ihr rauskommt!*"

Another prisoner joins him and both begin to push the boxcar crowd out of the open doors. Many fall. I manage to jump down. So does David B. We are waiting for Debra, Aunt Rose and David R. The SS man now comes closer screaming at the top of his lungs:

"Line up. Women before men. Quick. Schnell."

Just then, Debra and Aunt Rose appear in the doorway. We help them down, but as soon as they hit the ground the prisoner police pulls them up front, ahead of the men. I don't even get a chance to say good-bye. In no time, the female queue grows long. I can still see Debra with Aunt Rose. The men's queue begins to form quickly behind the women, and bends so that my field of vision improves.

Chapter 45
SELECTION

To say that I am totally confused would be a huge understatement. I went through an awful lot in the ghetto, and I somehow learned how to survive. This, though, is a completely new game. What should I do to get out of the SS sight? In the ghetto, I somehow always managed to avoid direct danger when confronted with a new situation. Now I am totally lost.

Way ahead I see a bunch of SS men keeping order, and making certain that only individuals approach the man in uniform. Is this Dr. Mengele, I wonder, and if so what is he doing there? As the first woman approaches he looks her over and motions to her to go over to one side. Another older woman is waved onto another side. After a while it becomes clear to me that sick, old, and children go onto one side while the stronger-looking women go to another. Mothers who do not want to part with their children are told to go with them. The queue moves forward very fast.

I see Debra approaching the man in uniform, and he motions for her to join the sick. Aunt Rose, who is right behind her, grabs her by the hand and says something to the selecting German officer. He stops for a second, and then motions for both of them to join the healthier-looking group. Once the selection of women is complete they are quickly led away. The sicker group moves toward a cluster of buildings distinguished by tall stacks. The group of people who appear to be in better shape is marched over to a group of buildings close to the camp gate.

After the women come the men. The two Davids and I stick together. As we approach the uniformed selector, I see a handsome man dressed in a newly pressed uniform. He must be of a higher rank, judging by the insignias on his shoulders. A death head adorn his military cap, the letters SS resembling more the sign for lightning than actual letters, are pinned onto his collar. In his hand he holds a riding whip and very nonchalantly points the whip in the direction he chooses for the approaching individual. As we near, he begins to exhibit signs of boredom. He yawns for a long time, covering his mouth with his gloved hand. What a gentleman, I think. He surely knows his table manners. To me, this gesture demonstrates the arrogance and abhorrence for the pathetic crowd passing in front of him. After all, he is the Arian, the member of the Master Race, and we are cattle, not humans.

David B. faces him first, followed by me and my uncle David. At the instant I come face-to-face with him a picture of a slave market flashes through my mind. I have read books about Negroes being sold in North Africa to slavery. This, too, is a slave sale. Without money exchanging hands, it is organized with the order and finesse befitting the masters. All three of us are motioned in the direction of the healthier-looking people.

We are urged now to hurry up and join the end of the female crowd being prodded toward a big, one-story garage-type building. The building is almost filled to capacity. At the front there is a door to another wing. I see naked women going through this door. An order to undress is heard. I hesitate for a while since the last of the female line are still shedding their cloths, but a couple of bangs with a policeman's stick over my head remind me quickly this is no time for hesitation. I begin to undress. Soon, we are all naked and being pushed toward the open door. The pace is now very slow. We have to wait until room for more people is made in the next room.

"What's going on in there?" someone shouts.

"You are gonna get shaved. We'll get you really clean in this place," I hear a loud German voice reply.

I turn around and right behind me an SS man is trying to make his way into the other room. We part before him as, I imagine, the waters must have parted before Moses. As soon as he gets to the door he is heard shouting "Schnell. Get going. We want to close this transport before nightfall."

I move toward the door, and see a row of men and women sitting in chairs. They rapidly shave people with clippers. Wherever hair grows it gets quickly, and judging by the expressions of some of the faces, painfully, removed. We line up now behind a shaver, a mix of both men and women. In front of me is the back of a fairly well-built and filled-out girl. Her body has the form of a woman, not like most of the others that look like skeletons with empty water bags hanging from their chest. She turns her head and lets out a terrible howl. "Mania," I call out. She covers her eyes with her hands and quickly disappears into another, more distant line overcome with shame, not saying a word.

I am glad she did that. I wouldn't want her to see me in my Adam's suit that fits me so closely that every rib and bone of my body can be readily distinguished. There is no time to reflect upon what just happened. We are prodded on. I reach my barber, and am quickly shaved clean, but not without having to bend and stretch.

As soon as I am through with the shaving, I move into another huge room.

Before entering, we are each given a small bar of black soap. In the room there is a large number of showerheads built into the ceiling. All are working, and we are urged to wash quickly and thoroughly. Soon we get into another room where we are handed towels, a shirt, underwear, a prisoner's suit, a blanket and a pair of shoes with wooden soles. Because of our shaven heads, it is now hard to distinguish the women from the men. We are all bald, and dressed the same way. I do not see Mania anymore. Orders come for the women to fall in, and they are quickly marched away. I finally find the Davids, who had lost me in this horrible shuffle.

"Thank God, we found you," says Uncle David with relief.

"Let's make sure that we don't get separated again," I say as I begin to breathe air through my nostrils for the first time since leaving the train. Towards the end of the train trip my sinuses plugged up, mercifully depriving me of the sense of taste and smell. Now they slowly open up, and fresh air rushes into my lungs. I smell something. It is the smell of burning coal or wood mixed with another stench which I cannot identify.

"What's that smell?" I ask.

"We smelled it as soon as we got off the train. I don't know," says my cousin.

We look around at the compound towards which the sick, young and infirm were led, and see tall stacks emitting plumes of smoke mixed with sparks.

"What are they burning there?" I ask in my constant curiosity.

"Remember, it is curiosity that killed the cat," says a voice behind me. Turning, I notice a camp policeman, who admonishes, "Don't ask questions. You'll find the answers yourself soon. I will take you now to your new block. This will be your new address from here on. Line up and let's go!"

As we march away, I turn around once more to look at the stacks. Could they possibly? Noooo. The Germans wouldn't do that. They are civilized and highly cultured people, I remember father's words.

On the way to our "new address," we pass through an arched wrought iron gate. On top of the gate are the words "Arb*eit Macht Frei*" made from wrought iron rods. "Work Liberates." What an ironic motto. I ponder to myself, if this place comes in any way close to the ghetto, "Work Kills" might be much more appropriate. The barrack we are led into is large. It looks like a sporting arena in comparison to the boxed car train enclosure. Wide bunk beds are stacked up against the walls, much too wide for one person to sleep in. Fresh straw covers the wooden planks. It smells good, and almost overrides the smell from the stacks.

As soon as the last group destined to stay here arrives, a man dressed in a prisoner's uniform with a black beret on his head steps onto a wooden crate placed in the center of the room and shouts out, "All of you form a circle around me, and listen very carefully. I am not going to repeat myself, and should I have to, you can start feeling sorry for yourselves right now."

We press closer to where he stands so as not to miss a word. The Davids are on each side of me.

"My name is Ivan," he begins in Polish. "That's all you need to know. I am your *Blockleader,* your *Blockaeltester,* in our jargon. You belong to me and must be ready to briskly fill my orders no matter what. Though I don't have to, let me introduce myself. As you see I wear a black triangle. You will soon wear red and yellow triangles which form the Star of David. Black means that I am being held on criminal charges. Red is political, and yellow Jewish."

He looks around as if to make sure that his words are sinking in. "I am a Ukrainian who lived, after World War One, in a small town next to Lvov, under Polish rule. Next to us was a Jewish town. I hated and still hate everything you Yids stand for. You took from us our land and built your little villages, from where you exploited every poor Ukrainian peasant. I hated you for that. You practice your strange religion, that of Antichrists. You used blood of our poor farmer's children for your leavened Passover bread. I hated you for that. You taught your kids to read, while my father never did. I hated you for that. Your parents were never drunk, while my father lived off alcohol. I hated you for that. Your kids never got beaten by their parents the way I was. I hated you for that. You helped one another, while nobody helped us when we were in trouble. I hated you for that.

"As you can see, I do not harbor much love for you, you bastards. I have waited all my life for these days of revenge. This may be your hell; to me it is heaven. You see you belong to me. You are my slaves and I can treat you the way I see fit. I can beat the shit out of you. I can even kill you and get praised for that rather than reprimanded. So watch your rotten steps, and make sure you don't get in my way or step on my toes.

"This is Igor," he continues, pointing toward a corpulent man. "He is your *Stubendienst*, or room-help. This doesn't mean that he is here to serve you. He is my right arm. You have to obey him as you must obey me. He will give you your orders for tonight. Tomorrow morning we all will congregate in front of the door, and you will be sent away for the day to a selected place of work. In the evening, upon return, I will give you your daily rations. Igor will help me with that. That's all I have to say. Igor, take over." He jumps off the crate and heads toward the door.

"Welcome, welcome to the workers' paradise, you dirty kikes. My name is Igor. I, too, am a Ukrainian; see the black triangle? Criminal charges. You should call me "Schtubendienst Igor." Also, be careful to always call our boss Ivan "Blockaeltester." I will be in charge of feeding you, bringing in the food from the commissary. I will watch you, and see to it that you guys don't goof off while in the barracks, heh?" Igor is a broad-shouldered, stocky guy with a wide face displaying an expression of soul emptiness, a stupid smile on his rather fat lips, and big bulging blue eyes. The fully shaven head gives him the look of a moron. "Line up against the wall and you will get your bunk assignment. Each bunk is identified by a number."

We meekly line up as ordered. What else can one do? I make sure that both Davids and I are together, and count the people ahead of us. There are four people assigned to a bunk. We skip two people in line, and are given the same bunk.

"Spread out your blankets," shouts Igor "No mess. No straw spilling. Otherwise I will make you clean the entire barracks four times over. Tomorrow morning, at four fifteen sharp, you will be given an order to assemble in front of the barracks. Everyone must be there. No washing or latrine after that. Otherwise darkness will be with you." I guess it comes from the German *Ich sehe schwartz fuer dich,* meaning you are on the shit-list. "Your latrine is located behind the barracks." He points in the direction of the back wall, opposite the door.

Our blankets are quickly spread, and the order is given to go to sleep. The only light bulb in the room, which hangs from the ceiling, is turned off. I lie between my uncle and cousin. It is a little cramped in comparison to our ghetto accommodations, but we had the train ride and after that anything seems comfortable. I am so exhausted that it doesn't take long for me to pass out.

As sleep consumes me I get the feeling of descending into a dark pit. It is frightening here. I want to scream, but no sound emanates from my mouth. Suddenly a dim light brightens the sullen darkness. In the center of the pit is a table dressed up for the Sabbath meal. Four candles are mounted in shining candelabra. Slightly slouched over the candles I see a woman's figure. A dark shawl over her head, her face is covered with her hands. She appears to be doing the candle blessings. After a brief while, two of the candles rapidly burn out. A third slumps, and gets close to extinction, while the weak flame produced by the fourth candle reaches up, and sparkles slightly in the darkness. The woman's shawl falls off onto her shoulders. Her hands recede from the face. My mother's face is in front of me. She smiles and tries to reach out to pet my head. I quiver, and the image disappears. I wake up covered by sweat. Only snores are heard all around me. I lie for a while with my eyes open thinking about my dream. Soon, exhaustion takes over and I am back, submerged in deep sleep.

In the past few days I have learned more than in my four years of ghetto internment, and all that knowledge comes from old inmates. What have I learned? Well, let's start with the place I am in. It is a concentration camp called Auschwitz. I am in a section of this camp called Birkenau. Auschwitz was formed around 1941, basically designed as a slave labor camp, but the Birkenau addition was built as a proficient and very efficient death factory. It kills people fast, gassing them, and disposing of the bodies in huge crematoria. The Germans tried it out on Gypsies first. Hence, to the insiders, Birkenau is known as the *Zigeuner Lager* or Gypsy Camp.

The buildings to which our sick and infirm were led are the gas chambers. Inside, they look similar to the shower rooms we passed through on our way in, but instead of water, poison gas is released, and the people die an agonizing death. The bodies are then transported to the next building, where they are burned in huge ovens. All those details I got from a member of the prisoner guard who work the ramp and buildings. For some unknown reason his outfit is called Canada. The Canada have been coerced to do the work, but improved rations, and a sense of false security help them stay in the outfit. It's a horrible job, and they are convinced that they face certain death. Now I know why the man at the ramp wanted me to remember the name Mengele, the name of the monster who determines who is to live and who to die. He wanted to make sure that if he doesn't make it, there will be others who will remember the names of the perpetrators. The Canada are the only ones who are permitted to work the place, and thus know all details. They will make excellent witnesses, either at trials or simply for history's records. That is, if they survive.

There is a camp police force here as well. It consists of prisoners who managed to survive a couple of years in this hell. They can be identified by armbands on which the word KAPO is imprinted. KAPO stands for *Kameradschafts Polizei*- comradely police. After all, in the new Germany you address people as comrades. I guess this is a remnant of the socialist philosophy that has been so badly distorted by the Fuehrer.

Geographically, we are in the south of Poland, not far from the city of Krakow. I am told by an old-timer not to feel too confident. One day I, too, may be sent to the gas chambers. The inmates who get sick and cannot perform the work they are given eventually wind up in a barrack specifically designated for collection and final disposition of these poor souls. I listen, and take mental notes of everything I hear.

Chapter 46
GETTING OUT OF HELL

I have been in close situations before, but never in one resembling, even remotely, the one I am in now. There is no doubt in my mind that this is the place that may finally end my existence. I must get out of here. The war is coming to an end and I want to be alive when that happens.

The first few days I worked in fields digging holes in the ground, it seemed to me just for digging's sake, and no other purpose. My Uncle David managed to squeeze himself one day into a group that worked in a factory. They were one man short, and he succeeded. The factory's name is Buna. He tells me that they make artificial, or as we call it ersatz, rubber for tires. Natural rubber supplies have dried out. Besides, he says the synthetic rubber, although ersatz, is in many ways better than natural. My cousin David works on a building site. He carries bricks all day long.

On the fourth day, it was pouring buckets out of leaden skies. The holes we dug quickly filled up with water. We were told to assemble, and marched off to the barracks. That afternoon on my way to the latrine I met another prisoner whom I knew from the ghetto. His name is Moishe. He used to work with me in the tailor shop. Moishe has been working in the camp taking care of the latrines. He advised me that my chances of getting out of here are better if I can manage to stay in camp, and not go to work outside. He says that every once in a while announcements for transports to other locations are being made. He is certain that these are calls for work, perhaps in factories located in Germany. But how can I stay n the camp and I get away with it? My Blockleader will kill me if he finds out I did not report to my work group, and have been goofing off. "Don't worry," Moishe says. "Since I have been here, everyone left behind has been put to work doing something. Sometimes the Blockleaders are glad to have more people at hand to perform various chores, otherwise they have to do it themselves. Most importantly, try to stay close to the food distribution chain. Eventually some benefit will come of it."

The next day I did not line up in my group. Instead I lined up with another group which was filled to capacity. After the count I was found to be redundant and sent back to camp.

Following my return to the barracks I was greeted by Igor with, "Why didn't you go to work?" I told him that there were too many workers in my group and that's why I am here. "Do you have any work for me to do?" I asked diligently. He had plenty of it. First, I will start sweeping the inside of the barracks and then continue sweeping around the barracks. At noon I will join four others to fetch food rations. In the evening he will need me to bring kettles of soup to the barracks for distribution to the prisoners. When the kettles are empty I shall have to return them to the kitchen. At first, my sweeping effort wasn't good enough for him. After a couple of hard kicks in my behind I tried to be as thorough as I could, and worked fast, especially when he was looking. I even tried to soften him up saying that he keeps his barracks cleaner than anyone in the compound. He liked that. "You know why?" he asked and without waiting for my answer added, "Because I know how to make you bastards work. I am smarter than you are. I always was."

From that day on I stayed behind cleaning the barracks and dragging food. Out of all of my daily chores the most rewarding one was the carrying back of the empty soup kettles to the kitchen. Frequently, there was more food left on the bottom and sticking to the walls than I would get into my soup can. So on the way back to the kitchen I stopped in an inconspicuous place, and scraped out the inside of the kettle with my spoon to the point where it hardly needed any washing.

One day, what I had been waiting for so eagerly happened. It was the seventh day, just to the week of my arrival. I was sweeping the ground behind the barracks when I heard the camp loudspeaker announce: "We need bricklayers and carpenters for transport. Anyone with experience register at the main *Appel Platz*", this is the main square on which major assemblies take place, either for countdowns, dispatches to local work sites or for deportations. I dropped my broom and rushed over. There, at a table set up in the open, sat a uniformed girl with a long list. Next to the table stood two SS men.

As I approached, a small line had already formed. At my turn I was asked for my prisoner camp number, but I had none. In earlier transports prisoners were given a number which was then tattooed into their arm. We did not get any, nor were we tattooed, because there was so little time left for the German Masters to finish their plans for extinction. In their hurry, they disposed with registration. One of the SS men asked me about my experience. I told him I was laying bricks in the ghetto, building factories. "*Gut, sehr gut,*" he said, pointing towards a group of prisoners already assembled a few yards away.

Before night fell they had their quota. We were marched towards the train ramps where boxcars were already waiting.

Here come the trains, I thought to myself, as I was prodded, kicked and pushed on board. Once in the car, a familiar sight: straw on the floor, buckets, water barrel. This time each one of us was given a full loaf of bread, perhaps two pounds, a piece of cheese, margarine, and our soup cans were filled with what seemed to be a nourishing meal. This was more than I had been given as rations in a long time. My original apprehensions gave way to hope and optimism. If they were sending us to die they wouldn't have wasted this much food on us. Besides, why send us to other places for the purpose of extermination when we were already in a very efficient death factory?

The train began to move. At first very slowly, then gradually accelerating its rhythmic beat. I decided to lie down and take a nap, holding on to my latest rations. Who knows how long we will ride and if we will get new supplies on the way? Better leave eating for later, when the situation has become a bit clearer.

Chapter 47

IN GERMANY

It has been five years, almost to the date, since this insane war began to consume our lives. It struck like a tornado, leaving nothing standing in its path. It destroyed everything, tearing apart our families, culture, tradition, beliefs, and ethics. We have been brought down to a sub animal level. I say that because animals at least are free to roam. We don't even have that. And, as if to "celebrate" our anniversary, we just arrived at a new site.

Upon disembarking, we are commanded to form units of forty. The ramp on which the train has stopped swarms with uniformed SS men. Upon taking stock of those present we are told to follow a group of soldiers. The march is brief. Soon a new vista opens in front of our eyes. New, and yet familiar; the double rows of wire fences are similar to those used in the other places we have been forced to occupy. The pronouncement that "Work Liberates" looks familiar, but this time the sign is made of wood, and adorns a huge wooden gate. The camp, however, is different. It is brand new, and composed of small huts. Only the roofs of the huts can be seen rising above the ground level.

There are many of them. Perhaps a hundred, perhaps two hundred; I really don't care to count. Outside the fences I see a number of wooden structures.

We are led onto a large field, apparently the makeshift *Appel Platz*. We line up and count off at the order of an SS man. Soon a group of prisoners appears. They are dressed in the same striped uniforms that cling to our emaciated bodies. They take up places ahead of our column. Some wear KAPO armbands. Our group is led by a uniformed SS man to a prisoner with an armband marked *Blockaeltester* or Block Leader. On the command of *"Achtung"* the Block Leader quickly jumps onto the spot pointed out to him by the SS man and springs to attention, stretching his body straight up as best he can, and trying to get his heels to click at the same time. I cannot help but grin; the wooden heels of his shoes do not readily click, at least not as sharply as the officer's leather boots. He looks embarrassed, although no one seems to be paying particular attention.

I notice our Block leader is about five feet eight, broad chested, and a bit on the corpulent side. His protruding pot belly and hefty behind do point to a better food diet than the one I have become accustomed to. The beret he wears hardly fits his head; probably couldn't find his size. His head is enormous, and seems to be mismatched with his body as his beret is with the head. I notice his narrow eyes are deeply set in sockets which are surrounded by baggy wrinkles. His nose is broad, like a boxer's, his hands big. I view him with interest because it seems that he will be in charge of our group, and may have some say over my future in this camp.

New orders to form single lines are announced through the camp microphone. We fall in and follow our Leader to a large hut located on the camp grounds. Inside the hut there are tables with benches. At each table sits a prisoner in striped uniform who will apparently question the newcomers. Is this some kind of interrogation, or registration; I wonder. In Auschwitz there was no registration. The camp leaders didn't worry about it, perhaps because the time was rendered short by the approaching Red Armies. The main emphasis had to be placed on disposing of prisoners rather than keeping them on the account ledgers. Here at least they seem to care who we are. That must be a good sign.

The waiting stretches out, but after the long train ride I don't mind. My bones are stiff and standing for a while gives me a chance to loosen up what's left of my muscles. "Next," sounds a command as my turn arrives. I see somebody waving me on and pointing to a spot on the bench next to him.

"Sit down, please."

I am flabbergasted. The man said, please. I haven't heard that word in years. This is a great start.

"Your name, place, date of birth," he asks, and I quickly oblige.

CRY...IF YOU CAN

"You are, I presume, like the rest from the *Litzmannstadt Ghetto*, right?" "Yes, sir."

"You don't have to sir me. I am a prisoner like you."

"But you are different. You aren't Jewish, are you?"

"No. I am a member of the so called Arian race, and ashamed of it."

"May I ask what brings you here?"

"My family lives in Munich. I have been attending the Technical School there. After the latest unsuccessful attempt at the Fuehrer's life, they put me in prison under suspicion of having been sympathetic to the insurrection. They were right. I was all for it. So here I am."

"Where are we?"

"I have come from Dachau to register the newcomers. This camp is under the jurisdiction of Dachau. This place is called *Kaufering*, Camp No. 4. You are now in Bavaria, not far from such famous places as *Landsberg*, where the imprisoned Fuehrer wrote *Mein Kampf*, and Munich." He keeps on filling out the sheet as he talks.

The entire conversation takes a minute or two, but it has a terrifically refreshing effect on me. He behaves like a civilized being, the likes of which I haven't seen in a long time.

"Your name is meaningless here," he continues. "From now on you will be known as prisoner 95110. I must ask you not to worry. This is not Auschwitz, where you people have come from. Dachau is one of the first, if not the first, concentration camp built in Germany. It was originally built to isolate, and if possible, eliminate the Fuehrer's enemies. But there are no gas chambers here. You will find in Dachau communists, socialists, priests, homosexuals, a really exotic mix. Most of us work. You may not be as well off as I, because I get parcels from my parents, but your chances of survival are much better here than in other camps I've heard off. Good luck." He shakes my hand, giving me a cloth tag with my number on it, and two triangles, one red and one yellow, one to be sewn onto on my uniform. The red one is meant for political prisoners, the yellow for Jews. They are to be sewn onto my coat and made to overlap to form the Star of David. Yellow on top.

Following this little pep talk, I feel much better. My legs have become springier, and I jump up. "Thank you," I utter and leave the place to return to my group.

The registration proceeds smoothly. All Kapos; (I have learned in Auschwitz- Birkenau what *Kapo* stangs for) and Block Leaders must have been issued wooden clubs while I was inside. Or didn't I notice them before? They wave their clubs and force us into line. Once the last man of our group has been cleared, we walk away toward our new accommodations.

Chapter 48

ANOTHER LEADER, ANOTHER CAMP

He said we can call him Comrade Z. His welcoming speech differed from the one we received in Auschwitz like day differs from night. He spoke Yiddish, and introduced himself as a prisoner with a similar background to ours.

Comrade Z arrived in Auschwitz in 1942. Before the war he lived in an old Jewish section of Paris which known in Yiddish as the *Pletzl*, or Little Square. He didn't always live there. He was born in a small town in Poland, and left as soon as the Spanish Civil War erupted, to fight with the republicans. He was a communist, so he said, and the call to arms to save the socialist system in Spain moved him to action. After the fall of Madrid, he escaped to Paris, where he married a Jewish girl and settled down working in her father's bakery. When the war broke out he fought in the French Army, and returned to Paris after the armistice with Germany was signed.

Following the French surrender to the Germans and the formation of a new French government under the leadership of Marshal Petain orders were issued to arrest all foreign citizen of Jewish dsecent. The place where the Jews were assembled was called Drancy. From Drancy he was sent to Auschwitz, things were different then than they are today; much different. He became foist a KAPO and then a Block leader. In those days he had quotas to meet. Every morning he had to deliver some dead prisoners. How they died didn't matter; as long as the quota was met all was well. The SS monsters were satisfied and so were their commanders. Comrade Z told us we are lucky people! He doesn't have to kill here. He was told that this will be a bona fide working camp. In a way, it is too late for killings; the steam of the killing engines is losing its power and has considerably cooled off. The war will soon end. Why did he kill? He had to in order to survive. He was brought here from Auschwitz together with a large group of old inmates. Their job is to organize the new camp.

He wanted us to remember his political leanings. He would favor children of the proletariat. In other circumstances I would have found this amusing. As he talked, it sounded crazy, totally unreal. "Are there any proletarians here?" he asked. All of us raised our hands. He chose a strong, muscular fellow, who looked extremely good for an ex-ghetto inmate named Szymon, as his assistant, his *stubendienst.*

And so, with this introduction, we settled down to lead the life of concentration camp inmates. No more deportations. This, most probably, is our final residence. Here we will be liberated or die; there is no other way out. At least this is how I saw it. The next day, however, I discovered that others did not necessarily agree with me; three bodies were pulled off the electrified fences in the morning. Did they try to escape? Commit suicide? No one really cares. It is all the same; they are dead.

Our new life has, after a while, become quite predictable. We live almost underground, with only the roof sticking out. The inside of our barracks has been dug out, and with the sole exception of wooden boards placed on the sides, and the roof supports, it is all earth.

The "door" is an opening which faces the camp street. A blanket is hung over it to keep out the cold winds. A ditch, running through the entire length of the barrack, has been dug into the ground. When I stand in the ditch I just about reach the apex of the roof. On both sides of this ditch are elevations, or elongated, continuous bunks. These bunks, at ground level, are wide enough to accommodate a stretched out man. There are no partitions. We sleep there touching one another, like canned sardines. At the barracks center is a cast iron stove whose pipe extrudes through the roof. In the back wall, there is a window. On both sides of this window are bunks separated from the rest of us by a wooden wall. These bunks are wide enough to sleep two to three people. This is where Comrade Z sleeps, and opposite him, the *stubendienst* Szymon. Above Comrade Z's bunk is a large shelf where he keeps our rations.

We wash outside in a small fenced-off compound where there are a few water faucets. The water runs off into the latrine ditch, as do the wooden urinal troughs. The latrine ditch has a long, frequently supported pole running along its full length where we sit to shit, bunched like birds on a telegraph wire. What a nice, torturous, simple, and cheap arrangement. I must give the Germans credit for it. I think this must be the cheapest little concentration camp ever invented. I imagine in the winter time, these little barracks of ours will feel like Eskimo Igloos; the snow will cover the entire structure and it should be pretty warm inside. Why, the heat and gasses emanating from the people should be good enough to prevent us from freezing.

Chapter 49
A NEW ORDER

The first couple of days we spent getting organized. New SS arrived. One of them is called Lager Kommandant. He was announced as the camp commander by another SS man, who showed him a lot of respect. The "commander" is short, stocky, wears silver-rimmed glasses, highly-polished boots, and gloves. Judging by the horse whip in his hand, he probably delights in beating up prisoners. The announcing officer is referred to as *Oberscharfuehre*r T. (The T ironically stands for Temple, a Jewish house of worship). He is supposed to be tough. Very tough, says Comrade Z, who had a couple of run-ins with him before we arrived. Z advises us to stay out of his way. The prison guards seem to speak with an accent. Our Blockleader says they are members of the SS foreign regiments…

The kitchen is located in a nearby woman's compound. The female prisoners are mostly Hungarian Jewesses. Their heads are shaven, and many of them are difficult to distinguish from male prisoners. They say that they have come here from Hungary via Auschwitz. This we got from comrade Z, who goes there often to fetch food supplies and sometimes, when the SS guard isn't looking, gets to exchange a couple of words with them. As of now, Z tells us, we have yet to get a camp leader. That is a prisoner like us who will interact with and carry out the orders of our jailers.

Last night we were told that by four in the morning we must all be lined up on the Appel Platz. The time for work has arrived. So, here we are at four a.m. standing, shivering in the dark. We watch lights go on in the military barracks outside the camp perimeter. Some time passes by. Oberscharfuehrer T (that's what his men call him) jumps out of an open barracks door, seemingly eager to start off the day. He calls for two SS men who open up the main gate, and he marches in with the air of a conqueror. "*Eintreten*" yells the head Kapo. We quickly fall in, forming rows of twenty each.

"Achtung," rings out another command as we stretch out to attention. "*Muetzen ab*," and we pull off our berets.

By this time, T is receiving the daily report from the head Kapo. "*Oberscharfuehrer,* we have," he gives a number, "of *Schutzhaeftlinge,* ready for a countdown."

The word *schutzhaeftling* isn't exactly new to me. I've heard it before, but here this, apparently, is our official designation. Literally translated, it means something akin to "prisoners in protective custody," and the SS is our custodian.

"*Abzaehlen*," shouts T.

"*Eins, zwei, drei,*" ring out the voices of the prisoners. The countdown is to confirm that the number specified has been assembled.

While we are still at attention, the chief Kapo approaches Oberscharfuehrer T and reports, "My Commander, the given number of prisoners is at your disposal."

"*Ruehrt Euch!*" Screams out T, and we relax.

As we are standing there, a group of SS men enters the compound. Some of them have slips in their hands. They approach T, who looks at each slip and orders them to pick the number of people they need. I get picked, with another forty-nine prisoners. Four SS men call on us to line up in rows of four, and we are marched off. I really don't care where I am going as long as it is out of the camp.

After about fifteen minutes of marching, we reach a train. This time it is a passenger train, which had obviously been shot up. All the windows are gone and many of the seats are battered, as are the roofs of the cars. A puffing locomotive is already waiting and anxious to move. Its siren keeps sounding off every few minutes. We board the train to the shouts of "Schnell" issued by the SS. We must be late to work if they are in that great a hurry. All are finally aboard, the train machinist waves a flag and we move off. It is a cool September morning, and I feel it in my barren bones. My uniform, made of some cellulose fiber, is stiff and cold. My shirt offers no warmth, either. The shoes with their wooden soles do not feel too bad, aside from their lack of flexibility. I wonder if they will ask us to run. What then? I don't think these shoes are made for running.

As the train works its way through fields and woods edged at the horizon by majestic mountains, it is hard not to be touched by the beauty of nature. This is the first time in years that I have traveled in a passenger train with windows, offering an unobstructed view of the moving scenery. Life seems to be so normal out there. The farms we pass are dotted with farm hands cutting hay or digging out potatoes. Some of them raise their heads to look at us. Here and there a combine is doing its chores. Cow pastures. How I envy the cows. It looks like they are free to eat as much as they wish! They too may be enslaved, but they are truly cared for until the farmer determines their destiny. We are starved, beaten, dehumanized, and treated worse than cattle. As for our destiny, it seems to have long been determined by our jailers.

After a fifteen-minute ride, we enter dense woods. The train stops and shouts to disembark ring out, echoing throughout the place. We quickly get off, line up, and another countdown ensues to make sure we are all here. From the depth of the woods emerge the silhouettes of three uniformed men dressed in brown and black. They don't wear arms. They salute our SS guards with the all too familiar *"Heil Hitler"* that sounds to me like *"Hatla,"* raising their right arm

far enough to merit an arm raise. After a brief conversation with the SS men, we are ordered to follow with the SS guard behind us at a distance. Presently we reach a small clearing camouflaged with netting covered with branches and leaves. Three openings leading to what seems to be an underground tunnel are alive with people and vehicles moving in and out. On the outside, a domelike structure made of concrete reinforced with steel is being completed. The structure covers the underground tunnels.

There are a couple of cranes and trucks present in the clearing. I can read the names of the contractors, or owners, one says MOLL the other HOLZMANN. Our group stops. There is a brief exchange between our SS guard and a man who seems to be a leader here. I hear him say, "Use them to unload the trains with cement on the southern ramp." In no time we are marched off to another train ramp, and ordered to unload bags of cement.

The paper bags are heavy; very heavy. At the first try at lifting one bag my knees buckle and I collapse, dropping and ripping the bag which now spills all of its contents onto the ground. In no time I see the wild face of one of our SS guards over me.

"You sow, you pig, you loused-up Jew," he fumes, his eyes practically bulging out of his head. "Do you want to sabotage the work here?"

"No," I manage to reply, although I am now so scared that I have trouble saying anything. "I..I..I..I couldn't handle it."

Now I feel the point of his boot digging into my rib cage. "I will show you how to handle it. You will never forget it. Hear me?"

"Y..Y..Yes sir." I not only hear him, I feel the monster. His ire is growing with every kick. All of a sudden, relief. It seems that others have done the same thing. He and the other guards are running amok. They shout, scream, hit, kick, and use every means at their disposal to express their disappointment with our performance. Alerted by the noises, the man in brown who gave the assignments comes running.

"Was is los?" He approaches the SS. "Shouting and beating will get us nowhere. We have a job to do. Let me show those bastards how to carry a cement bag."

He orders us to assemble at one train car, jumps on it, lifts a bag, and stands it up at the car's edge. He then jumps off, gets close to the bag, bends down slightly and flips the bag quickly onto one of his shoulders, stiffening his body at the same time.

"Keep your legs stiff; do not bend your knees. See that? It's easy."

Our work starts. I promptly run up to the train and pick one sack. It is easier than the first time. Before we know it we are running with bags as if we have been doing it all our lives. So this is what they needed bricklayers for, I think as I carry out my job.

My ribs hurt. The pace is unsustainable. On one hand, if I don't slow down I will drop dead right here. On the other, if I am to survive I have to find a new strategy, otherwise the SS will maul me into the ground. Looking around, as I carry my load, I notice the SS, now somewhat pacified with our improved performance; have sat down under a tree. Their rifles on the ground, they seem to be relaxing and in a good mood. Perhaps this is the time to slow down. As I unload my bag I pretend to be dusting off my uniform, not losing sight of the SS guards. As soon as one turns his head I start walking faster toward the train.

The strategy seems to be working. I have used it before: work when they look, relax when they don't. At lunch time, the hectic pace has slowed down and I manage to relax ever so slightly. Our lunch consists of some rations we got last night and brought with us. The food is somewhat better than in the ghetto. We got a chunk of bread, some margarine and a small piece of cheese. I ate part of it with the evening soup. The rest I consume now. After thirty minutes of rest it is back to work, back to the game I am getting better at by the hour. Finally, a whistle blows. Work stops, the day is over. We assemble and march off to the train that takes us back to the camp. On the way back to the camp our guards suddenly develop a musical urge. "Ein Lied," shouts one of them, "Sing". The four of us up front quickly decide on a song that we all know. It is the Battle Hymn of the Republic in Hebrew. We put a marching tempo to it. The rest pick up the well-known tune. When we reach the "Hallelujah" portion, I can see the satisfied grins on the soldiers' faces. We keep on singing the same song, repeating the refrain, up to the gates of the camp.

Back at the camp, we rest for a while, get our soup and evening rations, and sit in long rows on our bunk with our legs dangling in the ditch which we now call the aisle. We are asked to sing again, this time by Comrade Z, our Blockleader who requests proletarian songs. We oblige. He likes a few of them, he also likes a couple of voices, and before I know it I, together with four others have become the choir of our block, comrade Z's entertainers. Night falls, and we finally, totally exhausted after this first trying day's work, literally hit the hay.

Life in the camp is hard, but predictable. There are no major surprises: the food is more or less the same, the workplace has remained the same. Sometimes we carry cement, at other times steel bars, sand, water. I have learned that we are working on the construction of an underground aircraft factory. There seems to be no end to the layers of reinforced concrete that are being poured on top of the protruding dome. Daily beatings by our guards are now par for the course. The main idea is not to get them mad to the point where they will impart serious damage. Once you are impaired, you are left to slowly expire in the camp's "hospital," a place where the entire medical staff consists of one old Jewish doctor, and the main prescription available is ersatz coffee.

A week ago it was announced that a new prisoner had arrived. He will be our Camp Leader. One evening we all assemble at the Appel Platz to see him introduced by none other than Oberscharfuehrer T. We were surprised. T, quite openly, despises us. He has been exhibiting ever-increasing sadism lately. He calls on us to fall in early, especially when it is cold and rainy. He threatens, curses, and publicly whips prisoners, I presume to show his superiority. We named him Tiger, to remind us of the predator he is. To introduce a new prisoner should be below his dignity, but there he was introducing a tall, handsome, lean man with a Clark Gable mustache, dressed in prisoner uniform. The introduction was brief, "This is Raul, your Camp Leader. All Kapos, block Leaders, and prisoners are to strictly carry out his commands. His command is our command. He will be the only person permitted to stay in touch with the camp's military leadership.

A couple of weeks went by. Raul has so far turned out to be a decent chap.

Comrade Z tells us that in his first meeting with the camp Kapos and Block Leaders, he introduced himself as Lieutenant Raul, and explained that he was sent here from the Eastern Front after it was discovered that he carried a Hebrew prayer book and prophylactics in his bag. His mother was Jewish, and his father Austrian Catholic, he says that he secretly stuck to the faith of his mother. They lived in Vienna where he studied to be an actor before the war. We feel encouraged; as a soldier he probably knows how to handle military personnel, especially the SS, which is also present on the front lines. Perhaps his experience will help to alleviate some of the problems we have been having with Tiger.

1945

But the Lord will pardon Jacob and will again choose Israel.
And will settle them on their own soil and strangers shall join them
and shall cleave in the House of Jacob.

Isiah 6.

Chapter 50

STAYING ALIVE

A new year has arrived and we are wondering what tidings it brings. We know that the German military situation has drastically deteriorated, but our own cannot be bragged about either. It is so bad that most, if not all of us, have serious doubts whether we will ever see the end of this war, and that of the satanic hell we are in.

Last night I couldn't sleep. It got terribly cold when the fire in the stove died out, and my feet were frozen stiff. I sat up and as I was looking around for some way to warm them up, I noticed a figure rise from the bunk and move towards Z's bunk. I looked closer at the outline and recognized one of the young men in our block as he slipped into Z's bunk. After a while Z got up, reached above onto the shelf and pulled down what I thought was margarine left over from our rations, and promptly retreated behind the partition.

Now, it was no secret that the Germans did intern homosexuals. But in our camp there was no one that displayed a pink triangle on his uniform, and Z always bragged about his beautiful wife. Could it be? In the morning I discussed this with my choir buddies, Moniek, Heniek, Slamek, and Mietek. They had seen this before. As a matter of fact, Moniek was directly approached, but refused in spite of the promised bigger bread ration. He wouldn't talk about it because he was, and still is, scared. We decided to shut up, and not to discuss it anymore, lest we draw the ire of Z and his stubendienst on us, which is the last thing we need right now.

The nights are so long and the waiting each morning for dispatch to work becomes a bigger chore than work itself. We freeze in the cold wind that blows down from the mountains, in spite of the long coats we've been given recently. Yesterday I noticed that Moniek disappeared into the latrine with an empty cement bag. This morning, on the way to work, he is not complaining as much of the cold as he used to.

"What did you do with that bag yesterday?" I ask. "Keep quiet."

"Why? Did you eat it?"

"No. Try to bring one home, and I will show you tonight what you can do with it."

The guards again request a song. "Das Hallelujah Lied," one shouts. So off we go, singing our Battle Hymn in Hebrew. At work there is plenty to do. A new train with cement arrived. We unload it faster than usual to keep ourselves from freezing. Our SS guards huddle around a fire they kindled early in the morning, and try to keep it going, merely to keep warm. One of the guards, I notice, has a small bottle, for which he reaches every few minutes. At lunch time as we sit and consume our meager ration, the same guard comes over.

"Get up! *Aufstehen.*"

We jump to our feet. What does he want now? He lines us up and looks us over. I can smell alcohol. He looks a bit shaky on his feet as he walks over to the top of the line. "Hey you," he commands, pointing at the first man standing there.

"What will you do to us when the war is over?"

The man is perplexed and doesn't answer. Out comes the butt of the rifle and lands squarely on the prisoner's head. He topples and falls to the ground.

"What will you do?" He asks the next man. "Nothing, sir. Absolutely nothing." "You liar you." The SS man's fist lands in his face and. I see his head swing. A couple of teeth find their way to the ground. I am fourth in line and my anxiety begins to rise. "How about you?"

"Well, sir," the next prisoner begins to stutter, "It-hmm-is too early t.-t-t-to think about that. I haven't g-g-given it any thought."

The SS man doesn't even wait for him to finish the last sentence. Out comes the boot, and lands on the man's groin. He grabs himself by the crouch and bends to the ground in pain. The gears in my mind keep on speedily turning. What should I do? What should I say?

"Hey, you," my turn has arrived. "What will you do to us when the war is over?"

He has made up my mind for me. He wants the truth so I will give it to him. Otherwise he will send me to our horrible block called "hospital" for the rest of my miserable life.

"Sir," I answer, and hesitating for a split second I continue, "The same thing that you do to us." As I finish the sentence I am ready to be instantly mauled to death.

"Du bist ein braver Kerl." Is he talking to me? I am a brave fellow? His eyes lose their wild look as he reaches into his chest pocket, and pulls out a wrinkled pack of cigarettes. "Have one. You deserve it because you are telling the truth."

That one was pretty close, I think as I resume my work. My fellow prisoners think I am a crazy hero. Crazy, perhaps, but no hero. I said what I said out of fear, not heroics.

In the evening someone must have told Z about it. He comes over to my place on the bunk and hands me an extra piece of cheese. "I heard you were pretty gutsy today. This is for you. Remember though, if you want to survive don't play the hero. The next time around you may get shot like a stray dog."

"I know. I had no other way out, that's why I said it."

Moniek is already leaving for the latrine as he motions to me. I join him outside. "I saw you got caught up today with that crazy maniac. I smuggled in a cement bag for you." He says as he opens up his coat pulling out a folded cement bag. "All you have to do is tear an opening on the bag's bottom for your head, and two openings, one on each side, for your arms, and you have the best windbreaker money can buy."

I carry out his instructions: Remove my coat and jacket, and pull the sack over my head tucking the bottom into my pants.

"Gee! I'm warmer already. It really feels good. Wonder how the lice will take to it."

"Let them eat cement rather than your blood."

"That's what you think. They'll find their way to the skin, no matter what you put on," I say, but I am happy to have the sack. "Thanks for remembering me."

On the way back to the barracks we hear distant sirens. It is dark by now, and the sirens howl like hungry wolves. We stop and listen.

"Well, finally things seem to be moving again," I say, my hopes rising.

"Look," Moniek points to a faint red cloud on the horizon. The color of the cloud becomes more intense by the minute as the rumblings of dropping bombs become audible.

"They're bombing Munich," I shout.

"Keep quiet! Don't forget where you are." Moniek's scolding brings me back to reality. They may be bombing Munich, but that doesn't mean that we are about to go free. Nevertheless, it is music to our ears. A beautiful symphony that beats anything any composer ever wrote. We walk slowly back to the barrack listening to the growing intensity of the explosions. The red clouds are spreading along the horizon. What a sight!

There is obvious excitement in the barrack. Z and Szlomo are trying to keep us under control. Z is warning us to lay low. Even when gunshots are heard, and we are far from any battle field, he advises we should keep our noses close to the ground and our mouths shut. Otherwise we are risking not only our own lives, but those of everyone in the camp. We oblige. I fall asleep to the accompaniment of the distant explosions which affect me as the lullabies that mother used to sing to me when I was a child.

Raul, our camp leader, decides to put on a show in a couple of weeks.. He hopes to be able to invite the camp brass, make them smile, and perhaps somewhat loosen their strangle hold on us. He sought and received permission from the camp authorities. In return he invited the entire front office and guards, and promised them lots of fun. Now he must deliver. The show is being written, directed, and to a large extent also performed by, who else but Raul.

The cast is recruited mostly from the Block Leaders, Kapos, and Stubendiensts. These people are always available in camp for rehearsals, and are also most presentable on stage. According to Z, who, by the way, will have no part in it, four people will actually perform on the stage: Pepe, a Kapo of Greek-Jewish descent; Gaston, a Jew from Paris; Pierre, a Moroccan Jew, and Raul. New songs written by Raul will be introduced by him. One of these will be called the Anthem of Kaufering. He wants all prisoners to become familiar with it and sing along. The performances will be primarily in German, interspersed with French, Greek, and Italian songs.

On the Sunday after New Year's Day, all of us gathered in the evening on the Appel Platz. In the center was a stage, put up in a hurry by the Kapos. In the back of the stage was a dressing shack, assembled from empty crates. In front of the stage, benches were set up for the front office personnel and military. Two huge bon fires were lit on the sides, and the mood became real festive.

The show was opened by Raul, who cracked a few jokes about camp life. Not funny to us but the people in the front benches laughed. Good start, I thought. Then came Pepe, who sang a Greek song about fowl, roosters, hens; there was a lot of quacking and crowing. He did some encores. The Germans liked it, and applauded. Raul reappeared dressed as a Spanish woman with improvised castanets. He sang and danced. The song was about a lady from Castille who tried to induce a soldier to come to Spain. He objected but was finally seduced by the beautiful Castillian maiden. Lots of applause from the front benches. While Raul was changing, Gaston sang in Italian *"Mama soltanto felice,"* a song announced as being about a nice Italian mother, missed by her son. Then again came Raul again, this time with a song about Kaufering:

Kaufering, Du bist fuer mich das schlimste Arbeitslager
Kaufering, den jeder Kapo ist by uns ein Schlager
Muessen Wir, Schon einmal fort von Dir....etc. etc.

I was amazed that he dared to compose and sing something like that in front of the military camp brass. It talks about our camp as being the worst working camp; about our Kapos who are beaters, this is why we must once and for all leave you, and on he went. When he finished, the front benches were quiet, but the prisoners erupted in a storm of applause that quickly died out when Tiger turned to look at us. This song was followed by a number by Pierre, some kind of a funny Arabic song. It was funny because he told us so. No one understood a word, but he made up with motions and faces what we missed in words. We all laughed.

The grand finale came when the performers filled the tiny stage, and Raul began announcing that he composed an anthem for the camp. He asked the prisoners to rise, but we were standing already, so everyone laughed. Then came the anthem,

> O! Kaufering Ich kann dich nicht vergessen den Du mein Schicksahl bist
> Wer hier nicht ist, Der kann auch nicht ermessen
> Wie teuer die Freiheit ist
> Wie teuer die Freiheit IST.

In rough translation it says, O! Kaufering I cannot forget you, and the mean Kapos, because you are my fate. Who hasn't experienced you cannot possibly appreciate how dear one's freedom is, how dear one's freedom is.

The show ended. We went back to the barrack. The night was quiet, interrupted only by faint, distant rumbling thunder reminiscent of the one we have been hearing lately.

Monday morning, the morning after the show, we are called out early and lined up. The Tiger enters, apparently in a bad mood. He screams at the SS guards accompanying him. When he reaches the prisoner contingent, he yells at Raul, the Kapos, at almost everyone in his way. His behavior doesn't bode well for us. We know, from experience, this kind of mood usually means our downfall.

The entire protocol is messed up. It is now Raul's fault. He whacks him over the back with a stick he has in his hand. Raul does not lose his composure. Instead he jumps to attention, and shouts out:

"Oberscharfuehrer T, the camp is at attention ready for the countdown."

"Then start," yells Tiger.

No sooner has the countdown begun when Tiger spots something apparently not to his liking, "Stop counting," he commands.

He slowly looks first at his hands, pulls up his gloves, straightens out his jacket, and a strange smile appears on his face as he approaches the first row of prisoners.

"You! Step out," he motions at one man.

The man steps out. I look at him and become horrified. A paper bag hangs out from underneath his coat.

"Open your coat." The order sounds ominous.

As the man opens his coat, two cement paper bags drop to the ground. "Take off your coat." Tiger is now slowly building up his wrath.

The man takes off his coat and it is now apparent that underneath his jacket there are more bags. This time he wears them the way I do. "Take off the jacket" comes a new order.

The prisoner takes off his jacket and exposes a double paper bag worn as a shirt.

"Undress."

He drops off the rest of his clothing, and stands nude, shivering in the January morning cold. Tiger is now raging mad. His stick begins to fall on the man's head, shoulder, arms, in a rapid succession. Tiger's boots find his groin and rear. Blood is beginning to redden the white carpet of snow under the man's feet. As T rages he calls on the SS guard, "All hands on deck!"

"All undress. If you have bags on carry them over to the front." Tiger is now totally out of control.

We begin to undress in a hurry. To my surprise most of us have managed to get sacks. Even those who worked in other locations, not connected with the aircraft factory. Five SS men assume positions close to Tiger. All men with bags have to pass through the men. The pounding is severe. I have a bit of luck. By the time my turn comes to turn in the bag, the SS man is tired and barely manages to raise his open hand and whack me in the face.

"You louse-infested Jews. If I catch anyone stealing national property I will shoot you on the spot. This is sabotage." Tiger is now tired but determined to enforce his laws. "Now, back to work."

It is cold without the bags. I am frozen stiff, but begin to move around carrying cement, and this warms me up a bit. The SS are more active than usual. They follow our working activity rather than sitting on the side by their bon-fire. For one reason or another, Mietek has become a focus for their attention. They follow, kick, and harass him on every occasion.

Mietek is my roommate and singing mate; that is he sleeps next to me and is one of the five choir members. He is a very bright and intelligent person who has managed to retain a good deal of civility in spite of the cruelty around him. He is tall and very slim. His ever-present shy smile gives him the appearance of being somewhat helpless. He comes from a well-to-do family. His parents and grandparents were teachers. It is obvious to me that he has grown up totally sheltered from the evils of street life.

Even in the ghetto, he lived on the grounds of the school complex that R built, protected from the ghetto elements, and better fed than most of the inhabitants. In this camp he is lost. He is clumsy at work, and attracts the fury of our guards. I feel for him, and have tried to teach him how to work so as not to be picked on.

After the last beating he begins to cry. I move closer to him.

"What happened?"

"Don't know, but they have been picking on me all day."

"You are not too steady on your legs today, do you feel OK?" "Not sure. My head aches, and I feel chills all over my body."

"I too, am freezing. They took my bag away. Now it is really cold. Take it easy. I'll see you in the barracks."

Mietek made it through the day. Back in the barrack, I touch his head. It is glowing with fever. As soon as the daily rations are distributed, I drag him over to the hospital. The doctor is busy. There is a long line ahead of us. We finally reach him. Mietek undresses. The doc looks at his body. His back appears to be covered with little red freckles. The doctor's diagnosis is firm, "It is typhoid. My fifth case today."

"What can he do?" I ask.

"Nothing. Rest and drink lots of boiled water. If you wish you can give him hot compresses."

At our return to the barrack I start boiling water on the stove. Szymon, the Stubendienst, is angry. He didn't get much wood today. The water is boiling anyhow, and I fill Mietek's soup can with hot water. He takes a sip, and pushes it away. I ask him to lie down, take off my shirt, dip it in the hot water, and start giving him compresses. He lies there hardly reacting to my efforts. The commotion attracts Z's attention.

"What's going on?"

"Mietek is sick. He has typhoid. That's what the doctor said. He cannot eat, nor does he want to drink."

"Get him out of here!" he calls over Szymon. "Take him over to the hospital and tell the doc to take good care of him. He is one of my proletarian kids. He is my singer. Tell him also that if he cannot eat, I want to see all of his rations here in my barrack. We will safe-keep them for him. When he gets better, he will have something to recover on."

CRY...IF YOU CAN

Szymon and I pull Mietek up, throw his arms over our shoulders, and drag him off to the hospital. On the way he keeps on singing, hallucinating, and vomiting. We hand him over to the doctor with the instructions we got from Z.

By this time the camp leader has authorized a special barrack to be cleaned for the typhoid cases, who must be quarantined. We put Mietek up in fresh straw. The latest count is eight cases, according to the doc.

Mietek died a couple of days later, and not long afterward, I, too, entered the quarantine barrack. Szymon accompanied me with the same instructions from Z. I do not know what transpired in the next four days, it's all a blank. All I know is what I was told by the doctor later; that I was found late one evening outside in the cold and snow. A guard in the watch tower saw me with his spotlight, lying there motionless. He alerted the front office, which in turn made it known to the Camp Leader Raul that someone had dropped dead in the snow. When the burying detail arrived to remove the body they were surprised that I was still breathing and took me to the typhoid barrack. A few days later the crisis had passed, and I was released back into Z's custody.

While I was sick the camp was closed and a general quarantine was declared. No more outside work. We are shut in for the time being. Z has kept his word and collected my rations while I was sick, otherwise they would have been stolen. For a full week I enjoy double rations, which helps me to get back on my feet. Alas, while I was delirious with fever, and for the next four weeks, the camp has been decimated by the disease. Many of the acquaintances I made aren't here anymore. Luckily, Moniek, Slamek and Heniek have survived. Moniek was also sick but he somehow recovered, although he keeps on constantly coughing. Our camp Kaufering IV has now been quaranteened and designated as a camp for sick prisoners.

Our SS guards are, in a large measure, gone. Rumors have it that they have been sent to the eastern front, which is now on German soil. They have been substituted by Ukrainian SS Unit members. Tiger is still here, as are most of the brass. And we now have new prisoners who were brought by a military guard and installed in some empty barracks. They are Russian soldiers. My Russian is very poor, and limited to the similarity between Polish and Russian. It is good enough, though, to make myself understood, and to understand the soldiers. They tell me that they were taken prisoner early in the war. That they were frequently tortured, and made to work hard in special prison camps. They say that their treatment was not in compliance with the Geneva Convention, whatever that is. Ours has been out of compliance with any basic human rules.

The day following the Russians arrival, three were missing. How they managed to escape no one knows. Unfortunately for them they were soon caught, brought back to the camp and shot in front of the full camp assembly on the Appel Platz. Tiger himself did the shooting.

I like the Russians. They seem to be naive, good natured, and romantically inclined, despite the barbarous fate that brought them here. They constantly talk about home, their mothers and girlfriends, and sing beautiful ballads. One of those songs, in particular, appeals to me. It is a beautiful ballad about love, called *"Tschomnaya Notch"*, which means: The Dark Night. I have learned it and now know it by heart.

March is usually very unpredictable. In the same day it may rain, snow, freeze slash. The sun may shine only to be covered by clouds. Not this year. This year March is different. It is as cold and snowy as January. It feels like the Almighty has poured out his wrath on our heads; that he is trying to finish us off before the final spring of peace arrives. And peace is not far away. We know it. We heard it from some guards, soldiers, and the Russians, who have been brought here from the east to avoid the advancing Soviet troops. We heard that all of France, Italy, and Poland, including our ghetto, has been liberated. But as far as we are concerned, war goes on forever. I am constantly thinking of Paul, the prominent figure in Remarque's *"All Quiet On The Western Front."* I wouldn't want to meet his fate. I want to live. I must live.

Today, at our Appel Platz meeting it was announced that we will have a visit from the Swiss Red Cross. After five years of incarceration the world has suddenly become interested in our fate. How ironic. Or is it the presence of the Russians that brings them here? We are told that we will be issued new prison garb, including wooden shoes. During the visit we have to appear spotlessly clean and shaven. We are given soap and toothbrushes.

A couple of days prior to the arrival of the Swiss we kept on cleaning, cleaning, and cleaning. Everything had to be in order. The latrines were emptied and scrubbed clean. A new pole was put up for our toilet seats. The barracks were refurbished with new straw. Wood was brought in for the ovens. The camp alleys were combed clean of refuse. Finally, the place assumed a decent look. The night before the visit, the camp commandant and Tiger inspected every barrack.

When the Swiss arrived we were lined up in front of our barracks. A big truck laden with parcels arrived with them. Four Red Cross representatives, looking like well-fed, prosperous burghers, sat on the truck and handed out parcels. At times they would ask whether we were being well treated. With fear choking our throats, the answer was almost always "yes." The whole affair took about an hour. After they left we rushed back into our barrack. I opened up my parcel, and to my surprise I found it loaded with goodies that I hadn't seen in years. There was a bar of chocolate, a can of sardines, crackers, a can of condensed mild, candy, and a pack of cigarettes. I sat down with my bounty, and slowly began to taste a bit of everything. What delight! This is heaven on earth! Or is it heaven in hell?

After two weeks the parcels were forgotten and we were back to our starvation diet. Now, if I were to die, at least I could tell myself that I had tasted heaven.

Chapter 51

THE LAST GASP

What a dreary morning. We got up, as usual, at five and assembled at the Appell Platz for a countdown. It is moist and cold, and a freezing spring wind adds to our misery, cutting through our thin striped uniforms with merciless vengeance. My sockless feet are stiff and numb in the cloth-covered wooden shoes. Aside from the line-up commands, the most prominent noise seems to be coming from the rattling of our teeth. I feel like a dried leaf left by chance desperately clinging to the bare branch of a tree, after its time to fall off and disappear has long passed.

The past week brought a lot of changes. Tiger is gone. He departed two days ago with most of his guards and all prisoners capable of walking. Z with his Stubendienst, Szymon, went with them. The rumors, lately plentiful in our vegetating environment, had the marchers walking towards Austria, away from the oncoming Allied armies. The Tiger made it known that the prisoners left behind will be shot. In spite of the threats I selected to stay behind. I pretended that my leg was limp and that I couldn't walk. That decision was not easily reached. After careful consideration of the overall state of my physical and mental being, I came to the conclusion that I would probably die on the road anyway, and decided to remain in the camp. So did my pals Moniek, Heniek and Slamek.

The Tiger's job was taken over by another Obersharfuehrer who had been in charge of the camp's food distribution. He was rumored, in the prisoner circles, to be having an on-going affair with the head of the Women's Compound, who supposedly came from a nice, orthodox Hungarian-Jewish family. This obviously was taboo since the Nuerenberg laws imposed a strict prohibition on inter-racial intercourse. How he was getting away with it was totally incomprehensible to us. Now, it really doesn't matter since the women prisoners moved out to another location a couple of months ago. We nicknamed him the "Fox."

Fox was, in a way, if not outright liked, at least tolerated by the prisoners. Unlike his peers, he never cursed, and never hit anyone; nor did he ever try to impress his superiors by spewing expressions of hatred and disgust at the prisoners, as was the case with all other military personnel in our camp.

Somehow, Fox also managed to retain the respect of his peers and superiors in the SS.

For the past two days we have been continuously working on the disposal of corpses under Fox's direction. Of the fewer than two thousand inmates left in the camp, following the departure of the men capable of walking, about half were already dead or dying. The thankless job of piling up bodies, left to the remaining crippled and sick prisoners, seemed to be never-ending. We have been piling up bodies in pyramid-like stacks. Egypt comes to mind again; the intriguing pyramids. Alas, this time not of stone, but of our own corpses. Perhaps, when the war ends, and the Nazis are finally defeated there will be a new Passover holiday dedicated to preserve these dark pages in our history. What consolation!

Yesterday the Camp Commander received replacements for the departed guards. They seem to have come from a general mobilization. They wore Wehrmacht rather than SS uniforms, and were obviously much older than the departed crew. Since their arrival, the camp activities have markedly increased. It is now apparent that some kind of preparations are being made to raze the camp to the ground and burn the dead inmates. Cans of gasoline can be seen outside the camp administration buildings, and at least two earth- moving machines and two fire engines are parked by the main gate.

Our food rations have decreased to a small piece of bread and a chunk of cheese. Instead of soup there is salty hot water fattened with margarine. Last night, to suppress the hunger I went to sleep earlier than usual, but could not sleep at all. On one hand, I was agitated by the thought of the war finally coming to an end. On the other, I could not help but wonder whether I would be privileged to survive. The fatalistic ending of Eric

Maria Remarque's war novel haunted me, and would not leave my mind. The strong passion for life and wish for survival, which possessed me all through the five years of this horrible ordeal, are wearing thin. My friends, whom I formed strong bonds with, slept next to me in the filthy mauled up straw. Moniek kept on coughing and also could not sleep. Slamek started cursing when his brother Heniek got up to go to the outhouse and stepped on him. Soon, we were all awake and talking about the exciting new possibilities.

"Strange," I said. "The end of the war seems to be so near, and yet our chances of survival are probably very low."

"Don't be a pessimist," answered Slamek through a broad yawn. "The war is ending. Soon we will be liberated, and on our way home."

"Home?" asked Moniek. "Where is home? My parents and siblings are all dead. I know because I buried them myself in the Ghetto. Some died of starvation, some during the typhoid epidemic."

"So did mine," I stated rather matter-of-factly. "Only my sister may possibly be alive. I saw her walk onto the working side at the Auschwitz selection."

"Boy. And how do you think we will survive in a normal world after this ordeal?" added Moniek. "We have lived like dogs and been treated like vermin for all these years. In a way we have become animals worrying only about our hour-to- hour existence."

"Listen you guys," Slamek adds, becoming a bit agitated. "This kind of talk will get you nowhere. Think positively and you will make it. Remember, after five years in this hell you are not going to give up at the last minute. You hear me?"

"We hear you. Let's stick together when we leave this place, and think in terms of escape at the first opportune moment," I reply.

My suggestion is well received. The four of us agree to support each other and escape as a group at the first given opportunity. A couple of minutes later the sirens went off followed by a barrage of bomb explosions. For the past two weeks the city of Munich appeared to be under constant bombardment. The exploding bombs acted like a magic sleeping potion. They offered deep sleep. And dreams of liberation, food, wine, clean clothing.

That was last night. Now, we are again lined up waiting for the commanding officer to arrive and take count.

"*Achtung*," screams one of the newly arrived soldiers. "*Muetzen Ab!*" The call of "Attention" and "remove your caps" means that the Camp Commander is here and ready to start the process of accounting for every camp prisoner. Soon he emerges out of the cold, foggy air, and proceeds to take his place at the top of the assembled prisoner columns.

"Abzehlen," rings out, the command followed by the standard "Eins, zwei, drei..." response of the prisoners. At the end of the count the Commander checks his list.

"Two hundred and ten are missing. Where are they?" The question is directed to Fox who quickly responds that the remainder is all accounted for. They are either sick in the barracks or dead. Dead men don't talk.

"Now listen carefully," the Commander's voice booms with authority. "Today is the last day of your imprisonment in this camp. We have orders to liquidate the camp, and move you to a safe place, closer to our main offices in Dachau, where you will be shielded from any kind of war activity. The sick among you will be taken to hospitals soon after arrival. There is nothing to fear. You will be well cared for. A train, which will take you to your new destination, will arrive at ten o'clock a.m. sharp. By this time, you should all be assembled at the railroad pass. You can take your blankets and any food you might have, or will receive, with you. Have a good trip." This speech sounds very familiar. How many times have I heard this before? That beast of a man, who in the past eight months presided here over our gradual extermination, wishes us a good trip.

"God help us," I quietly pray while awaiting the order to disband.

"*Ruehrt Euch*," screams Fox, finally ordering us back into the barracks. "I ask that only the remaining block leaders and Kapos remain standing. I will give you more detailed instructions regarding the evacuation."

On the way to the barracks, we pass the pyramids of corpses ready to be sent to heaven via the ultimate conversion; to fire and smoke. Somehow I am still alive, and cannot wait to leave this God-forsaken place, no matter what happens.

Where we are going doesn't matter anymore. At least we'll be given a train ride. This is bound to save me some energy. Maybe I'll survive after all. The war is coming to an end, and the Nazis may have softened their attitude towards us. Maybe the Commander was telling the truth. All these thoughts reel through my mind as I enter the barracks.

A few more inmates have died. We carry them to the nearest pile and heap them on by grabbing the legs and head, swinging, and releasing the carcass at the count of three. This is how our guards want us to toss the bodies. It makes for a tighter and neater pyramid.

Chapter 52

ESCAPE

It is ten in the morning, and all inmates are lined up by the railroad crossing. Many cannot stand up by themselves. They either lie on the ground, or are propped up by other inmates. We fear that the ones on the ground may be left behind and shot, and try to keep as many standing as possible. A couple of hours ago we received some hot ersatz coffee, a slice of bread, and a piece of cheese. I quickly consumed my ration fearing it may get lost on the train. Besides, I need all the energy I can muster. Our blankets are hanging either off our shoulders or our heads. We look like a bunch of starved sheep being led to slaughter; pitiful, lost, helpless, and powerless, infested with lice and flees.

The threatening sky above us opens up with a fine, cold drizzle when the whistle of an oncoming train pierces the air. Shouts of "The train is here!" rise in the crowd. "*Ruhig*," scream the guards. The locomotive slowly moves towards its designated stop at the crossing. The first three cars just past the locomotive are loaded with machine and anti-aircraft guns, and soldiers in position ready to use them. I cannot believe my own eyes.

"What the hell is going on?" Slamek cannot hold back from whispering into my ear.

"I don't know, but they must be out of trains and this is their way of moving soldiers while also transporting prisoners," I answer.

"You know, they may be using us to camouflage the military aspect of this transport," says Slamek, who seems worried.

"There's nothing we can do. So let's stick together and wait," I murmur back to him, so as not to be overheard by our guard, who stands only a few feet away.

Following the military cars are about ten cattle cars ready to take on their new load. The train, slowly grinds to a squeaking halt. The soldiers in the front cars jump off to stretch their legs and take a sip of what appears to be hot coffee from their canteens.

Fox assembles his guards and issues instructions. Apparently every guard is assigned a wagon and told how many people to load on. The guard nearest us begins to assemble his group of prisoners. Counting to eighty, he huddles us together and separates from the others while awaiting his car assignment. During that time I get a chance to observe him a bit closer. He appears to be in his fifties, probably somebody's father or grandfather. His round face is adorned with bag-like cheeks that were once filled with fat, but are now hollow and slumping down past his chin. A Hitler-style mustache separates the tip of his nose from his thin, bluish lips. Steel-rimmed glasses hang off his running nose which he attempts, ever so frequently, to dry with the sleeve of his uniform. His legs are wrapped in straps made seemingly of old soldier uniforms. His leather boots are civilian. He frequently jumps and pounds his arms against his chest, trying to keep warm. He looks sloppy, totally different from the neatly dressed, always perfectly trimmed, tall, stiff, and well-fed SS men which manned our camp not so long ago. Of all the guards, Fox is the only one still wearing his SS uniform.

A couple of minutes pass and we are beginning to board the train cars. As previously agreed, the four of us try to stick together and attempt to board the same car when the command to move to the next car is given. I and Slamek are the last ones to board our car. Moniek and Heniek will be in the adjacent car.

Our wagon is so full that one cannot possibly stand up. Being last to board puts me on top of at least two layers of people. I maneuver with my feet trying to find a mooring but this only pushes me downward, and another inmate climbs on top of me. Fox's voice commands the guards to check if all are aboard. I can hear him, but cannot see him. All I can see is a strip of sky directly above my head. Suddenly the sky turns gray with smoke.

"Is this the camp burning?" I hear a guard ask.

At half past ten the train begins to puff hard, its penetrating whistle goes off, and the wagons are shoved off their static position. Soon the train moves. We are in motion, riding toward some unknown destination. I should be used to it by now having had this experience at least twice before but with each experience I feel more helpless and apathetic. There is nothing we can do now. If there is a God in heaven we are in his hands. May be this time he will hear us and put an end to our persecutions. I close my eyes and try to sleep,

The train moves very slowly. We have been in motion, now, for about an hour when a sudden jolt shakes the train and all the cars seem to be banging into one another. The train has come to a screeching halt.

There is a lot of commotion, and the sound of quick orders fills the air. Fox shouts and the guards repeat after him: "All prisoners stay in place. Do not move or you will be shot." At the same time I hear boots trotting in a hurry into the surrounding woods. I sink an inch deeper into the wagon's hold when I distinguish a distant sound of approaching airplanes. Yes. It is not a single plane. No. There seem to be many. The sounds grows louder and louder; the planes seem to be right over our heads.

Living hell erupts. Machine gun and rifle fire seems to be coming from the woods. After a while the planes respond. Small bombs begin to erupt ahead of our wagon.

"American planes are here," yells Slamek. "I recognize the white stars under the plane's wings."

A few seconds pass and it seems that the planes had left. For an instant in time I hear only the "flak, flak, flak." of the guns on our train. Then another plane approaches. This time the eruptions seem to be much closer. I do not dare to raise my head. The plane departs. The "Flak" is silent. I feel liquid running down my cheek, and reach up and wipe it off with my hand. It is blood. "Is it me?" I wonder. Recollections of my boyhood and the lessons I learned in the scout movement come flashing by like lightning. "You do not necessarily feel when you get shot. It takes a while." I remember my instructor's words. These words trigger an immediate reaction. My mind is made up. I must jump overboard, and don't care if I get shot by the guards or not. With the whole strength remaining in my frail body, I stand up, shaking off the man above me. He slumps down.

Part of his head has been blown off, I note, as I jump over the wagon's wall and run towards the woods. Once covered by the trees I take time to stop and quickly examine the situation. Looking around I realize that I am not alone. There are people jumping off every car over the entire length of the train. As I reach an embankment before the edge of the forest I notice another plane lining up in the sky and getting ready to attack. "My God there must be about ten or more of them. Can't they recognize our striped uniforms? They're flying so low!" I mumble out loud to myself, and head towards the nearest tree. Once under the tree, the words of my scout master again flash through my mind. "Lie down pressing your upper body against the trunk. Pull in your feet, and watch the sky if you can." I quickly assume that position and wait. Time is going by very slowly. It seems I am trapped in eternity. Finally, the sound of aircraft grows weaker and fully fades.

After a while the soldiers and our guards begin to assemble and move towards the train. If I ever had a chance to escape, this is it. But without my friends I probably would not get very far, and a promise is a promise. I have to look for them.

I emerge from the woods and approach the train. My God! The destruction is total. I look at the train. The locomotive is shot to pieces and every car has been badly mauled. The screams for help coming from the open cattle cars are unbearable. Fox apparently survived in good shape. Only some dirt smears mar his flawlessly pressed and clean uniform. He is gathering his guards. Next to him a young Lieutenant is calling for his men. Most of them seem to be here. One or two got wounded. I don't know if any died. As I approach the wagons I can see limbs, torsos, and heads thrown around all over the place. I climb onto the wagon I was in. It is apparent that whoever remained and did not run got ripped apart. I wonder if my friends survived and begin to scream out their names.

A half hour has passed and Fox managed to organize some semblance of order. At first he assembled the prisoners who were whole; all of my friends showed up unharmed. They all had the same idea and jumped off the train in between bombings. Then Fox ordered us to remove the striped uniforms off the dead and tear them into long strips resembling bandages. Even though they were filthy he thought they would at least stop the flow of blood. He organized the prisoners who could move into three groups. One, composed of prisoners with some medical training, tended to the needs of the wounded. Another group assembled the corpses. The third formed a living chain towards the nearest water well. Fox went to a nearby village and requested help. The inhabitants refused to cooperate. He then grabbed two water buckets off a commode, formed a line, and we are passing water buckets to the wounded. My friends and I have been assigned to that line.

It has been a long and exhausting day. Now, as night approaches it is getting cold again. I do not know whether there is enough strength left in me to survive another cold night. Fox found some shovels and we began digging graves for the dead inmates. This is slowly turning into an insurmountable task. Fox notices our strained and useless efforts. We are weak and going only through the motions, accomplishing very little.

"The four of you. You, you, and you," he says, motioning to me and my friends. "Come over here."

We slowly abide and approach him. He is sitting on a rock and consuming his evening meal.

"I have been watching you work. Under the circumstances you have done as good a job as you possibly could. It is evening now. The train is shot. The war is almost over. Here is a piece of bread." He breaks off half of his bread ration. "Disappear into the woods. All I can say is good luck."

We would have done it anyhow, but now we do not have to fear him anymore. Quickly we grab our blankets, divide the piece of bread into four pieces, and head for the woods.

Chapter 53

LIBERATION

Forests have magic. In early childhood I listened spellbound to the Grimm and Anderson tales of little children lost in the woods read to me by my mother. Their fears and anticipations captivated my young mind. This fascination carried over into my adulthood. Now, the woods look foreboding. The descending darkness seems to be lowering a curtain on their secrets.

Frightened and disparaged, we slowly keep moving forward on a small, but well trotted, path. We have no idea where that path leads to, but keep pushing ahead with all the strength that is left in us hoping to find some friendly spot where we can wash up and get some sleep. We encroach upon a thick growth of young pine and spruce trees. It is hard to see ahead but the path is still well defined.

Suddenly, "Stop," proclaims a loud German voice. The young trees part and a silhouette of a man emerges from behind the growth. "Who are you?"

Startled by the unexpected appearance of the stranger, my first tendency is to run. I look at my friends. They appear to be frozen to the ground by fear. "We are inmates of a concentration camp which was closed this morning. We were bombed on the way to a safer place. The train was blown to pieces, so our guards let us go," I respond, playing it safe.

There follows a moment of silence while the figure moves closer. It is now clear that the voice belongs to a man of about twenty-five. He wears an army cap and jacket, and baggy civilian pants. He drops the rifle he was holding to the ground.

"Where do you hail from?" the soldier inquires with a befuddled look on his face. "Where are you going to?"

"Originally we lived in Litzmannstadt Ghetto. We were sent to a number of different camps," I answer in German. "Where are we heading? God only knows."

"What a coincidence," utters the soldier, visibly becoming more comfortable with the strange group he has encountered by accident. "I too was born and lived in Litzmannstadt. I am no Nazi, believe me. I was forced into the Army.

You people must have been through some ferocious times."

Now, we all begin to feel somewhat more at ease. He seems to be genuinely puzzled by our appearance.

"Are you hungry?" he asks. "You look so skinny and starved."

"Off course we are. We have had only some bread, cheese, and water to eat this morning. Since that time there was not much we could find."

"Wait a minute." The soldier reaches into the undergrowth and pulls out a knapsack. In it is a thermos, a large loaf of bread, and what appears to be butter wrapped in waxed paper. "I don't have much, but you are free to have half of it. I can always get more food easier than you."

He breaks the loaf in half, smears some butter on the top of it and hands it to me.

"Thank you officer," I respond, noticing a Lieutenant insignia on his uniform. "Do you know by any chance where we are, and where we can safely go to?"

"You are in upper Bavaria not far from Munich. I would not advise you to try to walk very far. The nearest spot is a farm about 500 meters from here. Just follow that path it will lead onto the farmer's field. I must go now. As you can see I am ready to defect. *Aufwiedersehen,* and all the best".

"*Aufwiedersehen,*" we answer in a subdued chorus, certain that we will never meet again.

The soldier disappears into the bush. We sit down on the cold, damp ground and divide the food into four parts, which we consume in a jiffy. Moniek's cough has worsened. He coughs almost incessantly, spitting up dark phlegm. I also have stomach cramps, and so do my comrades. Having consumed our "meal" we quickly rise off the ground, wrap our blankets over our heads and continue toward the farm referred to by the soldier.

Sometime later we finally see a clearing in the woods. The night has not yet fully covered the area. The sky is becoming darker and the stars are beginning to sparkle. Visibility is good. Maybe too good for us to emerge into the field opening up before us.

As we near the field the sound of voices reaches our ears. Someone is shouting. But the language is not German. The sounds are familiar, as we come closer to the woods' edge they become clearer. Soon it is apparent that the conversation is in Polish. We select Slamek to crawl over and examine the situation. We watch him anxiously as he moves towards the edge. Suddenly he stands up and shouts in Polish, "Poles, we need help." At the sound of the Polish language, two men come running over. We do not waste any time and also approach the group.

"Who are you?" asks one of the Poles.

"We are Jews who were held in a nearby concentration camp," Slamek answers. "We need help very badly. As you can see we are all sick. Especially this guy." He points at Moniek, "Please help us."

The two Poles appear moved. "We have been brought here by force following the unsuccessful uprising in Warsaw," they explain. "We have been working for this farmer ever since. We would like to help but there is a limit as to what we can do. We, too, are prisoners."

"All we want is someplace where we can spend the night shielded from the cold and German soldiers," I answer. "There must be something you guys can do."

"The war is almost finished, and our farmer knows it. Let me talk to him and see if he will let us accommodate you until it ends."

"May God bless you," replies Slamek. "Try your best. We are dying." The two Poles drop the hay forks they are holding and run towards the farmhouse which stands out in the dark with its well-lit windows. We sit down and wait without uttering a word. We all realize that this may be our last chance to find a place that will allow us to survive.

A few minutes pass by which feel like hours. Soon the men emerge from the farmhouse. They are in the company of a third person, who, upon closer examination, seems to be a female. As they come closer it becomes apparent that the female is a girl of about sixteen dressed in the Hitler Youth uniform.

"We have been betrayed," whispers Heniek, who is obviously trembling. The rest of us are inclined to agree, but are willing to give it a chance and stay put. After all, where can we run to? The group approaches the place where we were waiting.

"What can we do for you? You poor people." The girl is obviously shocked by our appearance. "My father sent me over to tell you that you can stay in one of our farm buildings until it is all over. We will give you all the food you need, but for the time being we cannot extend to you any medical help."

"This is all we need," I answer in German. "You are very kind. Please thank your father for us."

The Poles are not waiting for the conversation to end. One takes off. We are asked to follow the other who slowly leads us towards a shed. The girl rushes back to the main house.

As we enter I notice bales of hay all over the ground. A ladder leads towards an elevated platform which forms an upper level. From my vantage point it also seems to be full of hay. The Pole climbs the ladder and asks us to follow. Once on top he unravels a couple of bales of hay. We lie down to try out the new beds. It feels great, after all we have been through so far.

"Are you hungry?" asks the Pole.

"No, thanks. But would you have some water? We have had very little to drink today."

The Pole disappears and shows up in a few minutes with the farmer's daughter. She carries a large jug of milk and four glasses. She climbs the ladder, pours the milk, and hands everyone a glassful to drink. We grab the milk, something we haven't seen in years, and drink as if it were champagne. After a while the farmer's daughter and the Pole leave. They remove the ladder.

"What are you doing?" shouts Slamek "We may have to go out to the outhouse, you know!"

"You cannot go anywhere now. It is not safe. Although only I, my friend, the farmer and his daughter know of your presence here, there are lots of other farm workers around, and roaming German soldiers are everywhere. I have to hide the ladder so that no one can climb up and discover you. We can all be shot if they do." He motions with his right hand, pretending to hold a gun. "Bang, bang, and we are all gone."

"Would you have a bucket that we could use over night? We will empty and clean it in the morning." I interject.

"Fine. I will get you one, but remember be as quiet as you can."

He leaves and soon returns with a large steel bucket, which he hands us with the aid of a long pole.

"Good night. I hope this is your last night under the Germans," says the Pole as he closes the huge barn doors, and places a crossbar to keep them shut.

"Amen. Good night," we sigh, exhausted.

The Pole is gone. I begin to feel dizzy and try to sleep. It is difficult. The fear of being discovered, and the mistrust towards the German farmer and his daughter continuously haunt me. My friends also have trouble sleeping.

Moniek's condition is growing worse from hour to hour. He seems to have a very high fever and the coughing spells are more persistent. To make matters worse, all of us seem to have been adversely affected by the fresh milk we drank, and the bucket is hardly given a chance to rest. The obnoxious smell doesn't bother us; we've grown used to it.

A few hours pass. No one keeps time. We all gaze at the door clearance to see if dawn has yet broken. Suddenly, the noise of a truck's engine disturbs the quiet of the night. The truck seems to be coming closer to the building we are in. Soon the headlights shine through the door cracks. The truck stops, and a number of German voices are heard. One of the voices sounds very familiar. It is the highly pitched voice of the farmer's daughter. We look at each other frozen with fear. So this is it. The German girl must have notified the SS. We lie there helpless and quiet as we hear the crossbar over the doors drop, and the doors swing open wide.

"The ten of you will find enough room here to spend the night," says the farmer's daughter. "Poor soldiers. Are you hungry? Thirsty?"

"Thank you. We are tired. All day long we have done nothing but run. We need some rest," replies one of the men.

"I understand. Things are really rough now. Good night. Heil Hitler." The farmer's daughter leaves, shutting the doors behind her.

The soldiers make themselves comfortable, and after a while the sound of snoring rises up to the roof and seems to shake the trusses of this flimsy farm building. Moniek, who has been trying to suppress his nasty cough, suddenly breaks out with a loud, continuous coughing fit. Terrified, we quickly cover his head with our blankets, trying to at least muffle the sound.

"Hey, who is coughing so loud?" calls out one of the sleeping soldiers. "Is it you Hans?"

"Shut up. Mind your own business, and stop snoring so loud." It must be Hans answering his comrade. The sound of snoring erupts once again, filling the building with noise. It is so loud that Moniek's coughing provides only a weak accompaniment.

The day has dawned, but we still lie there, not daring to move. We are all sick. It must be dysentery. We did not dare to go to the bucket since the soldiers' arrival. Instead, we relieved ourselves on the spot into the loose hay.

The rising sun wakes up the soldiers. They get up and leave. Soon one of the Polish workers arrives. He carries a pitcher with ersatz coffee, some bread, a chunk of butter, and a paper bag. Upon entering the building he digs out the ladder, and we slowly climb down. Moniek is very weak, and the Pole carries him down on his shoulders.

"Listen closely," he says once we are assembled on the floor. "The radio announced this morning that the German Army is readying a counteroffensive. The farmer is worried. He gave me orders to remove you from these premises. Here is some food to keep you from starving for another day. You need medical attention or you will all soon die. Not far from here is a monastery where monks used to live in seclusion raising sheep and manufacturing cheese. Today, it has been converted to a field hospital, and is full of soldiers. You must be careful, and avoid people in uniform as you approach this place. Try to talk to the monks. I think they can be trusted. I had contact with them before, working for our farmer. They may be able to extend to you the medical help you need."

"Where is this place? How can we get there?" asks Slamek.

"Follow me." The Pole exits the building. Once in the clear, he points to a hill rising on the horizon. "The monastery is located on the top of this hill. It is not far; it takes me fifteen minutes to get there. It may take you a couple of hours. Be careful, though, there are soldiers all over. Do you see the cluster of trees forming a small wood like pattern? It originates right here. I will take you there. Stay covered until you reach a field. You can see the clearing from here. Stop and look for a civilian or a monk. I wish you all the luck."

As we follow the Pole, Heniek assumes the role of food keeper. Once we have reached the tree cover, the Pole turns back, waves us off, and we are on our own.

The walk takes a long time. After a while it turns into an upward climb which is very exhausting. Our dysentery has left us completely dehydrated. The coffee has been quickly consumed, and we yearn for water. We stop and rest frequently. The sun has risen, moved across the sky, and is about to set when we finally reach the clearing at the edge of the field. We are totally drained. Moniek falls down, and is incapable of going farther. Heniek's food bag is by now empty. Slamek and I approach the edge of the field.

The field, located on a slope of the hill, is filled with sheep. We look closer and discover a man's figure dressed in monk's robes. The monk has a stick in his hand with which he tries to prod the sheep into one group. As if by a miracle, one sheep breaks away from the flock and heads in our direction. The Monk follows.

"Father! Father!" I whisper loud enough to be heard by the monk. "We need help!"

"Who is this?" inquires the monk with a touch of surprise in his voice, as he moves in our direction, "My God," he exclaims at the sight of me and Slamek.

"You poor creatures. Where are you coming from?"

"A concentration camp," we reply.

The monk is clearly agitated and bewildered. "You look so young. Why were you interned? What crime did you commit?"

"One, sir. We were born Jewish."

The monk's face turns pale and he begins to tremble. "Poor children. You must be helped right away." His eyes are tearing. "I know little about medicine, but there is a man here I trust. His name is Ferdinand and he is a nurse. I will send him over as soon as I get back to our place. In the meantime lie down and rest. Try not to be visible. There are still many monsters around this place. You know what I mean: the SS."

He quickly turns around and practically runs toward the largest structure, leaving his stick and his flock of sheep behind.

We lie down and wait. Time goes by as we anxiously look at the evening sky, hoping to hold back the onset of darkness. We want to have at least enough light for the nurse to examine us. Finally, the outline of a figure accompanied by our monk appears in the distance. They are rushing toward our refuge in the trees. Not far behind them is a group of five or six men. They too are moving in our direction, holding forks and shovels in their hands. All are dressed in civilian garb.

Ferdinand and the monk reach us first. At the sight of us, Ferdinand gasps and bites his lower lip, perhaps to keep from crying out loud. He stoops down near Moniek first. He removes his jacket exposing a skeleton-like body.

"*Herr Gott!* What have they done to these people?" Ferdinand cannot hold himself back from shouting, "This man is near death!"

"This is ghastly," utters the Monk. "Shame!"

At this moment the rest of the group arrives. They stop and look us over. "*Mon Dieux!*" They yell as if on command. "*Quel malheur.*"

"*Parlez-vous francais?*" asks one.

"No," I answer "*Polonais? Allemand?*" I have learned a few French words during one visit of my uncle from Belgium.

"*Bon,*" says the Frenchman. "Let us speak German. You poor people. We are prisoners of war. We have been here for four years working as field hands and performing various chores at the hospital. We knew of concentration camps, but never imagined them to be this bad."

"You are not unique," I reply in German. "We were there, and cannot fathom that fact. You just met us and wonder. Can you imagine what it took to get us to this point?"

"Let first things come first," interrupts Ferdinand, trying to assume some authority. "You, Francois, come back with me. We shall get some medication for the dysentery these people are suffering from, and tea to ease their dehydration."

"Jean," says another Frenchman. "You stay here with them. We will all go back to see what we can do to help those poor souls."

Jean is a tall fellow in his late twenties. He wears civilian clothing embossed on the back with a big K for *Kriegsgefangene* or prisoner of war. He tells us he thought he had seen everything, but our appearance is beyond anything he anticipated from the Germans. He speaks a broken

German but we have no problem understanding each other. The war is coming to an end, and very soon, he consoles us. Maybe tonight- the latest by tomorrow. He knows from some German hospital employees that the Americans have been seen only about ten kilometers away. The German Army is falling apart. There is hardly any resistance. He tells us to hold on to our lives. Soon the whole thing will be over. We will be taken care of and nursed back to our old selves. We are lucky, he says, to be in this place at this time. This is a military hospital filled with the personnel and medication required to nurse us back to health. But it is still dangerous out there, he warns. The only people he trusts are Ferdinand and a couple of Monks. We were extremely fortunate to encounter one of the trustworthy monks. A few others are real sons-of-bitches. He also tells us that in the last couple of days they managed to get hold of some rifles and ammunition. When the right time arrives they will fight.

Soon three of his comrades arrive carrying toasted bread, which they say is good for our diarrhea, boiled water, and some raisins. One of them pulls out a bottle of white wine, removes the cork, salutes us, and takes a gulp directly from the bottle. The bottle gets passed around, but we beg off from drinking. We do not feel well and worry that wine may raise havoc with our sick intestines.

Ferdinand and Francois arrive carrying medication, a bowl of water, and civilian clothing. Ferdinand helps to wash our hands and faces. We discard the smelly old striped uniforms and put on clean pants, shirts, and jackets with the letter K. The French prisoners pulled the clothing out of their stock room. There are also socks and slippers. Our old stuff gets rolled up into one bundle, and buried beneath one of the trees.

The French also brought some clean blankets, but they have a problem putting us up in a safe place. They think that the place we are at is probably the safest at this time. They will leave a man with us, and alternate every four hours, Francois explains.

Night has covered the terrain with a dark, impenetrable cloak. We wrap ourselves up in blankets and fall asleep totally exhausted, but stimulated by the day's events. I do not know how long I slept but now that I am awake, I can see the sun rising in the sky, and hear gun shots and explosions all around us. Our French friends are here in full force. They tell us that the army battalion that was assigned the defense of the hospital perimeter has left an hour ago. It is now safe to move us up the hill closer to the field hospital.

Four strong guys are given the job of carrying us piggy-back style. We submit to their orders, being fully convinced of the friendliness and dependability of these people. They are our guardian angels in the full meaning of the word. Once on the hill, the men drop us by the main road that winds up the hill, encircles the hospital building and proceeds down the slope on the far side of the structure. One man, with a rifle in hand, is left behind to guard us. The others, accompanied by other prisoners with rifles and ammunition belts across their chests, proceed towards the main building. Soon some shots are heard, and someone screams for help. There seems to be a lot of commotion up there. After a couple of hours things settle down.

The sun is high over us when two Frenchmen arrive with lunch. They bring with them eating utensils and canteens filled with food and coffee.

"What happened up there?" asks our guard.

"Oh! Absolutely nothing," replies one of the Frenchmen. "We had a couple of accounts to settle, that's all."

"Did you get Helmut the Skunk?"

"Oh yeah! And a couple of his close collaborators. All is fine. We are now waiting for the Americans."

We are not interested in who Helmut the Skunk was. We hope and pray that we will make it. Moniek still coughs, but now the phlegm he spits up is full of blood.

All seems to be eerily quiet except for the occasional distant roar of engines that can be heard accompanied by some intermittent bursts of machine gun fire. With time the roar grows louder. Looking down at the road, we see many vehicles emerging from the cluster of woods where we spent the night, as well as from the streets of a small village at the foot of the hill opposite our hiding place. They form a column and begin to move up the road we are on. The Frenchmen quickly assemble near the place we are resting. Francois is apparently in charge.

As the first tank arrives he calls the group to attention. They drop their gun stocks to the ground and stretch out as tall as they can. Francois then pulls out a French flag, ostensibly made from some colored shirts, waves it

271

at the approaching tank, and bursts into the Marseillaise, *"Allions enfants de la patrie', le jour de gloire' arrive.."*

The song is quickly picked up by the rest of the group. A soldier, manning a machine gun on top of the tank, smiles and responds with a salute. All of this looks somewhat grotesque and reminds me of old French classical movies with Jean Gabin. Be that as it may, we have survived the German hell.

I, too, want to sing out. This is a great and historic moment for us. We are free! But, neither do I know what to sing, nor could I utter a word if I knew. My throat is clamped. Tears are running down my cheeks for the first time in years.

The first tank stops near the main building. Soon a jeep with four American officers arrives. The officers step out of the jeep, and return a salute from a group of German officers assembled at the top of the steps. The Germans are dressed in their full uniforms as if they were expecting a parade. After a brief exchange they all enter the main building.

Meanwhile, the column of tanks moves on, followed by a line of jeeps. They stop for a while. Soldiers in the nearest jeep call on us to come closer. I stand up and walk over. They seem to be bewildered, as if they had just come across a wild monster.

One soldier asks me a question in English. "No understand English," I respond. My knowledge of English has not gone beyond father, mother, sister, hello, good-buy, I love you, understand, and a count to ten, all of which I learned primarily from the movies.

"French, Russian, Polish?" he asks, pointing at me.

"Jewish. Kazet. Mother, father kaput." I point to the heavens trying to indicate their fate.

"Schlekt, bad, Deutch kaput." He tries to accost me in his limited vocabulary. "Candy? Chocolate? Cigarette?" He asks, and pulls out a couple of chocolate bars and a pack of Camel cigarettes. He hands me the best he has to offer at this time. "Share with comrades. OK?"

"OK," I stretch out my arm to receive the goodies.

"Schlekt, very schlekt," the soldier can now see my skinny hand with the baked-in dirt that so far resisted removal. *"Deutch* bad people. Good-bye." The column has started moving. In no time, all the tanks had left the hill. Only a couple of jeeps are left behind. We are still by the road, as this euphoric day is drawing to an end. This is the day we have waited for over five years to come. Yet, when it has finally arrived we are still hounded by suspicion and fear. What will happen to us?

As if to answer my fears, the French, who for a while moved in the direction of the main building, return. Francois tries to tell us something, but stops as if to formulate his thoughts. After a few seconds he continues: "Didont, mes amies," he starts in French, but changes quickly to German. "We are all free now. I am sure that the Americans will take good care of you. My comrades and I are homesick; we have been away from our families for much too long. There is also a lot of urgent business to take care of. You know: Laval, Petain...all those crooks. We've decided to set out for home tonight. One American officer told us that there are many empty supply trucks moving in the direction of France." He thinks we should have no problem getting back home. He clears his throat and continues, "As far as you are concerned, we have tried to put you up in the hospital but were told by the German Director that there is no room. So, for the time being you will spend the night in the cow barn. We already prepared a place for you. Ferdinand promised to take care of you, and keep you supplied with food and medication. So, *au-revoir mes amies*. We wish you the best. Maybe we shall meet again in a free France."

They embrace each of us. It is hard to part with those decent people who may have saved our lives. But there is nothing we can do. We follow them to a barn. The wide, gate-like, barn doors do not fit well and large gaps remain at the threshold and door frame. The gaps between the boards from which the door has been constructed are wide enough to see through, which bothers us a bit. A place by the door is laid out with straw. There are a few buckets filled with fresh water. Next to the barn is an outhouse.

Ferdinand has arrived, and helps us wash up. He feeds us as best as he can. The French leave shouting, "Vive La France." The sympathy and understanding shown by the Frenchmen has a soothing effect on us. They may have left, yet we feel more secure and happy than we have been in a long, long, time. We fall asleep tired out by the events of the day.

I am awakened by the rays of the rising sun. They penetrate the barn through the open slits in the door and form thin light panes in which the barn dust particles dance merrily around. I lie there wondering what today will bring when the sound of approaching people reaches my ears. They speak German. God, I pray, help us. Frozen with fear I am incapable of awakening my friends. The voices come closer. Through the slits in the door I can see German military men. I cannot make out what is said, which further contributes to my consternation. The door swings open and the bright sun temporarily blinds me.

"*Wer ist das? Was machen die Leute hier?*" One of the military men questions. What is that? What are these people doing here?

"*Ich habe keine Ahnung,*" answers the other "I have no idea".

Slowly, my vision begins to adjust to the sun, and I shield my eyes with my hand. Now I can see them clearly. The man asking the questions in perfect German is not a German soldier. He is dressed differently, more like the soldiers I saw last night in the tanks. Could he be American? How come he speaks German so well, I ask myself. The other military men are German officers. In the rear of the group I notice Ferdinand. He steps forward.

"*Herr Kapitaen,*" he addresses the stranger. "I found them at the clearing the day before yesterday. They are concentration camp inmates. I and Father Eric decided to help them out. We kept them in seclusion until today. Besides us only the French prisoners of war, who left last night, knew about their existence. Herr Major, our commander, had no knowledge of them being here."

The American Captain enters the barn and moves in our direction. By this time Slamek and Heniek are on their feet. Moniek remains on the ground motionless.

"Is what this man tells me true?" he inquires.

"Yes," I am still amazed by the perfect accent of the Captain. "Ferdinand was very helpful. I am certain that the Herr Major did not know about it. Had he known we, probably, would have been shot."

"This is not true," cuts in the Major. "I would have ordered them admitted to the hospital. Why didn't anyone tell me? Ferdinand, you should be punished for insubordination."

"I am the boss here, and I will decide who should be punished," interrupts the Captain. "At this time, I order you to clean those people up and admit them to the hospital. You have two hours to carry out my orders. Understood?"

"*Yawohl, Herr Kapitaen,*" says the Major, who apparently is the highest ranking of the hospital crew. He jumps to attention and salutes the Captain. "I shall immediately assign two nurses to do it."

"OK. In two hours I will check to see whether my orders have been carried out." The Captain walks over to Moniek, who is still lying inert on the ground. "Is he asleep?" He bends over him, raises Moniek's arm and lets it drop. He checks his pupils. Tries to feel his pulse. "The man is dead."

We are shocked but have neither the strength nor the sense of awareness to show much emotion. We stand there motionless and speechless, when the Captain moves closer to us,

"Are you Jewish?" He asks in German.

"Yes."

"So am I. Let us say *Kaddish*." His voice is serious but a softness in it suggests the man's understanding of our plight. "Repeat after me: *Yisgadal, v'yiskadash shmei raba...*"

We repeat word for word in a deadly silent barn. It seems to me that the world has suddenly ceased to exist. Only our voices reverberate in my mind. The Captain has finished. The Germans stand there, totally perplexed, bewildered, and looking very uncomfortable.

"You probably wonder who I am," the Captain says to us after a minute of total silence. "I was born in Germany of Jewish parents. In 1934 we escaped to Argentina from where we made our way to New York. In Germany I studied medicine. I finished my studies in New York, and joined the US Army as soon as it became apparent that war is inevitable. This is my fourth year in the Army. During this time I have seen and experienced some horrible things, but what I witnessed in the last few weeks surpasses all my experiences in sheer terror and horror. Frequently I think it is a terrible nightmare; a chimera. I never in my life would have imagined that things like that could happen in this, the twentieth century. We knew in the USA that Jews are being persecuted. But this...?"

Without finishing the sentence, he turns to the silent Germans who stand there, uncomfortably shuffling their feet, with their heads bowed, and repeats his order to accommodate us ordering them also to find our friend a decent grave and properly mark it with a Star of David. He wants to assist with the burial. At that he turns and leaves.

Two hours have passed. The clock on the wall indicates ten. We have been shaven clean in all areas and dusted with DDT to remove the lice which have been pestering us all the time as if to help our persecutors. Dressed in clean hospital pajamas and slippers, we sit now at a large oblong table in the center of a huge room.

With the sole exception of the door passage, all walls are crowded with beds filled with sick soldiers. The headboards rest against the walls and we can easily read the tablets with the occupant's name and rank. Every other bed is filled with a member of the SS. Many sit up in bed and look us over. Others walk around and gaze at us with interest and suspicion. I am certain that the SS members know who we are. The rest may be surprised by our looks. We do look like walking skeletons. They watch us consuming some liquid cereal and tea. As we sit there observing one another, I wonder whether I will still make it, I feel terribly exhausted and weak. In comparison to the sick German soldiers we look like resurrected mummies that may fall apart when touched. After a while the doors open, and the camp director appears. He walks to the center of the room, leans on the table's edge and says:

"Soldiers. Comrades. Times have changed. These changes, to be sure, are not to our liking. I am forced to take orders from the occupational military authorities, and can do nothing about it. The men you see sitting at this table are concentration camp inmates." He is interrupted with boos and whistles, but continues. "I have been given orders to find three beds by the hour of ten. I have waited as long as I could, hoping that the orders may change. Alas, I am compelled to pass them on to you. Please, do voluntarily vacate three beds for these men."

He points at us, looking around for volunteers. No one moves. He begins again to ask for volunteers, explaining that he has an order to provide three beds, and orders of superiors must be followed. No one moves.

As he stands there contemplating his next move, the American Captain walks in. He stops at the door's edge, looks around as if sizing up the situation, glances at us still sitting at the table, and approaches the Director.

"I thought I gave you an order to have these three people in bed in two hours. The two hours have now passed. What's going on?"

The soldiers are startled. He speaks in pure German understandable to all of them. It is apparent from their looks that they do not know what to make of it.

The director remains silent, looking down at the floor.

"I am asking you like a gentleman, like one soldier to another; vacate three beds, voluntarily." The Captain sizes up each individual.

No one moves.

"OK. I have examined your facilities and found a large empty room with beds in the cellar. He turns toward the Director. You were probably holding it for an emergency, right? This emergency has arrived. It is here gentlemen. Since there are no volunteers, and to be fair to everyone, I order you to vacate this room in ten minutes. All of you. And to you bastards that are capable of running around, all I can say is, shame on you. You have made your less fortunate comrades suffer. I repeat, you have ten minutes to leave. The sisters will take you downstairs."

The room begins to empty out in a hurry. As long as there was an option, no one wanted to leave. Most of them are now perfectly capable of grabbing their bedding and personal effects and crowding out through the door. A few are wheeled out on beds or chairs.

Three nurses get busy preparing our beds. We are asked for preferences. We don't care. Before long three beds are all made up.

We lie down. Oh! How comfortable those beds feel. Our aching bones finally have a comfortable place they can sink into. And the pillows! Our heads are used to piles of straw, now they are resting on piles of feathers. If there is such a thing as Heaven, we must be right in its neighborhood. I never thought I would live long enough to experience this moment. It is all quiet on the western front. Paul, it looks like I did make it. Sorry, pal.

The Captain comes over and assures us that he will stay here for a long time. We have nothing to worry about. With this assurance I relax, close my eyes and fall into a deep, restful, and soothing slumber which buoys me up into the clouds like a fine feather. Higher and higher I fly when at once the sound of a voice reaches me.

"Wake up, please. We want to interview you. We are reporters from Stars and Stripes."

It seems the voice is part of a nightmare which is set to bring me down to earth. I do not answer. My sleep becomes so absorbing. It is deep, almost comatose.

Fluffy, multicolored clouds begin to swirl around in front of my closed eyes. They swirl in bizarre and fantastic circles, forming unusual patterns. Soon, the swirl abates into an orderly transformation out of which emerge the faces of my sister and parents smiling at me and saying, "You have made it!"

Epilogue

The year of 1945 began with an enormous Soviet offensive. In early January Marshall Zhukov attacked along the entire Eastern Front. Poland was cleared of all German troops. Auschwitz was liberated but not before the Germans evacuated. The ghettos and concentration camps located on Polish soil were no more. The Romanians joined the Red Armies, as did Tito of Yugoslavia to the south-west. The German Troops in Hungary were fleeing. The Russians approached Vienna and Prag.

The main contingents of Russian troops moved on Berlin with an enormous mass of men and equipment, Allied troops advanced to the East and South liberating in their drive, to their own surprise and dismay, concentration camps such as Dachau, Bergen - Belsen, and Stuthoff.

By the end of January Hitler's Capital City of Berlin was threatened. By about the same time the Allied Armies managed to cross the Rhone River. The US Third Army under Gen. Patton began a race to the East. They met up with the Soviets in Saxony late in April. By that time the Red Army had finally taken Berlin, but not after leaving the city in shambles, and registering the loss of tens of thousands of soldiers.

On the 30th of April it was announced that Hitler committed suicide after marrying his long-time sweetheart Eva Brown a day before. His master propagandist Goebels followed his Fuehrer's lead killing not only himself but also murdering his own wife and children. The Germans surrendered. On the ninth of May the war was over. Germany was divided into parts occupied by the US, USSR, Great Britain and France. The capital of prewar Germany, Berlin, was also divided into sections occupied by the Allied partners. All Nazi criminal leaders (with a few exceptions) were caught and jailed. A couple of months after the surrender of Germany, they were sitting in jails awaiting trial.

While war in Europe was finished. The pain of the few Jewish survivors had just begun. Very few managed to find a relative or two. The realization that they were all gone was hard, if not impossible, to bear.

I admit not knowing exactly how many Jews died. I was in no position to count them. I am certain that out of my family, which includes the siblings, parents, grandparents, aunts, uncles, and cousins, very few survived.

Concerning the people mentioned in this book - my three grandparents, alive at the start of the persecutions, perished Bella B. and Yakov W. had a baby, but none of them survived; they disappeared without a trace. Aunt Hannah and her daughter Itka deported to Chelmno were never heard from again. .There were reports that they were gassed with carbon monoxide in special vans. Ita B. and Sara B. shared the same fate. Haim D., Hannah's husband, died in the Ghetto. David B. was killed in a camp in Silesia. My mother's cousins Zajvel R. and his wife Rachel died in the ghetto of starvation. His brother Julek R., with his family of five, all died in Sobibor extermination camp.

On my father's side, the entire "W" family, with the exception of Heniek, was gassed in Auschwitz-Birkenau, including Aunt Bajla, Uncle Wolf, and cousins Lajb, Dvora and Aunt Rose.

My own parents died of starvation in the Ghetto of Litzmannstadt.

My sister Debra was gassed in Birkenau on the holiest of holidays, the Day of Atonement.

Of the major figures listed in this book, Mr. R, otherwise known as Chaim Rumkowski, the leader of the Ghetto, it is said, died with his entire entourage upon arrival in Auschwitz-Birkenau. He apparently was told by the German Ghetto manager, Mr. B or Bibov, which was his true last name, that he and his entourage would continue their rule over the Jews in another place. Instead, the entire group was immediately dispatched to the gas chambers. An equally gruesome fate awaited Mr. T, real name Targownik -the Gestapo informer, and his entire family. It is said that they were killed by the co-habitants of the box wagon and arrived dead at Auschwitz.

One thing is certain and that is that millions of Jews died. It is of interest to note that the toll of Jewish victim mounts whenever German troops or Nazi officials were directly involved. There were instances when

German orders to hand over Jews were not followed, and many Jews were saved. Thus, when Bulgaria, an Axis partner, received orders to hand over the Jews, the King refused. In Denmark the King refused to follow German orders and in the cover of night dispatched the Danish Jews to neutral Sweden. France, an original Allied partner turned into a partner of the Axis, following the loss to Germany, managed to save fifty percent of its Jews by rendering a deaf ear on their presence in the unoccupied Vischy territories. Italian Jews, some of whom belonged to the Fascist Party, were in a way shielded by the Fascist government. Many Italian Jews died after the Germans took over the government following the coup d'État against Mussolini. In Hungary, Jews were treated badly, Stripped of all their rights and wealth and forced to labor in special camps they still managed to survive until orders, given by the Germans, were allowed to be carried out. Adolf Eichmann, assumed command of the "solution" to their Jewish 'problem' and in the summer of 1944, dispatched most Jews to Auschwitz-Birkenau Romanian Jews were persecuted, but a great many managed to come out alive.

The disasters that struck the Polish, Lithuanian, Dutch, Check, Slovak, Yugoslavian and Ukrainian Jews, have no parallel in history. For five years they were beaten, hanged, shot, starved, worked to death, and when the time came to accelerate the process of their extinction, gassed with carbon monoxide or Zyclone B. There was no organized Allied resistance to stop this. Some Jews were saved by good Samaritans who for various reasons felt it their duty to do so risking their own life. And Gypsies. They were subjected to persecution similar to that of the Jews.

Many years have passed since the end of World War Two. Many countries have risen, many have fallen, and though the legacy of World War Two lingers on, the survivors of that catastrophe are dying out. Whether the world has learned any lesson from this cataclysmic event is doubtful. With the proper scenario and set of circumstances, this catastrophe can again be replayed on the world scene, maybe even on a larger scale. Perhaps this time the origin, or race, or religion of the persecuted may change. Perhaps not.